BUSINESS
BEHAVING WELL

ALSO BY RON ELSDON

Affiliation in the Workplace: Value Creation in the New Organization (author)

Building Workforce Strength: Creating Value through Workforce and Career Development (editor)

RELATED TITLES FROM POTOMAC BOOKS

The Politics of Gratitude: Scale, Place & Community in a Global Age
—Mark T. Mitchell

Strategic Thinking in 3D: A Guide for National Security, Foreign Policy, and Business Professionals
—Ross Harrison

Warfare Welfare: The Not-So-Hidden Costs of America's Permanent War Economy
—Marcus G. Raskin and Gregory D. Squires, editors

American Poverty: Presidential Failures and a Call to Action
—Woody Klein

Social Responsibility, from
Learning to Doing

BUSINESS
BEHAVING WELL

EDITED BY RON ELSDON

Potomac Books
Washington, D.C.

Published in the United States by Potomac Books, Inc. All rights reserved. No part of this book may be reproduced in any manner whatsoever without written permission from the publisher, except in the case of brief quotations embodied in critical articles and reviews.

Library of Congress Cataloging-in-Publication Data
Business behaving well : social responsibility, from learning to doing / edited by Ron Elsdon.—1st ed.
    p. cm.
Includes bibliographical references and index.
ISBN 978-1-61234-294-8 (hardcover : alk. paper)
ISBN 978-1-61234-403-4 (electronic)
1. Social responsibility of business. I. Elsdon, Ron, 1950–
✓ HD60.B882 2013
  658.4'08—dc23

                                                        2012036466

Printed in the United States of America on acid-free paper that meets the American National Standards Institute Z39-48 Standard.

Potomac Books
22841 Quicksilver Drive
Dulles, Virginia 20166

First Edition

10 9 8 7 6 5 4 3 2 1

*This book is dedicated to
the authors' and editor's families*

All I'm saying is simply this, that all life is interrelated, that somehow we're caught in an inescapable network of mutuality tied in a single garment of destiny. Whatever affects one directly affects all indirectly. For some strange reason, I can never be what I ought to be until you are what you ought to be. You can never be what you ought to be until I am what I ought to be.

—Martin Luther King Jr.,
Western Michigan University, December 18, 1963

CONTENTS

ILLUSTRATIONS

PREFACE

I remember many years ago in elementary school in England listening to the excited voices of other children at lunchtime seeing bacon on their plates. This is the only time they would have bacon, as their families couldn't afford it. I didn't understand that. It was only later I learned of the hardships of their lives, a contrast to ours of comparative comfort, though certainly not opulence. It was only much later I came to understand that this inequality in our school was a mirror of inequality in a much larger world community. The community we choose to create in this larger world is our legacy. That community, at a deep level, is a reflection of our beliefs and values, a reflection of our common humanity. And it is hurting.

Business has a big part to play in salving this hurt through socially responsible practices. Business organizations are part of a network affecting employees, investors, communities, and partner, customer, and supplier organizations. Successful business organizations embrace social responsibility for their constituent communities. Indeed, social responsibility is the essence of their longterm value creation. Recent economic turmoil calls into question a purely market-oriented doctrine with a narrow business focus on only financial return, a narrow manager focus on personal enrichment, and a narrow public policy focus on limiting strong government. Individuals, organizations, and communities suffer with this approach. There are alternatives, which we examine in this book. They involve socially responsible business practices, supported by enlightened public policy and thoughtful individual responsibility.

It is hard to know exactly where something begins but I think this book begins with that bacon and that school yard. It begins with a belief that all children and all people have a right to lives in which they have food and shelter, in which they have healthcare and education, and in which they can find personal fulfillment. It begins with the knowledge that we have far to go in reaching this ideal, but that it is reachable, and business has an important role to play. And so began my exploration of our social condition and the influence of business, particularly in the United States, which has been our home for many years. Some of this found expression in *Affiliation in the Workplace* and *Building Workforce Strength*, where the primary focus was the relationship of individuals to organizations. Some found expression in the social and community commentaries in our newsletters. Now, in this book, it has been a pleasure to find fellow travelers on this journey who bring deep experience and concern for social responsibility. Our contributors share their wisdom about the interface between business and the broader community, bringing primarily a practitioner and citizen perspective. We each bring our own perspective, and the views presented by each chapter's author(s) do not necessarily reflect the views of other chapters' authors. Moreover, any errors in this book are solely my responsibility.

We offer this book for you, mindful of the Native American tale Joan Chittister recounts.* She writes of an elder speaking about tragedy saying, "I feel as if I have two wolves fighting in my heart. One wolf is the vengeful, angry, violent one. The other wolf is the loving, compassionate one." And on being asked, "But which wolf will win the fight in your heart?," she replies, "It depends on which one I feed." We hope that we feed the loving, compassionate one.

Ron Elsdon
Danville, California

* Joan D. Chittister, *Scarred by Struggle, Transformed by Hope* (Grand Rapids, MI: Wm. B. Eerdmans, 2003), 103.

ACKNOWLEDGMENTS

I am deeply grateful to those whose lives have touched mine with kindness; there are many who, by their example, illuminate the pages of this book, some directly and some in the spaces between the words. I so much appreciate our chapter authors—Zeth Ajemian, Allyne Beach, Andrew Domek, Aaron Hurst, Megan Roberts Koller, Barbara Langsdale, Jim Leatherberry, Deborah LeVeen, Laura Long, Emet Mohr, Bob Redlo, Pearl Sims, Richard Vicenzi, and Linda Williams—for giving of their time and wisdom. This book is an expression of their insights and caring voices. I have been fortunate to work with many people over the years who by their quiet and profound presence exemplify the principles of this book. Many are mentioned in *Affiliation in the Workplace* and *Building Workforce Strength*, and to all those I am thankful. We have been blessed with a marvelous team of people at Elsdon, Inc., who bring joy and profoundness into the lives of many clients and their organizations. This book is a celebration of all who have been part of our team, most recently Michele DeRosa, Anna Domek, Andi Edelman, Martha Edwards, Rita Erickson, Lisa Franklin, Dee Holl, Alia Lawlor, Beth Levin, Jeannette Maass, Darlene Martin, Michele McCarthy, Maggi Payment, Dave Rosenberg, Mary Van Hee, and Richard Vicenzi.

It has been a pleasure working with many people at Kaiser Permanente over the years, some of whom we are fortunate to have as contributors to this book. In addition to our chapter authors from Kaiser Permanente, I am so thankful to many people in the organization for their presence, insights, and support, in particular John August, Jessica Butz, Barbara

Grimm, Mark Malcolm, and Lynda Wagner. I am also glad to know as colleagues and friends Pat DeMasters and John Morel at the Haas School of Business of the University of California–Berkeley who bring the principles we describe here into the career world of students.

Many in nonprofit and faith-based organizations soldier mightily to meet community needs and to advocate for a just path forward. I hope that this book in some way is a testament to their dedication and commitment. Organizations whose commitment to social justice I have been privileged to see firsthand include Shell Ridge Community Church in Walnut Creek, the Food Bank of Contra Costa and Solano, Project Homeless Connect, the Taproot Foundation, and Healthcare for All in California. I am especially grateful to Hilary Claggett, our editor at Potomac Books. Hilary has kept faith in this book as its shape evolved and has been such a good advocate and source of encouragement and insight throughout. Each of the three books I have written or edited exists because of Hilary's editorial involvement or encouragement, and for that I am so appreciative.

I am very thankful to my parents, Barbara and Frank, for helping me see, in those early years, those things that are important and matter in this world. My mother-in-law, Mary Bowey, reached 100 years of age when this book was written; I am thankful for her presence and all of the Bowey family in my life. I am so grateful for our family today and the light they bring. For our children, Mark and Anna, and their spouses, Erica and Andy, whose beautiful presence and lives are a light to us all. For our grandchildren, Claire, Emma, and Sophie, whose joyful grace is such a gift. May this book in some small way soften our world for them and for all children. Finally, this book is given with much love for my wife, Linda, whose gentle, life-affirming presence means so much to me.

INTRODUCTION

Ron Elsdon

He walked over slowly, a bit reticent, his bag of food waiting on the table by the door. He was in his seventies; originally perhaps from Eastern Europe, English didn't come naturally. I was one of many volunteers conducting a survey on food insecurity (a euphemism for hunger) at a local agency. When we came to the question about whether he was sometimes hungry because he couldn't afford to buy food he answered yes, almost apologetically. There was a tear in the corner of his eye, and in mine. There was something about his quiet grace that was deeply moving. I found myself wondering how can we live in the United States, one of the most prosperous societies on earth, and leave people behind so they depend on sporadic, charitable support for something as basic as food. This one person with his bag of food brings us face-to-face with the core issue of social justice framed by David Miller: "How the good and bad things in life should be distributed among the members of a human society."[1] Recognizing that on this subject there are different views and that, as Miller puts it, "the pursuit of social justice in the twenty-first century will be considerably tougher than it has been in the last half of the twentieth . . . we will have to think much harder about . . . what the universe of social justice should be in a world in which economic, social and political boundaries no longer neatly coincide."[2]

What can we do differently so that we don't leave people behind? How can organizations be socially responsible as one aspect of social justice? This will be the focus of our book: specifically, the role of business often in collaboration with nonprofits and the public sector. While our focus will be

1

mainly on the United States, we hope that our perspectives will be valuable to those living and working elsewhere. We recognize that our need is particularly pressing in the United States given our ranking as twenty-seventh out of thirty-one developed countries in a recent index of social justice.[3] Our book is written by people active in business, nonprofit, public-sector, and educational settings with a heart for social responsibility. It is this heart that is a source of encouragement for the path we can take as a society in the future. We offer our learning to all seeking to collaborate and find a better path forward.

In considering the role of business, it is helpful first to look at societal conditions that speak to the importance of social justice and therefore social responsibility. The emergence of the Occupy movement in 2011 brought important issues to the surface, which are intertwined with social responsibility. At their heart these issues are about gross, sustained, and growing inequality, evident in many places, and particularly in the United States.[4] Decreasing inequality helps us live longer, reduces murder rates, alleviates mental illness, reduces the size of our prison population, cuts down on teenage births, and increases the proportion of our population who feel they can trust each other.[5] There is growing evidence that inequality in a society brings many social ills, which include lowered educational performance among children, reduced life expectancy, higher infant mortality, more obesity, increased crime, lower levels of trust, and less social mobility.[6] Measures of social distress increase directly as inequality increases, whether comparing among countries or among states in the United States. This affects all of us, and it is not about the absolute level of prosperity; it is about the level of inequality.

We have a particular challenge in the United States since our society is so unequal.[7] Here is David Shipler's view: "The forgotten [in America] wage a daily struggle to keep themselves from falling over the cliff. It is time to be ashamed."[8] In the United States our level of inequality has increased significantly over the past forty years.[9] There are many measures that shed light on inequality.[10] One measure broadly accepted is known as the Gini coefficient (see figure 1). It ranges from a value of 0, where there is complete equality in a society, to a value of 1, where one family or individual has everything.[11] Figure 2 includes the Gini coefficient for family income in the

United States from 1950 to 2010. From 1950 until the late 1960s, the Gini coefficient gets smaller, which means we were becoming more equal during that period. Then there is a dramatic shift to growing inequality, which took off in the 1980s, as shown by the rapid increase in the Gini coefficient from that time on.[12]

FIGURE 1. Gini Coefficient

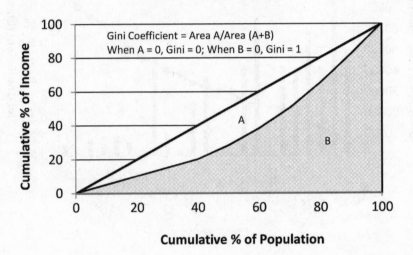

Cumulative % of Population

FIGURE 2. U.S. Family Income Inequality over Time

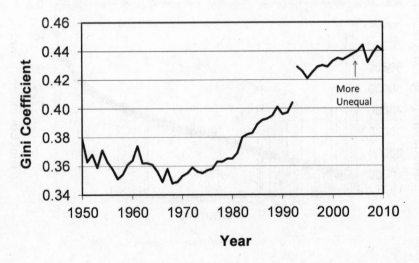

Year

How do countries compare? Figures 3 and 4 illustrate income inequality and economic strength for a number of countries.[13]

FIGURE 3. Income Inequality and Economic Strength (23 Countries)

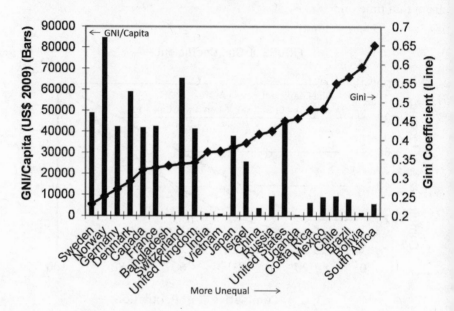

FIGURE 4. Income Inequality and Economic Strength (123 Countries)

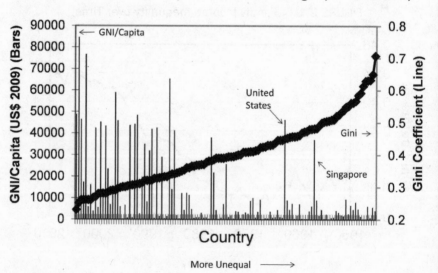

Figure 3 includes 23 selected countries; figure 4, 123 countries for which data are available (see table 2 in appendix A for additional details). The line with the diamonds on both figures refers to the Gini coefficient measures shown at the right of each figure. As we move from left to right across each figure, things become more unequal. So for the countries shown in figure 3, Sweden is the most equal and South Africa the most unequal. One myth that the figures dispel is that inequality is needed for prosperity. The vertical bars on the figures show gross national income (GNI) per capita referring to the measures at the left of each figure. GNI per capita is a measure of prosperity.[14] The majority of the most prosperous countries, with the highest GNIs per capita, are at the left side of each figure, where inequality is lowest. The least prosperous countries are concentrated more at the right and have much higher levels of inequality. The United States is an anomaly, being both prosperous and having high inequality. It is also worth noting that there are many countries as prosperous as the United States and some with greater prosperity. Looking at figure 4, we see that Singapore is the only country other than the United States with a high GNI per capita and high inequality. As we saw in figure 2, over the past forty years, the United States has moved from a level of inequality similar to other developed countries (Gini coefficient below about 0.35) to a level of inequality today that mirrors developing countries still trying to build their economies. This raises serious questions about the ability of our society to maintain its current level of prosperity if the level of inequality were to stay the same or increase. A critical question is, where would we like our society to move in the future? Is it to move toward further inequality and economic and social deprivation, or to greater equality and the benefits that brings? I suggest that the answer is clear: the path of greater equality is vastly preferable. And this is where business and collaboration with nonprofits and the public sector can make a major contribution.

The situation is not without its challenges. It is hardly surprising that in the United States we recently had the largest economic downturn since the Depression of the 1930s, as income and wealth inequality again reached levels not seen since then.[15] Consistent with the trend we have just seen, the share of total income accrued by the richest 1 percent of U.S. households increased from 10 to 21 percent between 1980 and 2008; this makes the

United States one of the most unequal countries in the world.[16] Income for the richest 1 percent increased at a rate 17 times that of the poorest 20 percent between 1979 and 2007, while tax rates have plummeted for the wealthiest households since the 1970s.[17] With income and wealth concentrated in the hands of a few, purchasing power of those in our broader community is so reduced that our economy stalls like a plane running out of fuel.[18] The poverty rate was 15.0 percent in 2011, or 46.2 million people, an increase of 2.6 million people from 2009.[19] That's more people living in poverty inside the United States than the entire population of Canada. Particularly alarming is the increase in poverty for children under age 18: more than one in five lived in poverty in 2011.[20] The number of people without health insurance was 48.6 million in 2011 or 15.7 percent of the population.[21] At the same time, 14.9 percent of households (17.9 million households) were food-insecure at least some time during 2011, and the number of children receiving subsidized lunches because of financial need rose to 21 million in the 2010–2011 school year, up 17 percent from four years earlier.[22] Levels of food insecurity in 2008–2011 were the highest since 1995 when the first national food security survey was conducted.[23] Meanwhile, the number of homeless youth and children increased by 41 percent, from the 2006–2007 school year to the 2008–2009 school year, to more than 950,000 students in 2008–2009.[24]

These problems might seem insurmountable, beyond our control. However, nothing is further from the truth since this is of our own doing. Taxation policy in the United States, which has favored the wealthy since the 1980s, is part of the reason for this growing inequality.[25] Moreover, Sarah Anderson and her colleagues note that in 2010 the average compensation for chief executive officers (CEOs) of major U.S. corporations was about 325 times the average compensation of American workers, and others have shown similar, disproportionately high CEO earnings in recent years.[26] With this degree of inequity, a CEO typically earns more in one day than an average worker earns in a year. By contrast, in the 1970s few senior executives made more than 30 times what their workers made.[27] The performance of the companies with the highest-paid CEOs was much worse than industry average in one study.[28] Executive compensation roared back in 2010. Total compensation for the top five executives in the Standard & Poor's (S&P) 500 companies increased by 13.9 percent from 2009 to 2010, while median total compensation for S&P 500 CEOs increased by 35 percent in 2010.[29] By comparison, average compensation for all civilian employees in the United States only increased by 1.9 percent in 2010.[30] Yet we see an organization like the U.S. Chamber of Commerce working against sorely needed social legislation such as healthcare reform.[31]

However, there are others who shine brightly. Warren Buffett displayed a refreshing perspective: "My friends and I have been coddled long enough by a billionaire-friendly Congress. It's time for our government to get serious about shared sacrifice."[32] And Muhammad Yunus, founder of the Grameen Bank and Nobel Peace Prize recipient, stated, "I strongly believe that we can create a poverty-free world, if we want to. We can create a world where there won't be a single human being who may be described as a poor person. In that kind of a world, [the] only place you can see poverty will be in the museums."[33] Another forward thinker, Tommy Douglas, founder of the Canadian public healthcare system (and a national hero for that), said, "Courage, my friends; 'tis not too late to build a better world."[34] The hope offered by the perceptions and examples in this book is that business can play a key role in creating this better world. A poetic view is provided by Sam Intrator and Megan Scribner who beautifully draw out the inner thoughts of leaders, for example, John Bogle, founder of the Vanguard Group: "My goals . . . to return capitalism to its original values, including trusting and being trusted. At the heart of that quest is the idealism that has permeated my life and my conviction that in these remaining years, I must give something back to the world that has given me so much."[35] It is with this conviction of building trust and giving back that we see the threads of social responsibility weave through our journey. And it is with this perspective that the voices of those writing this book bring their inspiring views and stories.

Our book is in two parts: part I addresses primarily principles, framework, and some applications; part II focuses on exploring examples, recognizing that our authors blend these aspects in their writing. In chapter 1, we examine the interconnection of business, nonprofits, and the public sector; the responsibilities of business to connected constituencies; and the implications for leadership. In chapter 2 Megan Roberts Koller, Emet Mohr, and

Pearl Sims build on a relationship framework to describe core principles of corporate social responsibility, focusing then on an educational partnership as an illustration of these principles. This partnership, between Chemonics International and the Republic of Georgia, achieves both private gain and public good. In chapter 3, Richard Vicenzi, with examples, provides perspectives on the ethical foundations of corporate social responsibility; he then explores how people typically measure the effective practice of social responsibility, as well as how we might enhance such measures in the future. Interesting to note is that these suggested enhancements point to the framework used in chapter 2. Barbara Langsdale in chapter 4 explores how to establish effective partnerships between for-profit and nonprofit entities. Barbara addresses how businesses can best plan to incorporate a philanthropic mission, and when and how nonprofits can engage with business organizations. Given the community benefits of socially responsible business behavior, government has a vested interest in supporting such actions. Andrew Domek completes part I in chapter 5 by examining strategies that governmental entities use to move business toward social responsibility and offers perspectives on efforts to increase such behavior.

Aaron Hurst introduces part II with chapter 6, describing examples of how companies offer nonprofit organizations knowledge through pro bono partnerships, where leveraging employee capabilities is central to community outreach. In chapter 7 Linda Williams explores the benefits of public and private sector collaboration. Linda describes an example of collaboration focused on employment needs in the community. We then move to three chapters that provide complementary insights into different aspects of healthcare in the United States. Universal, equitable access to healthcare is central to a socially responsible society. Our market-based approach to healthcare in this country is failing, excluding large numbers of people from coverage, incurring costs far in excess of other countries, and delivering worse outcomes. U.S. healthcare reform, by moving closer to providing equitable healthcare access for all, is a first step. In chapter 8 Deborah LeVeen explores the rationale and benefits of strong U.S. public policy to guide healthcare reform that will provide universal access. Deborah explores the structural problems that brought us to this point and shows how to build on the strengths of the 2010 healthcare reform legislation to address these structural issues; she then examines the implications for business. There are some bright lights in the healthcare sector, organizations that strive to serve their communities. Kaiser Permanente is one such organization. In chapter 9 Allyne Beach, Laura Long, and Bob Redlo explain how important an element cultural competency is in providing equitable access to healthcare as a socially responsible practice. They go on to consider the workforce implications of this factor and healthcare reform, using Kaiser Permanente as an example. In Chapter 10, staying with Kaiser Permanente and the healthcare sector, Zeth Ajemian examines labor-management partnerships and how they contribute to socially responsible workforce behavior, behavior that benefits individuals, organizations, labor unions, and the community. Zeth draws conclusions that are relevant to many sectors. We switch our focus in chapter 11 to the financial sector. In this chapter Jim Leatherberry addresses stakeholders and their needs, examining institutions and individuals successfully practicing social responsibility and those that have been challenged.

Finally we offer some concluding thoughts exploring foundation principles for the future, the connection to happiness, the importance of reversing growing inequality and how this might begin, and the role of business in building strong communities that honor all, including the least powerful. In our exploration of social responsibility in this book, we look through the lenses of different kinds of organizations, whether for-profit, nonprofit, or public/government; we look at different sectors and see connecting themes; and we embrace the relationships needed for social responsibility in business to thrive. We are glad that you are taking this journey with us, and we welcome you as a fellow traveler.

PART I

PRINCIPLES, FRAMEWORK, AND APPLICATIONS

I belong . . . to a privileged minority. Everyone reading this
sentence belongs, in fact, for only a small percentage of the
world's people has the ability and leisure to read and the
resources to buy a book. How do we, the "privileged ones,"
act as stewards of the grace we have received? We can begin
. . . by ripping off the labels we so thoughtlessly slap on others unlike ourselves. We can begin by finding a community
that nourishes compassion for the weak, an instinct that
privilege tends to suppress. We can begin with humility and
gratitude and reverence, and then move on to pray without
ceasing for the greater gift of love.

—Philip Yancey, *Soul Survivor**

---

* Philip Yancey, *Soul Survivor: How My Faith Survived the Church* (New York: Doubleday
Religious Publishing Group, 2003), 107.

1

Integrating Needs So We All Benefit

Ron Elsdon

"I wanted to be a blessing to someone." These moving words, spoken in one of our exit interviews by a person after leaving an organization, show the depth of connection people often seek in their work. This feeling comes up in other ways too. For example, when we ask people what kind of relationship they would like with their work, ranging from a job, which is only about material reward, to a vocation, which is about a calling in the service of a greater good, most say they would like to come closer to a sense of calling.[1] We seek a sense of purpose in our work and will contribute much to that end.

Socially responsible businesses provide such a connection. Here is how David Packard, one of the cofounders of Hewlett-Packard, puts it, "I think people assume, wrongly, that a company exists solely to make money. Money is an important part of a company's existence, if the company is any good. But a result is not a cause. We have to go deeper and find the real reason for our being. . . . A group of people get together and exist as an institution that we call a company, so that they are able to accomplish something collectively that they could not accomplish separately—they make a contribution to society."[2] Some other corporate leaders from successful companies—such as John Mackey, CEO of Whole Foods Market; Howard Schultz, chairman and CEO of Starbucks; and Jim Sinegal, CEO of Costco—express similar sentiments.[3]

This awareness of broad responsibility takes place in a U.S. society that, at its best, seeks to honor all, as in these words of Franklin Roosevelt: "We have always known that heedless self-interest was bad morals; we know now that it is bad economics. . . . The test of our progress is not whether we add more to the abundance of those who have much; it is whether we provide enough for those who have too little. . . . By using new materials of social justice we have undertaken to erect on the old foundations a more enduring structure for the better use of future generations."[4] Today, too, we have a duty to future generations to protect that foundation for it is threatened again by similar forces of greed and self-interest that brought on the Great Depression. Now, as then, government can create structures within which organizations can function well while protecting the interests of individuals.

What is missing from our landscape? So far it includes individuals, for-profit companies, and the public sector. We can add a final piece to complete the picture: nonprofit organizations. Nonprofits address the common good and do not distribute profits to owners; rather, income is used to further the organization's purpose. The many forms of nonprofit structures are governed by country-specific regulations. In the United States, a common tax-exempt designation, 501(c)(3), covers a broad range of nonprofits in areas like social, religious, educational, charitable, and scientific causes. For example, the Food Bank of Contra Costa and Solano, near where I live in California, has such a designation. Nonprofits satisfy important community needs. Although, as Larry Sly, the executive director of our local food bank, points out, "I wish we would agree that no one in our society should go hungry and we would take the necessary steps to make that true. But in the meantime, the Food Bank will continue to feed those in need."[5]

SOCIAL RESPONSIBILITY LANDSCAPE: INTERCONNECTED GROUPS

This brings us to how these various groups fit together and where the world of business fits in. Let's map out the landscape. Figure 5 illustrates the three types of organizations in service to individuals and communities.

As we explore how the three types of organizations—for-profit, nonprofit, and public sector—can work well together, the lens we use to assess success is that of individual, organization, and community benefit for individuals, organizations, and communities are connected to all three groups. The sizes of the three groups will change according to the type of economic system in place. In a market-driven economy such as that of the United

FIGURE 5. Types of Organizations

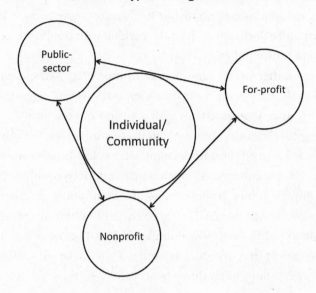

States, for-profit organizations account for much of the economic activity. However, more than 1.5 million nonprofits existed in the United States in 2010 with revenue of $1.7 trillion, and the public sector accounted for about 42 percent of U.S. GDP (U.S. GDP exceeded $14 trillion in 2010). Therefore, each leg of this three-legged stool is significant and a testament to the breadth of the economic base.[6] The balance shifts when moving to community-based economies; in these economies, there is greater economic equality and greater individual economic mobility, such as in Sweden or Norway whose public sectors account for 50–60 percent of GDP. In economies controlled by a small minority of people, unfortunately, the lens of individual, organization, and community benefit may seem irrelevant because of the inequities that exist. However, such a benefit is not irrelevant for the future well-being of those societies.

As we can see from the two-headed arrows in figure 5, organizations of each type ideally work together in partnership. For example, representatives of the food bank let for-profit partners know about financial and practical food distribution needs, while adjusting services according to resources given. And public-sector workforce investment boards must understand the employment needs of for-profit partners and change learning programs as needs shift. Moreover, based on changing public policy and population demographics, nonprofit healthcare organizations have to alter their structure and approach while working with public-sector agencies to help guide future policy.

Into this rather messy mix of organizations, agencies, communities, and individuals, each with their own expectations and agendas, we now need to introduce constituencies with a vested interest in what happens. By mapping the organizations and their constituencies, we can begin to disentangle their needs and understand where and how business can best contribute. Here are the main constituencies connected with our organizations: employees, senior leaders, investors, community members, suppliers, customers, and partners. The three types of organizations—for-profit, nonprofit, and public sector—are similar in how they work with most constituencies, except that investors are only in the for-profit sector and that customer expectations likely differ by sector.

THE CONSTITUENCIES OF FOR-PROFIT BUSINESSES

Let's focus on for-profit businesses and their constituencies. In table 1 each constituency lists social responsibilities for businesses to that constituency, business benefits from the relationship, and potential challenges and tensions that might surface. The responsibilities relate directly to socially responsible business practices.

We'll look at each constituency in turn, beginning with employees. In today's work world and the work world of the future, staying employable means continuing to develop new skills. The types of skills are shifting rapidly as new technologies emerge and work takes new shapes, for example, the use of electronic medical records in healthcare.[7] By 2018, one projection shows that about two-thirds of all employment will require some college education or better.[8] What role does business play here? Is it a matter of just letting everyone fend for themselves or does the organization have a role to play? Enlightened and successful organizations support individual growth and development. By honoring this important ethical responsibility, businesses gain affiliation, strengthened contribution, and, therefore, productivity.[9] Creating a place where people develop and prosper not only strengthens individuals, organizations, and communities, it is good business

TABLE 1. Business Organizations and Their Constituencies

Constituencies	Organization (Social) Responsibilities	Organization Benefits	Potential Challenges and Tensions
Employees	Support of individual development and growth	Increased affiliation and contribution	Sustainable employment with a changing economy, equitable compensation
Senior leaders	Establishment of appropriate governance practices	Growth and stability	Integrating the needs of different constituencies
Investors	Financial return	Resources for growth	Balancing long- and short-term needs
Community members	Services, products, employment, and investment returns; respect for the environment	Infrastructure and community resources	Equitable distribution of resources, environmental issues
Suppliers	Communicating needs, honoring commitments	Needed products and services	Quality and consistency of incoming materials/ services
Customers	Supplying evolving needs while meeting commitments	Payment and learning	Financial pressures
Partners	Honoring agreements	Support	Divergent objectives

practice. Yet it doesn't come without challenges and tensions. For example, creating sustainable employment through economic cycles is not easy; it likely means running lean at times, adjusting operations to handle profitability swings, and balancing permanent and contingent workforces. There is also the important issue of equitable compensation, which, as we have seen in the introduction, has been sorely compromised in the United States.

This brings us to the next constituency, senior leaders, and, in turn, to corporate governance. When we look at current corporate governance, we are confronted with an uncomfortable reality: many governance structures primarily serve the interests of a few (those at senior organizational levels) at the expense of many (employees and shareholders). So we are challenged to ask questions about governance and how to strengthen it. What do we mean by governance? The United Nations Economic and Social Commission for Asia and the Pacific (UNESCAP) defines it this way—"the process of decision-making and the process by which decisions are implemented (or not implemented)."[10] UNESCAP goes on to identify the characteristics of good governance as governance that is accountable, transparent, responsive, equitable and inclusive, effective and efficient; that follows the rule of law; and that is participatory and consensus oriented. We see a blend of characteristics that show respect for individuals and allow all voices to be heard in decision making. These characteristics are equally applicable at the organization or community level. They can become criteria for assessing how well a particular governance structure is working. We can acknowledge the challenge of meeting these ideals. In corporate failures such as Enron, most, perhaps all, of these characteristics are violated. Other crises of organizational confidence may stem from violation of one or more characteristics. So a key social responsibility of organizations to senior leaders is to establish the right governance practices. Such practices mean that the rights of all parties are protected and that senior leaders can focus on the organization's growth and stability.

Unfortunately, we have much to learn in this area as excessively high CEO compensation, divorced from both performance and average pay in organizations, has exposed the ruthlessness of some current approaches to corporate governance in the United States.[11] Fortunately, we do have some good examples like Jim Sinegal, CEO of Costco: "Having an individual who is making 100 or 200 or 300 times more than the average person on the floor is wrong."[12] Senior leaders are responsible for ensuring that businesses fully realize their long-term value contribution, namely, their social contribution.[13] So a particular leadership challenge is integrating the needs of various constituencies, which can include both people in the organization and those outside. This brings us to the next constituency: investors.

Investors include owners of the organization—the shareholders—and those who lend money to it, or the bondholders. Both groups provide resources for business growth. In generating financial returns to investors, businesses convert the work of many employees into economic value and then distribute it. In today's interconnected financial world, some people are employees and, as investors, they are also part owners or lenders. So when businesses create value, they transfer that value in part through investment holdings into the broader community. However, this transfer is not evenly distributed; those in the top 10 percent of income in the United States own close to 80 percent of all stocks.[14] If businesses only generate returns for shareholders, they exacerbate already large inequities. Therefore businesses also need to address other aspects of social responsibility. And in doing this, one challenge they may face is balancing long- and short-term gains, for example, giving up some profit today for future gain. Other aspects of social responsibility may include strengthening surrounding communities by supporting education programs in skill areas that will be needed for the future. This brings us to community members, our next constituency.

Businesses' social responsibility to community members is to provide services or products, employment, and investment returns while respecting the environment. Businesses share some of the value they create with the community directly by compensating employees and indirectly by not only addressing community needs with services and products but also generating returns on investment holdings. Social responsibility includes sustaining these activities over time, supporting employment practices that meet people's financial and work/life needs, and using business practices that honor legal, ethical, and environmental considerations. In turn, businesses benefit from community infrastructure in areas such as transportation, education, and communication. Exchange with the community can involve purchase of services from other organizations or tax payments to the public sector in support of the common good. All these factors underline the reasons the social responsibility of business is important: community prosperity is strongly linked to business success, and business success is dependent on vibrant communities. Potential challenges comprise ensuring that operating practices protect the environment and managing resources effectively, such as limiting pay inequities as we described earlier, so that all employees receive a living wage. Operating practices also include paying attention to relationships with suppliers, our next constituency.

The social responsibility of businesses to suppliers includes selecting suppliers with ethical operating practices, explaining needs well, and honoring commitments.[15] Accordingly, suppliers grow stronger so that they, in turn, can operate in a socially responsible manner. In return, businesses seek needed products and services at competitive prices while meeting quality requirements. Similarly, businesses must meet the requirements of their customers, the next constituency. This means keeping commitments and flexing with changing customer needs. Customers are integral to the value creation process through their purchases, which generate cash flow used to fund operations and provide benefits to other constituencies. Customers are also central to learning and collaborating around changing market needs. Social responsibility includes a willingness to stop serving customers who violate ethical employment or operating practices, for example, environmental requirements. Potential pressures include financial and pricing issues.

This brings us to the final constituency: partners. Partners can include a wide range of organizations: nonprofits, public-sector groups, or other firms that may offer complementary services or products appealing to customers; they may also include those that offer access to different geographic regions. We will explore some of these potential partnerships in later chapters. For the moment we can acknowledge that social responsibility includes selecting partners that share values and honoring commitments to those partners. Businesses benefit by receiving support. A potential challenge is that the objectives of partners, which may be closely aligned at the start of a relationship, may diverge over time. For example, if one organization is focused on growth through reinvestment and the other is focused on short-term profits, it may be necessary to redefine or terminate the partnership.

STRATEGIC ASPECTS AND ORGANIZATIONAL STEWARDSHIP

We can see that firms and their constituencies are connected by a combination of giving and receiving, with social responsibility interwoven into these relationships. What does this mean for business leadership, strategy, and operating practices? Simon Zadek and his colleagues describe a framework for corporate responsibility linking business practices to social policy, in the process creating a national corporate responsibility index. The factors within organizations that contribute to the national index relate to corporate governance, ethical practices, and human capital development (for example, worker rights and training and employee development). Zadek and his colleagues also describe five learning stages firms go through in adopting socially responsible practices.[16] The five learning stages are as follows:

• Defensive—Deny practices, outcomes, or responsibilities.
• Compliance—Adopt a policy-based compliance approach as a cost of doing business.
• Managerial—Embed societal issues into core management processes (daily operations).
• Strategic—Integrate societal issues into core business strategies.
• Civil—Promote broad industry participation in corporate responsibility (collective action).

As businesses mature in the area of social responsibility, they move from denial to ultimately a stage of broad industry participation, for example, companies participating in global climate change initiatives.[17] Furthermore, Zadek identifies the evolution sequence of social issues as: latent, emerging, consolidating, and institutionalized.[18] For a given organization and a particular social issue, socially responsible business practice and strategy is built at the intersection of the organization's learning stage and the evolution of the social issue.

William Werther and David Chandler point out that such socially responsible business strategy needs to incorporate a range of stakeholders, similar to the constituencies we introduced earlier:[19]

• Organizational stakeholders—employees, managers, shareholders, unions
• Economic stakeholders—customers, competitors, creditors, distributors, suppliers
• Societal stakeholders—government/regulators, communities, nonprofits and nongovernmental organizations, environment

This perspective reinforces how broad the constituencies are that are influenced by business social responsibility and therefore its significance for individuals, organizations, and communities. Given such breadth, effective leadership is central to embracing and implementing the principles of business social responsibility. Let's examine what this means, recognizing that leaders can be anyone in the organization, not just those vested with formal authority. Leaders have a key role in letting others in the organization know about socially responsible practices, and about constituencies affected by those practices, while creating ethical and operating frameworks within which these practices can be implemented. This means demonstrating leadership courage.

LEADERSHIP

There are some aspects of organizational stewardship, such as generating consensus about the ethical framework for a firm's operations, that are mainly senior leaders' responsibility. Overarching ethical frameworks can build on a values-based approach, a compliance-based approach, or a combination of the two.[20] On the one hand, the values-based approach emphasizes important goals for the firm, the means to achieve those goals, and motivations. The compliance-based approach, on the other hand, emphasizes rules and limits that need to be respected. For example, Southwest Airlines strictly enforces a compliance code when it instructs pilots precisely on how to fly planes to ensure safety standards are met. However, in meeting customer needs, Southwest uses a values-based approach, encouraging flexibility by pilots and flight attendants in making the flying experience as entertaining as possible.[21] After creating an ethical framework, it is then a matter of leading in a way that engages, includes, and inspires others. This brings us back to social responsibility and how leaders behave, again emphasizing that everyone in the organization carries leadership responsibility. Since there are many approaches proposed for effective leadership, it is clear that this is more a subjective art than an objective science, which is not surprising given the many factors that influence leadership success. However, there are helpful views on leadership that stand out as either based on comprehensive analyses or as intuitively appealing. We'll look at some of these views and what they mean for socially responsible leadership. Daniel Goleman, Richard Boyatzis, and Annie McKee identify personal competence (how we manage ourselves) and social competence (how we manage relationships) as key domains of emotional intelligence for leadership, with associated competencies:[22]

- Personal competence
  - Self-awareness
    - Emotional self-awareness, accurate self-assessment, self-confidence
  - Self-management
    - Emotional self-control, transparency, adaptability, achievement, initiative, optimism
- Social competence
  - Social awareness
    - Empathy, organizational awareness, service
  - Relationship management
    - Inspirational leadership, influence, developing others, change catalyst, conflict management, building bonds, teamwork, and collaboration

The authors go on to identify different styles of leadership in two broad categories—resonant, which are most successful, and dissonant, which should be used with caution:[23]

- Resonant
  - Visionary (most effective overall), coaching, affiliative, democratic
- Dissonant
  - Pacesetting, commanding

The resonant approaches to leadership are consistent with the human capital aspects of Zadek's corporate responsibility index mentioned earlier. Jim Collins offers a similar view of leadership to Goleman and his colleagues observing that "Level 5 leaders [the most effective] display a compelling modesty, are self-effacing and understated. In contrast, two thirds of the comparison companies had leaders with gargantuan personal egos that contributed to the demise or continued mediocrity of the company."[24] We see similar ideas expressed by Robert Greenleaf about servant leadership, built on the principles of listening, empathy, healing, awareness, persuasion, conceptualization, foresight, stewardship, commitment to the growth of others, and building community.[25] Again we see the direct connection between these characteristics and social responsibility.

Another view, well aligned with social responsibility and the principles of servant leadership, is based on the roles of effective leaders.[26] These roles include the following: guide, mentor, coach, conductor, artist, visionary, entrepreneur, innovator, general, change agent, and connector. We can also learn from the insights of the Management Research Group (MRG), which assessed effective leadership behaviors in North America by linking feedback from others about senior leaders to their perceived effectiveness. MRG found the most important leadership behaviors to be a combination of strategic capability and interpersonal skills, such as communication, empathy, persuasiveness, and an ability to generate excitement.[27] The combination of foresight and interpersonal skills is fundamental to the effective practice of social responsibility. Further insights are provided by an IBM study of global senior leader effectiveness, where the attributes of creativity, listening well to customers, simplicity, and speed rose to the top.[28] And we are reminded by the words of Warren Buffet about how central social responsibility is to effective business leadership: "I do think that when you're treated enormously well by this market system . . . I think society has a big claim on that."[29] This brings us full circle to socially responsible business leadership embracing strategic insight, operational effectiveness, interpersonal sensitivity, and openness to the inclusion and welfare of others.

In summary, we have looked through the lens of individual, organization, and community benefit at the interconnection of three groups: for-profit companies, public-sector organizations, and nonprofits. We have explored how for-profit businesses relate to their constituencies and what this means for social responsibility. We have linked business strategic direction and social policy and examined what this means for effective leadership practices. Now we continue our journey, guided by thoughtful and experienced practitioners, exploring social responsibility in a variety of settings. We begin with an educational setting outside the United States and examine a framework for assessing the contribution of socially responsible relationships.

2

Corporate Social Responsibility: Lessons from Educational Practice in an Emerging Democracy

Megan Roberts Koller, Emet Mohr, and Pearl Sims[1]

In 2004, after a thirteen-year period that included the fall of the Soviet Union, the outbreak of civil war, and increasing economic hardships, a new government in the Republic of Georgia was birthed through the Rose Revolution with the explicit mandate for systemic governmental change. Georgia had not accomplished these drastic moves toward democratic reforms alone. The United States has provided over $3 billion in assistance to Georgia since its independence in 1991. Much of the assistance had come through U.S. corporations and nonprofits committed to helping the struggling democracy in its ongoing transition to a free, prosperous, market-oriented nation firmly anchored in the Euro-Atlantic community.

Many of those helping Georgia after the Rose Revolution were organizations committed to modeling corporate social responsibility—a difficult task given the history of the country's corruption under the Soviet Union. Few examples existed for the nation on how to conduct business in ways that produced both profit and social benefit, and even fewer on showing how businesses could relate responsibly to the world around them. Into this void, the U.S. State Department sent U.S. organizations. This chapter is the story of how one private sector corporation, Chemonics International, carried out its social responsibility through relationship building.

As corporations pursue growth through global and international efforts, pressure on them has increased from shareholders and government regulators to prominently address their obligations toward society. In an effort to meet these obligations, organizations may understandably turn to the traditional corporate social responsibility (CSR) methodologies that have emerged over the past three decades. In 2008, Kunal Basu from the University of Oxford and Guido Palazzo from the University of Lausanne proposed an approach for analyzing the way a company's leaders and staff think, discuss, and act in building relationships with the organization's stakeholders.[2] Basu and Palazzo suggest that going beyond the more traditional approach of analyzing activities and projects "could help explain CSR behavior in terms of . . . what constitutes appropriate relationships with their [a corporation's] stakeholders and of the world in which they exist."[3] This analytical approach seems particularly relevant as U.S. corporations extend their reach into emerging democracies and into developing nations.

This chapter builds on Basu and Palazzo's definition of corporate social responsibility by exploring the relationships of one international development corporation (Chemonics International) in one sector (education) of one country (the Republic of Georgia), through interviews, field observations, and the analyses of project artifacts. Our aim is to understand what the leaders of the education management project in Georgia (funded by the U.S. Agency for International Development [USAID]) think, say, and do in relation to those it seeks to serve in this fledgling democracy. Using Basu and Palazzo's framework to better understand socially responsible relationships within one project of one international development organization can shed light on understanding how an organization's socially responsible relationships inform and strengthen its ability to engage with the world and ultimately to do effective and economically viable work.

CSR ACCORDING TO BASU AND PALAZZO

In their book *Reframing Organizations*, Lee Bolman and Terrence Deal explain the need for a sophisticated, nuanced, and yet practical way to describe organizations and the outcomes they create.[4] Focusing only on outcomes, such as specific metrics, or only on one viewpoint, such as middle management, does not provide enough information to fully understand what is happening and why. Effective frameworks and mental models need to be "powerful enough to capture the subtlety and complexity of organizational life, yet simple enough not to overwhelm the manager or leader."[5]

They describe frames as "both windows on the world and lenses that bring the world into focus. Frames filter out some things while allowing others to pass through easily."[6] Bolman and Deal also argue, not surprisingly, that companies tend to produce more of what is measured.

Therefore, if CSR analysis continues to focus primarily on projects, programs, and other outputs of a company's work, it may be tempting to view such activities as the entirety of socially responsible behavior. By using a framework that looks beyond outputs to the heart of an organization's interactions, we can begin to paint a more complete picture of corporate social responsibility. When a business is behaving well, not only will it produce profit through socially responsible programs, projects, or products, but it will also model socially responsible relationships. Approaching a deeper look at CSR may be analogous to viewing an iceberg. Icebergs are largely hidden below the waterline. Diving beneath the waterline takes skill and time. Most of all, it takes knowing how to ask the right questions once underwater. Regrettably, in a world rich with frameworks and examples of how to study CSR programs and activities (above the waterline), few methods exist for asking the right questions regarding relationships below the waterline.

Basu and Palazzo's research was propelled by their belief that examining what projects and programs a company may carry out to fulfill its social responsibility is a necessary but not sufficient step in understanding how the company's leadership thinks, speaks, and acts in socially responsible ways, that is, how it relates with all stakeholders. This framework puts forth three categories of critical questions that can aid in a below-the-waterline view of socially responsible corporations through the lens of relationships. The cognitive category asks questions about how an organization's leadership thinks. The linguistic view questions how an organization's leadership speaks. And the conative view seeks to understand how an organization's leadership acts and reacts to outside forces.[7] The three categories of questions are further described in the following.

Cognitive View: How an Organization's Leadership Thinks about Relationships

According to the cognitive view, a major part of describing a company's social responsibility is understanding how that company's leaders (recognizing that everyone in an organization can play a leadership role) think about the organization itself and the relationships with stakeholders, and how these leaders hope the stakeholders will think about the organization. Basu and Palazzo explain that how "managers view themselves . . . is likely to influence the type of relationships they would choose to build with their stakeholders and the wider world beyond their sphere of business interest."[8]

This aspect of the framework is intended to help organizational leaders better understand how to answer the following questions:

1. How does our organization go about adding value and usefulness to stakeholders?
2. How closely can or should the organization align itself to current stakeholders' views?
3. How can the organization go about partnering with stakeholders to forge new social norms and expectations, especially in times of significant change?[9]

Linguistic View: How an Organization's Leadership Speaks about Relationships

Once it is clear how a company's leaders think about the organization and others (cognitive view), we can look at the linguistic view, which addresses how and why information is shared with stakeholders.[10] A corporation's leaders must seek to answer two major questions regarding the linguistic view of the framework:

1. How does the corporation explain and justify its decisions to stakeholders?
2. How transparent will the organization be? How much and what kinds of information will the company choose to share?[11]

Conative View: How an Organization's Leadership Acts in Relationships

The final view (conative) describes how people within companies make and execute socially responsible decisions. Every company must respond to changes in external factors, and these reactions provide an important viewpoint of corporate character. This category is concerned with the following questions:

1. How should the company react (posture) to outside forces?
2. How consistent are decisions made in the organization over time and among different projects and activities, and how do decision makers at various levels of the organization support them?
3. How committed are people within the organization to acting in a socially responsible manner with all stakeholders?

Helping a corporation's leaders examine how they think, speak, and act in relationships is particularly relevant to those organizations that operate in fledgling democracies, such as the Republic of Georgia.

THE CONTEXT: THE REPUBLIC OF GEORGIA

The Republic of Georgia, located in the South Caucasus region of Eurasia, lies at the crossroads of Eastern Europe and Western Asia. It comprises an area that is slightly smaller than the state of South Carolina with a population of approximately 4.6 million people. Its capital, Tbilisi, located in the beautiful Mtkvari River valley, has a population of approximately 1.1 million people and is more than 1,500 years old. The country's recorded history dates back more than 2,500 years. Georgia has been historically situated on the margins of great empires, and Georgians have lived together in a unified state for only a fraction of their existence as a people. Since at least the first century B.C. through the eighteenth century, much of the country's territory was fought over by Persian, Roman, Byzantine, Arab, Mongol, and Turkish armies. In 1783, Georgia became a protectorate of Russia; in 1801 the Russian Empire began the piecemeal process of unifying and annexing Georgian territory. For most of the next two centuries (1801–1991), Georgia was ruled from St. Petersburg or Moscow.[12]

On April 9, 1991, shortly before the collapse of the Soviet Union, the Supreme Council of the Republic of Georgia declared independence from the USSR. Like other former Soviet republics, Georgia's newly declared independence was followed by ethnic and civil strife. Secessionists took control of parts of South Ossetia and most of Abkhazia prior to cease-fire agreements brokered in 1992 and 1994, respectively. Georgia began to stabilize in 1995. In 2004, when a new government came into power, officials took action against endemic corruption, receiving plaudits from the World

Bank. Further reforms from 2006 to 2011 aimed at fostering respect for, and strengthening, the rule of law, increasing media transparency, and improving the election process. In the educational arena, reforms included implementation of a fair entrance examination process for the university system. The World Bank has since recognized Georgia as one of the world's fastest-reforming economies. In 2011, it was ranked as the world's 12th-easiest place to do business, an improvement from 115th in 2005, and it now sits in the same tier as such countries as Australia, Norway, and Japan.[13]

As part of the change associated with the Rose Revolution, Georgia underwent a process of education decentralization. This process gave schools full legal autonomy (as independent legal entities), created individual boards of trustees for each school as a mechanism for school oversight, and eliminated municipal ministry of education bureaus, institutions historically plagued by inefficient management and corruption. To replace these bureaus, the reforms created educational resource centers to support schools but strongly limited their control over a school's actual operation. School funding also radically changed at this time from a Soviet-era model—funding school needs as determined by the ministry (the model continued after Georgian independence)—to a per-student funding model that provided individual students with vouchers usable at any educational institution, public or private. Finally, the system embraced student choice by removing geographic boundaries as the determining factor for school placement, allowing parents and students to choose which school to attend. These wide-scale reforms were designed to put the management of schools in local (and parental) hands. In addition, the Georgian government committed to significantly increasing education funding; education expenditures grew from less than 1 percent of GDP in 2003 to 3 percent in 2008. While these education reforms were undertaken swiftly at the legislative level, they were often not fully realized at the school level. An education bureaucracy ossified by decades of centralized command and control management often left principals, teachers, and board of trustee members unable or unwilling to make local decisions.

Above the Waterline: U.S. Efforts in Georgia

In light of these successes and remaining challenges, U.S. programs to help Georgians develop and reform the education sector are an important part of the efforts. U.S. education support in Georgia has been multifaceted, multipronged, and complex. During the time of transition after the Rose Revolution, USAID assisted the Ministry of Education and Science (MES) with national planning for decentralization and with regional implementation through support for education resource centers (ERCs). The World Bank also played an important role in supporting education reforms in many areas, including the creation of a teachers' professional development center to help improve instructional quality in the decentralized system. However, change was hard to measure and highly politicized, with uncertain results. What was certain was that rapid development and implementation of reforms allowed many individual education reformers to take control of schools and use the changed environment to significantly improve them. Although progress had been made, the improved policy environment (a result of the hard work of Georgian policymakers and international donor support) and localized success of individual reform efforts had not yet crystallized into the pervasive educational improvement across the country that policymakers sought. Therefore in 2009, USAID funded the Georgia Education Management Project (EMP) through Chemonics International.

Chemonics is an international development–consulting firm whose self-defined mission is to help people live healthier, more productive, and more independent lives by promoting meaningful change around the world. Chemonics works primarily with USAID and currently implements projects in more than seventy-five countries around the world; sectors are as diverse as financial services, private sector development, health, environmental management, conflict and disaster management, democracy and governance, agriculture, and education. Chemonics' website states, "As a for-profit firm, we strive to provide excellence and value. We set the highest possible performance standards. We innovate to create efficient solutions and make the best use of scarce resources."[14] While Chemonics is a for-profit firm and believes in creating value for shareholders, it operates by choice in a business environment alongside nonprofit and nongovernmental organizations, competing for business based on quality of work and cost. In July 2011, it also fulfilled one of its founder's dreams by becoming 100 percent employee-owned through an employee stock ownership program. This ownership structure allows employees to share in the company's growth through a retirement plan based on company stock and permits the company to remain independent and fully committed to its mission.

Beginning in 2009 Georgia's EMP worked with local educational leaders to solidify systemic improvement aimed at building the long-term capacity of educators and their institutions to manage the education system and ensure the effectiveness of education policies. Working with Ilia State University (ISU), the EMP helped establish a two-year master's degree in education administration and leadership and assisted the MES in creating a training program for education administrators based on standards developed in the United States for high-performing school principals. In addition, the EMP collaborated with MES and education resource centers to enable more effective regional planning and more equitable resource distribution for schools through a revised school funding formula. Finally, the EMP helped the ministry create information technology systems designed to provide data at the school, municipal, and national levels to inform education delivery and policy decision making.

At its core, the EMP looked to enhance decentralization efforts and help transform the legacy of a top-down, Soviet-style education management culture into one that is modern and decentralized. To accomplish this, the EMP focused significant effort on human capacity development within the education system (at national, municipal, and school levels) through on-the-job and course-based training efforts. Creating this link from policy to implementation was at the core of USAID's design and Chemonics' implementation of this project. For example, the project compiled and analyzed historic funding data, with Chemonics' staff working alongside ministry counterparts, to recommend a revised funding formula to promote equity and more efficient funding allocations in the MES student voucher program. Linked to this initiative, the EMP collaborated with the ministry to revise policies related to ERC oversight and support of school funding implementation, trained 146 ERC staff members, and trained over 1,000 school principals to understand the new funding formula and to more effectively manage their budgets in a decentralized environment.

As far as outcomes are concerned, Chemonics could be considered successful at meeting its contractual obligations and therefore at adding value to its own shareholders, USAID, and the people of the Republic of Georgia. However, the most important question is not what they did, but how they did it. The answer to this question lies below the waterline.

Looking Below the Waterline

According to Bolman and Deal, "Organizations are filled with people who have different stories about what is happening and what should be happening. Each story contains a glimpse of the truth, but each is a product of the prejudices and blind spots of the viewer. None of these versions of the truth are comprehensive enough to make the organization truly understandable."[15] Applying the relationship lens can provide a different picture of an organization and its work—one that can augment more traditional frameworks of corporate social responsibility that primarily compare and analyze a company's visible outputs.

To help understand the work of Chemonics' education management project using the three views of Basu and Palazzo, informal surveys and interviews with key stakeholders were conducted about how they viewed Chemonics' relationships with them. Also included was an analysis of a tool developed by Chemonics to guide and measure the projects' progress toward achieving a positive and lasting influence. Chemonics' standards for project excellence, AIMS (achieve, innovate, measure, and share), were created to ensure: that projects achieve their goals, that continual innovation occurs during implementation, and that results are measured and shared inside and outside the organization according to clearly defined standards. Use of these standards was woven into the EMP's plan from the project's beginning, including holding a workshop for all project staff to introduce and discuss the purpose and spirit of AIMS, as well as regular discussions with program staff about their progress in meeting or exceeding the standards at each level. Further, AIMS was used during annual work planning to facilitate the project's continual improvement both in meeting obligations to USAID and Georgian counterparts and in examining how this would be achieved. Following is an initial look at the EMP's work in Georgia, as implemented by Chemonics, through the three views of Basu and Palazzo's framework.

Cognitive View: How Chemonics' Leadership Thinks about Relationships

How an organization's leadership thinks about its stakeholders is one of the major forces shaping that organization's sense of corporate social responsibility. Because the EMP's work is primarily consultative in nature, the project strives to infuse the idea that developing relationships is not only important but also fundamental to providing valuable support to the education system in Georgia. Basu and Palazzo state that organizations with a relational identity "conceive of themselves as being partners in relationships with their stakeholders, often displaying strong personal ties."[16] This relational identity was integrated into the project's planning and implementation by project leadership, often by referencing key concepts from the AIMS standards. For example, showing evidence of the involvement of multiple stakeholders is one of the required criteria to earn the highest rating in project planning on the AIMS standards. Local Georgian education leaders were identified by EMP project leadership and were asked to participate in the first year, in subsequent work planning sessions, and throughout implementation phases.

From the outset of the project, the EMP's fundamental purpose was to help the Georgian Ministry of Education and Science with policy revisions to improve education management across the system and to assist the university in creating a master's of education degree that would help prepare education leaders for Georgia's future. EMP leaders put assurances in place that any suggested changes to the nation's policy or programs as a result of this project would be implemented through the system, not in opposition to it or outside of it. To this end, the project developed and utilized several working groups made up of a broad range of stakeholders as a fundamental tenet of its approach to implementation.

The project's leaders avoided aligning decisions with any one stakeholder's views by incorporating multiple stakeholder groups in the discussions. The focus was on helping stakeholders clarify objectives, analyze their views, and determine what additional decisions would need to be made to achieve the changes they desired. Principals, ministry staff, university professors, finance specialists, and representatives from local nongovernmental organizations (NGOs) all participated in the development of national standards for principals and in the creation of a new funding formula for schools. The EMP's primary purpose was to help guide them down the path of educational reform, not to support or marginalize any particular group's self-interest. By maintaining a keen eye on the outcomes produced by collaborative work, the results were seen as valuable and useful by all involved. More important, by attending to various groups involved in the projects, the EMP protected itself from being aligned with any one group. The success of the entire work group, including all stakeholders, helped forge new ways of thinking about education in Georgia. Because the EMP's project staff legitimized each stakeholder's role and contribution to the changes being discussed, Georgian educational leaders viewed the work as their own. The EMP project staff became known as the convener of the group's work, not as the sole owner of it.

Linguistic View: How Chemonics' Leadership Speaks about Relationships

Basu and Palazzo explain that "how organizations justify their actions to others might be viewed as reflecting how they interpret their relationships with stakeholders and view their broader responsibility to society."[17] Chemonics leaders are intensely focused on creating strong partnerships with stakeholders, and this has implications for how actions are justified. The company's leaders define success as not only fulfilling a contract with USAID but also fulfilling the AIMS standards. As another component of AIMS, the EMP is challenged to constantly innovate and look for new and better solutions to problems. This focus on innovation led to an extensive research program involving all key stakeholders about implementing a decentralized approach to education management in Georgia. Over the course of six months, the EMP conducted interviews, focus groups, and surveys across the system utilizing the Organization for Economic Cooperation and Development (OECD) Locus of Decision Making framework to characterize the state of decentralization.[18] At the end of the research, the stakeholders presented the ministry with detailed findings, shared these findings at a conference of mid-level education managers from across Georgia, and developed a condensed policy paper for circulation to the ministry's senior staff. The ministry chose to adopt three out of five policy recommendations. Its justification for adopting these recommendations was made easier because Chemonics chose to involve all stakeholders in an ethical decision-making process grounded in mutual accountability. Another reason the ministry moved forward in accepting these work groups' recommendations was their basis in solid research. Chemonics chose to guide the work group in creating this research project because its internal metrics require such an approach. The AIMS guidelines for successful planning and implementation of a performance management plan (PMP) demand extensive data, research, and analysis, and the sharing of those results. Several major stakeholders in the Republic of Georgia supported this perception; they selected the criterion "based on extensive research or evidence" as the leadership team's most important consideration when making a decision.

Generally, Chemonics strives to be a highly transparent organization. Again, the AIMS standards encourage individual project participants to share best-practice techniques with other organizations in their field. Moreover, Chemonics' employees take pride in this transparency and will share reports, training manuals, and even requests for proposals with other organizations. This absence of proprietary feeling is built into the corporate culture. Chemonics is not eager to help a competitor win a proposal, but it is interested in creating a better understanding of shared development issues and the challenges in a community. While the EMP is committed to transparency, there are times when information is not shared openly. Because of the often-sensitive nature of its work and close working relationship with local governments and USAID, the project must balance its general commitment to transparency and the reality that some work products contain sensitive data that cannot be released by contractual arrangement. Georgian leaders have sometimes been confused by this ambiguity in transparency. Chemonics recognizes this as an area of potential growth and development as they work to create stronger partnerships with local leaders.

Conative View: How Chemonics' Leadership Acts in Relationships

The conative category describes an organization's posture, consistency, and commitment regarding CSR. Posture expresses how an organization reacts to changes in its environment and differentiates itself from other organizations. Basu and Palazzo define an open posture as "the willingness to listen and respond to alternative perspectives offered by others."[19] Through the implementation of working groups and other key stakeholder meetings, the EMP works hard to understand the culture of its local stakeholders and will adjust its behavior as necessary to meet their needs. Because of this open posture, consistency becomes a more complicated issue. Specific behaviors within Chemonics may vary from project to project across the globe, but this reflects a consistent strategy of open posture in order to meet local needs. Chemonics' espoused behaviors intentionally relate back to its core business, which is demonstrated across its policy work in the EMP. The project's primary function is to support effective education decentralization through improvements in education management. A significant part of this work is ensuring that the project does not act as a centralized force. Instead, the project looks to create policies collaboratively that support the development of decentralized leaders and then works with the ministry to implement these policies in ways that affirm local leadership within education.

The final piece in the framework is commitment. Basu and Palazzo explain instrumental commitment as "derived from external incentives" and normative commitment as based on "largely moral considerations."[20] Chemonics is in a special position to reflect both aspects of commitment. Because their work in the Republic of Georgia is based on acting as an agent of USAID, Chemonics' largest client, EMP leadership works hard to guarantee that the project lives up to USAID's needs and expectations. This could be seen as an instrumental level of commitment. However, when Chemonics leaders partnered with USAID, they chose to align the organization with an agency dedicated to the public good and working to improve the quality of life for people around the globe. Chemonics' core business is helping people live healthier, more productive, more independent lives. Perhaps there is no better example of normative commitment than the EMP helping a fledgling democracy educate its children.

CONCLUSION

In looking at the EMP project, we can conclude that relationships do indeed matter. In fact, organizations cannot genuinely act in socially responsible ways without them. However, as Basu and Pallazo's work points out, few frameworks exist that can help organizations make sense of how to think, talk about, and act in relationships. Organizations such as Chemonics offer an opportunity to examine their corporate social responsibility through the cognitive, linguistic, and conative views. These views suggest that Chemonics strives to do the following:

- Be relationally oriented.
- Create moral and pragmatic legitimacy with its stakeholders.
- Base decisions on objective, evidence-based principles.
- Operate with transparency.
- React to challenges with an open posture.
- Maintain strategic and internal consistency, with a deep commitment to all stakeholders.

With the education project in Georgia, Chemonics sought to excel by forming strong partnerships with clients and providing economic and social value while implementing best-practice and well-researched techniques. These actions strengthened relationships between Chemonics and the Ministry of Education and Sciences in Georgia, between Chemonics and USAID, and, ultimately, between the ministry and the Georgian people. This analysis of Chemonics' implementation of the EMP project in Georgia offers only a glimpse of Chemonics' view of corporate social responsibility. But even a glimpse is enough to encourage others to measure CSR by the quality of their relationships and not only by the outcomes of their programs and activities. Certainly, there is much to be learned about CSR by looking below the waterline.

Lessons Learned below the Waterline
From a U.S. perspective, at a time when education in the United States has serious problems regarding student performance, there is much to be learned about how to build quality relationships among government, local communities, and other organizations seeking to influence student learning. The three-yearly OECD Programme for International Student Assessment (PISA) report, which compares the knowledge and skills of fifteen-year-olds in seventy countries around the world, ranked the United States fourteenth out of thirty-four OECD countries for reading skills, seventeenth for science, and a below-average twenty-fifth for mathematics.[21]

Reaction at senior government levels to the U.S. rankings, to critics throughout the nation concerned about the education performance compared with that of other nations, and to the long-term impact on the future economic viability of the country has been, as in the past, a call for more comprehensive reforms. Regrettably, literally hundreds of new programs and activities have been attempted over the last three decades in the name of reforms, mostly with disappointing results. Perhaps it is time to look below the waterline to consider how schools and their leaders can build effective relationships with all stakeholders, the kind seen in the EMP initiative in the Republic of Georgia, rather than try yet another program. Certainly the world rankings offer a wake-up call for the nation. The United States must seriously address education efforts, and where better to start than with a deepening focus on building effective relationships between the government and the communities served. In the next chapter we will focus both on the ethical domain of social responsibility and further explore how to measure social responsibility as practiced.

3

Understanding and Assessing Corporate Social Responsibility in Organizations

Richard Vicenzi

> The fact is that in modern society there is no other leadership group but managers. If the managers of our major institutions, and especially of business, do not take responsibility for the common good, no one else can or will.
>
> —Peter F. Drucker[1]

The introductory quote from Peter Drucker, although written in 1973, is even more cogent today. The ascension of capitalism in the intervening years as the dominant world economic engine underlines the increasing influence of business on social and cultural practices. Leaders of business powerfully influence societal values and behaviors. The nature of this influence in the future will be greatly affected by business leaders' responses to three key questions:

1. Does corporate responsibility extend beyond generating a return on investment to owners (shareholders) to include recognizing the interests of other stakeholders such as customers, employees, and the broader community?
2. Do we need to focus increased attention on resource consumption, particularly in developed economies, as emerging nations rapidly engage in the global economy?
3. Can we measure how all stakeholders benefit from business activity, not just measure return for shareholders?

The response of business leaders to such questions materially affects our future world. Furthermore, what we choose to measure and ignore will significantly influence the outcomes. In this chapter we will explore some fundamental aspects of social responsibility, first providing background perspective, then examining the ethics of corporate social responsibility (CSR), and finally exploring how to measure effectiveness.

A 2010 *Wall Street Journal* article (reprinted from the *MIT/Sloan Management Review*) referencing University of Michigan professor Aneel Karnani raised a firestorm of commentary.[2] In his article, Karnani resurrected the position expressed by Milton Friedman in 1970 that "the social responsibility of business is to increase its profits."[3] Friedman's position is best summarized when he goes on to state that "the responsibility [of the corporate executive] is to conduct the business in accordance with their [the owners of the business] desires, which generally will be to make as much money as possible while conforming to the basic rules of the society, both those embodied in law and those embodied in ethical custom." Karnani takes the argument further than Friedman. He states that managing a business in any way that does not maximize profits is either irrelevant because, naturally, increasing profits simultaneously leads to social benefits (where company profits and society's welfare align), or it is inefficient because companies have a fiduciary responsibility to shareholders to increase profits (where markets are not efficient and private profits and societal welfare are in conflict). Karnani's view is that this latter case would be considered a market failure, which it is not the company's responsibility to correct.

The shortsightedness of this position can be exemplified by the future costs to British Petroleum resulting from the Deepwater Horizon oil spill after a severe blowout of the Macondo deepwater well in the Gulf of Mexico on April 20, 2010. The commission tasked with investigating this disaster found that contributing factors to the accident included lax standards, insufficient training, and a series of decisions that were primarily made to save time at the expense of safety.[4] The report noted, "Corporations understandably encourage cost-saving and efficiency. But given the dangers of deepwater drilling, companies involved must have in place strict policies requiring rigorous analysis and proof that less-costly alternatives are in fact equally safe. If BP had any such policies in place, it does not appear that its Macondo team adhered to them."[5] The financial damage to BP as a result of the disaster began with the mandated establishment of a restoration fund of $20 billion for repairing the environment and compensating businesses in the Gulf. The damage will likely extend to potential civil and criminal penalties that could amount to additional tens of billions of dollars.[6] It appears that adhering to different values in decision making in this case would have been neither irrelevant nor inefficient.

The issues surrounding the social responsibility of business are just as intense today as in the 1970s when Friedman's article was published. Let's now begin to explore the question as to whether corporations have a responsibility beyond generating a return on investment to owners (shareholders). Friedman, Karnani, and those with similar views recognize that capitalism has raised standards of living, provided material conveniences, broadened education, unleashed talent, and created wealth. They fail, however, to acknowledge that unbridled capitalism has also imposed hidden costs and that it has sometimes been ruthless and exploitative and on occasion allowed the end (profit) to justify the means. Examples include using extraction methods that destroy a landscape and leave behind poisonous effluent or fostering extreme inequality that damages a community. It is therefore incomplete as an effective economic system.

There is a growing realization that now is the time to embed business conduct into a socially responsible ethos, one that leads to economic and social regeneration in advancing, vital societies. Examples of such a perspective include those of John Elkington (the triple bottom line, the chrysalis economy) and recent studies by organizations like the World Business Council on Sustainable Development.[7] These supporters of social responsibility argue that strengthened corporate social responsibility enhances customer support, corporate reputation, employee commitment, and investor confidence. Part of the rationale driving this perspective is characterized by what can be called dynamic markets, because these markets require capacity for rapid response to change. This movement is driven by the interconnected, global nature of today's business environment, which is accelerating the transformation of industries. Doing business in dynamic markets requires creativity, cooperation, coordination, flexibility, insight, resilience, integrity, and trust, attributes that extend outside the organization to external stakeholders. Such relationship-based interaction implies and encourages an awareness and respect for the interests and desires of multiple constituencies, which is central to corporate social responsibility. Thus creativity, to keep up with accelerated change, and ethical practice, to build trust with stakeholders, are fundamental to success. Since creativity thrives in environments that foster collaboration built on trust, common core values, and purpose, creativity and ethical practice are interconnected.[8] Success is not just built on efficiency and expediency; rather, it is built on ethical choices addressing a common good.

THE ETHICS OF CORPORATE SOCIAL RESPONSIBILITY

Corporate social responsibility is based on the premise that we consider the good for all stakeholders, not just the return for shareholders. CSR can be defined as the economic, legal, ethical, and discretionary expectations that society has of organizations at a given point in time.[9] Corporate social responsibility is related to, but not identical with, business ethics. While CSR encompasses the economic, legal, ethical, and discretionary responsibilities of organizations, business ethics usually focuses on the moral judgments and behavior of individuals and groups within organizations. Thus the study of business ethics may be regarded as a component of the larger study of corporate social responsibility.[10]

Fundamental shifts are occurring in the perspectives that we bring to the conduct of business that affect the ethical dimension of CSR. These shifts require more than a different approach. They require different assumptions about what underlies our values and thus what drives our decisions. Twenty years ago, Marilyn Ferguson described what she saw as a fundamental shift in the accepted business value assumptions and emerging presuppositions.[11] Lorin Loverde recently expanded upon selected elements of Ferguson's comparison, addressing dimensions such as customer needs, organizational decision making and design, and fundamental economic, psychological, and environmental assumptions.[12]

In a world of growing interconnections subject to this shifting paradigm, interrelationships among organizations and their constituents and stakeholders become increasingly important. This means finding new ways to work and to interact inside and outside organizations. For example, with many people collaborating to rapidly address challenges and opportunities, hierarchical decision making is ineffective. This prompts a need for creative, trustworthy, and resilient people, capable of making good decisions based on clear principles consistent with a company's perspective about stakeholder relationships. CSR is an important foundation for these principles. This includes transparency of operating practices and adherence to societal, legal, and ethical requirements. The consequences of violating such principles can damage or destroy companies, as we saw in the fates of companies such as Enron, WorldCom, Global Crossing, Arthur Andersen, Countrywide Financial, and Lehman Brothers.[13]

Even when company survival is not at stake, the consequences of ignoring broader social factors in decision making can be destructive. For instance, Toyota paid fines of almost $50 million for its failure to respond rapidly to unintended acceleration incidents; and additional significant future costs are likely.[14] The company dealt with customer questions and concerns with tactics that had served it well in the past. As discussed in "How Toyota Lost Its Way," a vehicle's chief engineer wields great authority, having total responsibility both for its design and business success.[15] As Toyota grew, the chief engineers became more insulated from market information. Important decisions continued to be made in Japan. According to Jim Olson, the company's chief American spokesperson for almost twenty years, "Division between decision making and execution slows the company down and prevents communication and planning."[16] Leaders underestimated the speed and intensity of both consumer and regulatory reaction. Technology problems erupted into serious quality, safety, and public relations issues. By the time Toyota was able to correct its response to a point where the furor subsided, a year had passed.[17] CSR policies and practices could have contributed to avoiding this debacle.

Apple, Inc., also dealt with a crisis emerging outside its U.S. headquarters, in this case initially more effectively. In early 2010, Apple received reports of a disturbing rate of employee suicides in some Asian factories where the company had outsourced manufacturing. Investigation led to the discovery of wide-ranging abuse toward employees: lack of appropriate engineering safety, hazardous chemical and air emissions practices, underage workers, fees charged to workers hired from distant locations for transportation and housing, and exorbitant recruitment fees for foreign work-ers.[18] Apple moved quickly, hiring psychological counselors and establish-ing twenty-four-hour care centers at the facilities with high suicide rates. The company even installed large nets on the sides of building to prevent impulsive suicides. An independent investigative team found that the quick response saved lives.[19] As a result of its audits, Apple terminated business with three suppliers who failed to show a serious commitment to Apple's supplier policies. It increased the number of both first-time audits and re-peat audits. In cases of underage hiring, Apple now requires the violating company to return the worker to school and pay for his or her education. Apple has forced the reimbursement of $3.4 million in excessive fees to workers from 2008 through 2010. Forty percent of the firms audited stated that Apple was the first firm ever to audit their facility for corporate social responsibility compliance.[20] Apple also found "a number of facilities that used discriminatory hiring practices such as medical or pregnancy tests; seventy-six facilities where records indicated workers exceeded weekly working-hour limits; sixty-four facilities with engineering safety violations; fifty-four facilities where workers weren't wearing appropriate personal protective equipment; eighty facilities which weren't properly storing or handling hazardous chemicals; and thirty-seven that failed to monitor and control air emissions."[21] Apple has suffered limited corporate fallout from this tragic situation, although issues continue to surface and require on-going vigilance. The quick and proactive initial response is an example of a commitment to CSR and the resulting benefit.

In their collaborative second-annual sustainability and innovation sur-vey of global corporate leaders, the Boston Consulting Group and *MIT/ Sloan Management Review* commented on reputations for sustainability: "If big-headline news stories can hurt leading brands, they are also facing a reputation landscape that has become more risky, since the instant and global nature of online communications means grassroots activists, blog-gers, and disgruntled consumers now have the tools to make their voices powerful. And as the world becomes more developed, growing numbers of its population have access to communications technology, increasing expectations of transparency."[22] This is a powerful statement coming from highly regarded sources in business. It endorses the view that managers must operate within principles that are aligned with the values and interests of all stakeholders in order to honor their fiduciary responsibility of maximizing return to shareholders in a societally responsible way. A well-integrated ethical and CSR framework becomes a necessary guide for an organizational environment of integrity, trust, and distributive leadership. Now we will focus on measurement of CSR and the strengths and shortcomings of current practice.

MEASURING CORPORATE SOCIAL RESPONSIBILITY

CSR adoption by organizations has led to the creation of indexes that rank business performance from an ESG (environment, social, governance) perspective—for example, the Dow Jones Sustainability Index and indexes from the Boston College Center for Corporate Citizenship.[23] Clarifying and developing transparency about the content and nature of ranking processes are ongoing issues that we will explore. Establishing effective executive sponsorship for CSR—for example, through a chief ethics and compliance officer (CECO)—is also a critical issue.[24]

Metrics Commonly Used

There are three well-established reporting and disclosure standards for companies submitting environmental, social, governance reports:

1. Global Reporting Initiative (GRI)—a standard that provides reporting on economic, social, and environmental performance through seventy-nine indicator metrics covering economic, environmental, labor and work practices, human rights, social, and product responsibility aspects of a company's performance.[25]
2. AccountAbility Principles Standard—based on three principles that together provide a foundation for accountability: inclusivity, materiality, and responsiveness. Inclusivity, the participation of stakeholders in developing and achieving an accountable and strategic response to sustainability, is the starting point for determining materiality.[26] The materiality process determines the most relevant and significant issues for an organization and its stakeholders. Responsiveness refers to the decisions, actions, and performance related to those material issues.

Standard AA1000APS was published in 2008. AccountAbility indicates that its standards are written for those that they directly affect, not just those who may benefit from them. They are based on Elkington's triple-bottom-line methodology and centered on assessing environmental, social, and economic indicators.[27]

3. London Benchmarking Group (LBG)—a collaborative group of more than 120 companies in fifteen countries working together to develop global measurement standards for corporate community investment (CCI), to benchmark and share best practices, and to develop and refine measurement tools.[28] Members benefit from an approach that is intended to provide a clear assessment of the scale and scope of community investment components of the ESG elements, including measurable results.

GRI indicators are used by over 40 percent of submitting companies for their reporting methodology, AccountAbility principles are used by about 25 percent of reporting firms, and LBG standards are used by more than 300 companies globally, according to information on each of the assessing organizations' websites in February 2011.[29] Companies prepare and publish CSR reports independently, mostly using one or more of these frameworks. GRI and AccountAbility are recognized as the two most commonly used reference tools.[30] The number of companies reporting has risen over the last decade. According to the Corporate Register, the total number of companies publishing corporate social responsibility reports increased from 26 in 1992, to 834 in 2000, to 2,453 in 2005, and to 5,525 in 2010.[31] GRI reports that submittals of CSR reports registered with GRI increased from 11 in 1999 to 1,793 in 2010.[32] The Boston College Center for Corporate Citizenship (BCCCC) user's guide summarizes the stakeholder data categories that are most often found in a CSR report.[33]

Some other aspects of CSR rating practices are as follows. The CSR rating indexes are often compiled as guides for investors who are interested in investing in companies that exhibit socially responsible practices. This focus may deemphasize the environmental and social elements of an ESG approach, as such aspects are often treated more superficially than the governance elements. Present measures of environmental and social aspects are largely quantitatively oriented (such as volume of emissions or philan-thropic donations) or focus on compliance or elements such as indepen-dence of board members and consistent application of articulated ethical standards. Where environmental measures exist, they are typically nonfi-nancial indicators of change with respect to items such as energy consump-tion, greenhouse gas emissions, water discharge quality, or waste generation.

Numerous institutions, including consulting firms, university-based bodies, and nongovernmental organizations (NGOs), are engaged in rank-ing companies based on their CSR reports, and they usually have their own methodology. The company being evaluated benefits by receiving a bench-mark comparison with other organizations. Participation in these surveys is indicative of a concern for the issues. However, this does open the or-ganization to additional scrutiny. Reviewing a sample of commentary and analysis on the CSR reports of various companies shows significant areas of missing information.[34] Some companies may be reducing their degree of participation. For instance, Rockwell Automation's 2009 report was 25 per-cent shorter than its first report in 2005.[35] The proliferation of sustainabil-ity surveys being conducted is an issue itself. Lack of standardization and the attempt by each ranking agency to create a proprietary approach place a heavy burden on participating companies, especially those that are recog-nized as CSR-conscious and are therefore frequently asked to participate.[36]

In a study that attempts to show how a particular rating agency's meth-odology illuminates the social responsibility aspects of a firm's behavior, Chatterji, Levine, and Toffel have identified four motivators that investors display when using these rankings as guides to their investment decisions:[37]

1. *Financial motivation*, for investors who believe that superior environ-mental performance leads to superior financial performance;
2. *Deontological motivation*, for those who wish to avoid investments in com-panies that act irresponsibly toward the environment because they consider it unethical to earn profits that have been attained through unethical behavior;
3. *Consequentialist motivation*, for investors who hope to direct funds to raise the cost of capital for misbehaving firms and lower it for respon-sible firms;

4. *Expressive motivation*, for those who base their social identity in part on investments and associations with good causes and seek to invest in companies perceived to be environmentally responsible.

All four types of investors desire to know how past performance and current decisions might influence future socially responsible performance. The study concluded that the ranking approaches appear to have a reasonably good, but imperfect, ability to predict bad investment outcomes. However, the study found little validation for predicting positive outcomes. The authors also identify the question of whether the act of being rated has an influence on corporate social responsibility as an area for further research.

The governance rating providers examined for this chapter all state that quantifying the link between ESG and investment risk is a primary, if not singular, objective. For instance, the stated mission of Institutional Shareholder Services (ISS) is "to enable the financial community to manage governance risk for the benefit of shareholders."[38] Yet there is wide variation in reporting criteria and methodology, including different and contradictory metrics (for example, lighting credits for buildings that may result in gaining points on one certification while losing points on another). Methodologies also vary from entirely self-reporting to third-party verification and from a heavy focus on financial metrics to generous incorporation of nonfinancial data. Agencies are, however, continually refining metrics and data-gathering methods (for instance, GRI released G3.1 in March 2011).[39]

A number of commonly heard critiques include:

- Quantitative data collected is not standardized.
- Rarely is qualitative data presented in a way that contributes to knowledge of how to enhance long-term and sustainable company value.
- Measurements tend to focus on activities rather than outcomes.
- The nuances of international cultural differences are generally reduced to a single global standard, which can obscure significant improvement by a company in a country where the normative category score is relatively low.

Bebchuk, Cohen, and Ferrell observe that some of the more popular indexes are based on a large number of governance attributes (more than 600). Among a large set of attributes, those of real significance are a limited and often small subset, and these may be given no higher weight than those of little significance. They conclude, "Firms seeking to improve their index rankings might be induced to make irrelevant or even undesirable changes and might use their improved rankings to avoid making the few small changes that do matter."[40] A more recent study by British academics found that "the benchmarking and league tables focus on ranking companies by overall reporting quality. . . . There is little evidence of benchmarking on performance in specific areas of concern. . . . In short, there seems to be a greater focus on benchmarking of reporting activity rather than on benchmarking of the results achieved."[41]

Surveys apparently have superficially addressed the realities of managing CSR in companies. One of the first national samplings on corporate citizenship issues was conducted by BCCCC during 2003 and 2004, with a survey that asked company respondents to answer several questions about management of citizenship in their firms.[42] As early as 2003, two-thirds reported that responsibilities for improving corporate citizenship existed at many levels of the company. The majority of larger firms surveyed (with more than 250 employees) addressed CSR in their employee communications (64%), public relations (58%), and company mission or vision statements (54%). However, far fewer had a process for measuring its effectiveness in their company, the contribution to the community, or the effect on their own bottom line. The number that incorporated CSR into their strategic plans (41%), work unit goals (36%), and manager performance appraisals (18%) was significantly lower. Only 24 percent provided any report on the company's social or environmental performance.[43] BCCCC's 2007 survey found only modest progress in embedding CSR principles into organizations.[44] Less than half of the large companies in a random sample reported that citizenship was an integral part of their business planning process or that they issued a public report on social responsibility. About the same percentage consulted regularly with either internal or external stakeholders on social responsibility issues.[45]

McKinsey conducted a survey in 2007 of companies participating in the United Nations Global Compact strategic policy initiative. It found that although 90 percent of CEOs were doing more than five years previously to incorporate environmental, social, and governance issues into strategy and operations, only 72 percent of them agreed that a corporate stance on ESG issues should be fully embedded into strategy and operations; but only 50 percent thought their firms did so. While 59 percent of these same executives agreed that their company should embed ESG issues into supply chain management, only 27 percent actually do.[46]

Wal-Mart Brazil is an example of supply-chain CSR. The company is making decisions about their vendors based on:[47]

- Not buying from companies with unfair labor practices,
- Not buying soybeans sourced from illegally deforested areas, and
- Not sourcing beef from any newly cleared Amazonian land.

There is strong evidence that companies are becoming increasingly aware about the shifting perceptions of the market. In a 2008 study, the IBM Institute for Business Value conducted a global survey of 250 business leaders and strategists.[48] In their introduction, the authors state, "It appears incontrovertibly true that business executives are starting to see CSR as a sustainable growth strategy." Three-quarters of these leaders admit that they do not have a good grasp of the social responsibility concerns of their stakeholders, which is reflected in the reality that only about one in five of these organizations collaborates with stakeholders on CSR initiatives. Even among those who are engaged at the stakeholder level, the number involved in collaboration ranges from 41 percent (with employees) to 25 percent (with government). These data are consistent with the 2007 BCCCC survey cited earlier. The authors of the IBM study go on to say, "It's equally true that the more advanced view of CSR demands significant long-term commitment, and definition (or re-definition) of corporate values. It can also require wholesale changes to the ways companies operate. Finally, it will require a finely honed appreciation of customers' concerns."[49] By implication, it will also require a more finely honed appreciation of other stakeholders such as employees, business partners (like suppliers), investors, the community, and government. This means a more engaged relationship with each of these groups.

What Metrics Could (and Should) Be Added

In an attempt to discern trends in publication activity about the environmental and financial performance of firms, Tekin and Kocaoglu conducted a bibliographic analysis of publications between 1990 and 2009 in the areas of green innovations, green investments, and green venture capital to assess the level of activity.[50] The analysis covered business, engineering, scholarly, and general interest publications. Trends in annual growth of publications in all three topic areas within all four types of publications showed a rapid increase. Since environmental issues are directly linked to CSR concerns, this is likely a proxy for growth in the study of, and interest in, other CSR-related areas. So we can anticipate an increase in the applicability and precision of additional metrics. Following are some areas they might usefully address.

One area currently missing, given the categories mentioned in the GRI Performance Indicators, is that of ethics. Ethics is a difficult category to measure for several reasons. As Edward Soule observed, "Ethics is not an activity. Rather, it is an intangible characteristic of conduct and a peculiar one at that. At least in the short term, the ethical dimension of behavior tends to go unnoticed unless it falls below a threshold of acceptability. Therefore, we have no straightforward way to quantify and objectively measure ethical performance, formulate goals and objectives in respect of it, hold someone accountable for the results, or use it as the basis for incentives."[51] It is important to understand the source for an ethical framework and to what degree it permeates the organization. Are guiding principles explicitly articulated? Are they communicated regularly and consistently? Do the same standards apply at all levels of the organization and are they uniformly enforced? Do executive and senior management walk the talk? Do people at all levels of the organization have the same interpretation of ethical principles? Can employees seek guidance and advice about ethical questions without fear of retaliation or punishment? Are employees comfortable delivering bad news?

Assessment of an organization's ethical culture is also difficult from the outside. Those who are in the trenches, making daily decisions in accordance with their understanding of organizational culture, are the best source for uncovering the in-place values of an organization. However, there is a challenge to delving into ethical self-assessment. People respond more honestly when asked to assess the behavior or values of others than when asked to reflect on their own ethical values.[52] This means that questions must be framed in reference to behavior of coworkers. In spite of these difficulties, it is important to incorporate an ethical dimension in measuring CSR performance. Recently, there have been unfortunate examples of high-profile companies whose espoused commitment to corporate responsibility faltered when faced with significant ethical challenges, namely, BP, Bank of America, and Goldman Sachs.[53]

Measuring the effectiveness of corporate social responsibility is further complicated both by the historical lack of broad information exchange between corporate management and other stakeholders and by a rapidly shifting business environment. Moreover, many of the key measures addressing sustainability and social responsibility tend to be qualitative and hard to obtain. And they tend to be subjective rather than quantifiable.

However, some business aspects that are already being measured and could link to CSR are as follows:

- Customer retention and satisfaction;
- Employee retention (voluntary and involuntary), satisfaction, and development;
- Supply chain standards and sustainability measures;
- Compensation practices compared with competitors;
- Proactively addressing potential customer issues (e.g., recalls);
- Energy use management;
- Level of engagement on climate risk and change;
- Level of impact on ecosystem and attention to minimizing it;
- Attitude toward employee health and safety (including wellness);
- Articulating a consistently communicated code of conduct and objective for value creation; and

• Proactive minimization and appropriate disclosure of risks to other stake-holders—customers, employees, suppliers, local community, investors, and environment.

These factors typically involve interactions among different stakeholders. Outcome measures then need to reflect the perspective of more than one constituency. A true measure of each factor would include the effect on each stakeholder group. Since most CSR ratings are compiled through company self-reporting, this kind of cross-perceptual analysis of value creation through socially responsible behavior requires a higher level of collaboration and transparency between multiple stakeholders than has typically been the case in the past.

Leaders of those organizations in the IBM survey who believed they understood their customers' CSR expectations well were more likely to engage their employees in the company's CSR objectives.[54] This likely means a higher level of collaboration with other stakeholders as well. Employees are the front line for this broad stakeholder engagement. Loverde identifies workforce characteristics needed to establish collaborative relationships among multiple stakeholders in terms of attitudes, human skills, operational skills, and organizational skills.[55] Creating an environment that benefits all stakeholders requires a sense of reciprocity that bridges relationships across the various constituencies. An opportunity to strengthen measurement of CSR in the future is that of linking internal workforce behaviors and attributes to relationships with multiple external stakeholders viewed through a CSR lens. Loverde describes components of internal behavior in areas that include cultural attributes, employee relationships, customer communication, and community engagement.[56] This provides a potential basis to extend measurement practice and, as a result, strengthen an organization's value-creating capability. Since these actions cross stakeholder boundaries, this approach would increase the recognition and enthusiasm for collaboration in environmental, societal, and corporate governance areas.

In closing, we can conclude that the interest of company officers in embracing CSR has steadily increased. Scrutiny by outside observers and critics has grown at an even faster rate, creating ever higher standards to be met. We have explored how evaluation systems of CSR effectiveness need to recognize both quantitative and qualitative aspects and examined some possible extensions of current practice. In addition, we have identified a number of areas that are foundational for a culture of attention and caring and that need to be considered in future CSR measurement methodologies. Perhaps one indicator of true commitment to CSR principles will be the degree to which companies that led recent annual rankings maintain that standing in difficult economic times. Another will be evidence that the leaders in these companies give as much priority to broad stakeholder relationships and longer-term community and social contributions as they do to the next quarterly earnings report. When that happens we will know that managers and leaders are indeed taking responsibility for the common good. In our next chapter, we will see examples of serving the common good as we look at partnerships between the for-profit and nonprofit sectors.

4

Partnerships between the For-Profit
and Nonprofit Sectors

Barbara Langsdale

In this chapter, we explore why and how businesses can include a philanthropic component (corporate social responsibility, or CSR) in their mission and direction. We examine what this means for effective partnerships between for-profit and nonprofit organizations. By corporate social responsibility we mean a business choosing to assume an obligation toward the good of society through direct contributions such as cash, payment in kind, loans, volunteerism of employees, and sponsorships, in addition to its profit-oriented business endeavors. Our focus in this chapter is on how to establish successful for-profit/nonprofit partnerships. We address the topic by first examining why partnerships between for-profit and nonprofit organizations are beneficial to both. We look at how corporations decide to incorporate a philanthropic mission into their operating practices. Then we explore how to lay the groundwork for creating successful partnerships and conclude by examining some suggested steps for implementation.

This review is based on my twenty years of experience in the nonprofit sector as a development professional. My involvement with corporate donors through their marketing departments and their corporate foundations has given me insight into why corporations decide to give back to their communities through their corporate social responsibility policies and practices. In building a foundation to address this topic, I interviewed people in a range of businesses that participate in CSR, both local and international corporations, and an array of nonprofits to highlight the partnership benefits to each entity. Five corporations were included in the interviews: Give Something Back, an office supply company; Hitachi Data Systems, a data storage and services company; PMI, a provider of mortgage insurance; R. C. Fischer and Company, an insurance company; and Tesoro Golden Eagle Refinery, part of Tesoro Corporation, a refiner and marketer of petroleum products. Having had personal involvement with all of these companies, I chose them because each has a belief in giving back in the form of both monetary support and company employee involvement, namely, volunteering in community or nonprofit endeavors. In addition, they have all developed an internal corporate social responsibility process that is part of their corporate culture. Within these organizations, I generally spoke with the corporate officer responsible for administering the CSR policy.

In the nonprofit sector, I interviewed either the executive director or the development director responsible for finding corporate partnerships and building successful relationships with business organizations. In determining the organizations to interview, I chose five that had a culture of building corporate sponsorships and developing a successful process for doing so: Habitat for Humanity, building homes for low-income families; Tony La Russa's Animal Rescue Foundation, animal rescue and adoptions; Youth Homes, residential homes and treatment for abused and neglected children; Contra Costa Crisis Center, twenty-four-hour crisis intervention; and my own organization, We Care Services for Children, early intervention services for young children with special needs.

WHY ENGAGE IN CORPORATE SOCIAL RESPONSIBILITY?

One national study points to the benefits of corporate social responsibility from a company perspective.[1] The study conducted by Walker Information, Inc., for the Council on Foundations, found that generous companies, which contribute to their communities, are more likely to have:

- Loyal customers who continue doing business with them,
- Employees who recommend the company as a good place to work and who continue to work for the company, and
- Shareholders who invest and may suggest the firm to other investors.

This study on corporate philanthropy was built on a survey-based process measuring the perceptions, attitudes, and opinions of employee, customer, and investor stakeholder groups as related to a company's philanthropic efforts. There were two sample groups. The first consisted of 1,273 people who responded to two separate surveys—first as employees responding about their employer and then as customers responding about an organization with which they did business. These survey respondents were adults (eighteen years and older) from the continental United States and were working full or part-time with a business that employed 2,500 or more people. The second sample group consisted of 426 shareholder respondents from the continental United States who were at least twenty-one years of age and had invested in individual stocks.

Using a measurement called the corporate philanthropy index (CPI), respondents were categorized into two groups, high CPI and low CPI, based on whether they perceived a company's philanthropic efforts as favorable or unfavorable. Results showed:

- Customers with high CPI ratings for an organization were three times more likely to be loyal than those with low CPI ratings. (Loyal customers tend to continue purchasing the company's products or services and recommend the company to others.)
- Employees with high CPI ratings for an organization were four times as likely to be loyal compared with those with low CPI ratings. (Loyal employees tend to have common characteristics: lower employee turnover, less absenteeism, greater efficiency, and work effort.)
- Statements from customer respondents showed that for one of every three customers, a company's giving record would be a reason for selection; for employee respondents, between one-third and two-thirds agreed that a good giving record is a main reason for remaining with an employer; and for shareholder respondents, one-third indicated that corporate generosity affects where they invest.

Further benefits of CSR are described in the 2010 Corporate Social Responsibility Perceptions Survey of a thousand consumers by Penn Schoen Berland, cited by Justmeans.[2] A majority of consumers, 70 percent, viewed

CSR as important despite the recession. The report also showed CSR contributing to enhanced perceptions of organization brands by consumers. The company officers interviewed believed that the true gain is realized in the health of the communities they live and work in.

This belief is reinforced by feedback from my interviews. Businesses that have made the decision to incorporate social responsibility into their practices believe this decision benefits both the company and society—their good work pays off. Answers to the question about how their company decided to incorporate a philanthropic mission into their business direction revealed some common philosophies in giving policies. Each company policy was reflective of the values of the company's leadership and the employees in the company, and their CSR policy was adjusted to align with the needs of the local community. Every corporate officer interviewed identified gains in multiple areas from their partnering with nonprofits, for example:

- *Employee morale.* Ken Dami, Government and Community Relations, Tesoro Golden Eagle Refinery, believes volunteering has a positive impact on employee morale: "Volunteerism is encouraged by Tesoro because we believe our employees' community involvement makes for caring people in our workforces, which transfers to a mutually supportive work place culture."[3]
- *Customer loyalty.* Michael Hannigan, president, Give Something Back, a socially responsible office supply company, states, "There is customer stickiness, as I call it, because customers feel good about our program of giving back to the local community they live in. This corporate giving program is effortless and at no extra cost to Give Something Back customers."[4]

In my interviews, not one company officer talked about their bottom line as a primary driving force. Here are two examples:

- "The value of a social responsibility policy is really about how a partnership between business and nonprofit organizations can improve the community they both serve; it's an investment to improve our quality of life"—Ken Dami, Tesoro Golden Eagle Refinery.[5]

- "Hitachi Limited believes Corporate Social Responsibility is one of the foundations of global management and contributes to building a sustainable global society with the realization that the resolution of social issues contributes to a better and more prosperous global society. This is a core value of Hitachi"—Greg Coplans, senior vice president, corporate affairs, Hitachi Data Systems.[6]

Now let's look at the benefits of CSR from a nonprofit and community perspective. The value of partnerships between for-profits and nonprofits flows through the companies' investments in nonprofits and to the community's collective good, improving quality of life. Whether it is feeding the hungry through local food banks, building homes for low-income families, providing job training for displaced workers, or educating children, investments by corporations strengthen nonprofits by allowing for additional programs, sustaining or enhancing current programs, and consequently enhancing vital community services. Even small investments can be significant. Nonprofits receive donations, and companies receive positive publicity and increased employee loyalty, making this a win-win for businesses, nonprofits, and communities.

In addition to monetary donations, nonprofits benefit from volunteers recruited from corporations, and the corporations benefit as well. Employee volunteer programs allow a business to strengthen the community while helping employees build leadership skills, create staff cohesion, and improve morale. Everyone interviewed in the nonprofits expressed their appreciation for corporate volunteers. "We thrive on volunteerism, we couldn't survive without volunteer participation," is how Daryl Lee, corporate development officer, Habitat for Humanity East Bay, described it.[7] John Bateson, executive director, Contra Costa Crisis Center, describes it this way: "In the first place, volunteers are essential to our work because they keep our costs down. More than that, though, volunteers infuse and enhance the culture of compassion that exists in our agency. Second, they don't have to be here; they want to be here, giving their time to help others. Third, volunteers often become our best individual donors. They see firsthand the value of our work and know how carefully we treat every dollar that is donated. Lastly, their involvement can lead to financial support from their employer."[8]

LAYING THE GROUNDWORK FOR CORPORATE SOCIAL RESPONSIBILITY

Having established the value of CSR and for-profit/nonprofit partnerships, we will now look at how to lay the groundwork for successful partnerships. Once a decision is made to explicitly recognize social responsibility as an important business practice, the nature and scope of this support for the nonprofit community needs to be determined. This may include the type of partnerships with nonprofits—for example, multiple-year support, a limited onetime cash donation, cause-related marketing (attaching a brand name to a nonprofit initiative that also provides for product promotion), in-kind product donations, or the loan of company employees to volunteer.

After a business has developed a plan for CSR, nonprofits can then assess their fit with the business, including when and how to apply for support. In my interviews, I found many commonalities in the social responsibility policies and implementation practices of large and small businesses. However, it became clear, not surprisingly, that for questions as to what suggestions to give to a company wanting to venture into corporate social responsibility and how to determine what form of philanthropic outreach fits the company's mission, there was no single answer. This process needs to be tailored to each company. It can be defined by leadership or more effectively created with employee involvement, as suggested by Charles Broom of PMI.[9]

Every executive interviewed underlined the importance of aligning CSR with the business's practice, philosophy, and mission. Give Something Back has an approach of building consensus through a voting process focused on involving employees and customers. Its president, Michael Hannigan, describes it this way: "The nonprofits are supported through a voting process involving employees and customers. We believe the community members know the nonprofits that are doing the best work. We also have a very successful co-branding partnership with Boise Paper Inc. where both companies each donate fifty cents for every case of 100 percent or 30 percent recycled Boise paper purchased through Give Something Back. The money is then returned to California county food banks."[10]

Some businesses may choose to use a community survey conducted by an outside research firm to make informed decisions about their corporate social responsibility focus, based on surveyed community needs. The businesses can look at the information and choose the focus areas that align with their core values. This information can then be communicated to employees to help build support for the businesses' CSR approaches and gain employee engagement in volunteer efforts at community nonprofits.

In the case of PMI, its charter focuses in part on supporting affordable housing and financial literacy through such programs as Habitat for Humanity and Junior Achievement. In addition, the charter's focus is to direct grant dollars toward social programs that contribute to communities in which PMI employees live and work. These programs include a range of causes that address education, at-risk youth, literacy, and supply of basic needs. The social programs are suggested by an internal community action committee, which also provides support through both monetary donations and volunteers.

Hitachi formed a foundation in the United States that developed plans for promoting employee community involvement among Hitachi employees. Hitachi group companies in the country partner with the Hitachi Foundation to establish and operate, on a volunteer basis, employee community action committees (CACs) that determine the focus of local giving and community projects. CACs encourage employee involvement and gather suggestions from employees about which nonprofits in the local community should receive donations or other forms of support. The CACs are in addition to other corporate giving programs that Hitachi group companies have in the United States.

Dirk Fitzgerald, the principal of one smaller local corporation, R. C. Fischer and Company, explained that its approach is based on the owner's involvement in such service organizations as Kiwanis and Rotary International. The approach includes supporting local nonprofits by sponsoring events to which they invite employees and clients. This broadens the participation and connection to the nonprofits. "I think that employers should concentrate efforts on key employees being involved in service organizations. Contributions can be identified and budgeted as ordinary business expenses. The company should also set up a matching program for employees who give to nonprofits."[11]

A significant benefit to having a corporate CSR policy published and readily available is that requests for support from nonprofits are more focused. Nonprofits that could easily review a business's CSR policy would naturally be drawn to those companies that have indicated an interest in their mission area. For small to medium-size companies that do not have a full-time staff person to review requests, publishing the CSR policy on the company's website can result in having only qualified nonprofits request support, thus greatly streamlining the request-and-review process.

IMPLEMENTING PARTNERSHIPS BETWEEN FOR-PROFIT BUSINESSES AND NONPROFITS

Having laid the groundwork for CSR, we can now look at implementation. Interviews with executives from both the for-profit and nonprofit worlds confirmed the importance of the partnership benefiting both entities and the importance of core values being aligned. For this to happen, nonprofits and for-profits must build a relationship and understand what each expects from the partnership. This alignment of expectations is a necessary foundation so that each party derives benefit.

For the nonprofit, establishing an effective partnership can best be accomplished with the following steps:

1. Complete a due diligence process about a prospective partner by answering the following questions:

    a. Does the company have a corporate foundation or a CSR policy (philanthropic giving history)? Does the company offer sponsorship opportunities through the marketing department? Many companies have this information on their corporate website. This is a good place to start looking.

    b. Do our missions align? Are there common values? "The process of alignment starts with research. I take a look at the organization's trends and interests. I specifically look at their interest in supporting affordable housing, sustainability, volunteer programs for their employees, and if they want to do something in a specific neighborhood. I determine that our missions are in alignment, and then I look for an entry point. This may be someone within my network who will help me champion my request. If there is not a point of contact from an introduction within my network, I find an executive from a company that has been a volunteer or I give a tour to a company executive I have identified. The tour includes an introduction to a client or another funding partner allowing for a personal story from the client or a success story from a corporate partner," per Daryl Lee, corporate development officer, Habitat for Humanity.[12]

c. Does the potential business have the capacity to give? Annual reports and the company's filed tax reports will indicate the company's financial strength.

d. Do we have a connection, for example, through a volunteer, donor, or board member?

2. Make the connection—build the relationship for now and the future. The volunteer manager, development director, and executive director should ask the question of themselves, "Whom do I know who could be a potential business partner?" This usually is a specific person they know in the prospective business partner organization. The question should also be one that each board member asks of themselves. In addition, the question should be addressed with the nonprofit's volunteers and donors, and with friends and family. Asking this question builds a list of potential supports and prepares for the next step of connecting. Connections to potential partners can be made in a variety of ways. Stu McCullough, executive director of Youth Homes, told me they have high-touch events for volunteer involvement. He also has ongoing contact with donors through calls and written updates, and he creates events to introduce potential funders to Youth Homes and their work in the community.[13] Elena Bicker, executive director of Tony La Russa's Animal Rescue Foundation, said, "It is not my determining if we have the right connection but through conversation with the potential partner that the common interest is found. We let the donor (corporation) decide."[14] As Daryl Lee of Habitat for Humanity describes it, "Invite potential contributors to tour, introduce them to clients or other funding partners."[15]

3. "Make the ask." How do you know when to make the ask? This decision comes from having built a relationship. During the relationship-building process, discuss values, goals, interests, and expectations with

the potential corporate partner. Then determine if the nonprofit program meets the needs of the company and if the nonprofit's mission is aligned with the company's CSR focus.

The for-profit organization should develop a plan for effective partnership. Questions to consider include:

1. How will our CSR policy be promoted to the nonprofit community?
2. Who has the authority to engage in a partnership and what form of partnership will we have? Will the decision be made by one person or a community action committee?
3. How will a decision be made about the partnership? What is the selection process? What criteria will be used?
4. How will we communicate our CSR contributions to our employees and the community?

GAUGING SUCCESS

How do you measure success? For the nonprofit, it is about linking activities, contributions, and outcomes to the organization's mission. How many volunteer hours did corporate employees donate, how many sponsorship dollars did the company donate, and did the donations further the nonprofit's mission? For example, how many lives were saved? Did the partnership improve a child's education or make the environment better in our communities? In addition, did the partnership meet the corporate donor's initial expectations? Did the nonprofit fulfill its promise?

Charles Broom of PMI states, "PMI measures the success of the various programs it supports by the number of lives the programs touch in a positive way, such as moving from poverty housing into safe, decent, affordable housing, or observing the number of people who have progressed from dealing with check cashing outlets that can have high rates of crime to establishing savings accounts at banking institutions."[16] Ken Dami notes that Tesoro Golden Eagle Refinery measures its public perception by conducting a survey every few years to calibrate the recognition of their community investments with public expectations of the facility's corporate citizenship. An increase in the number of people recognizing the value of Tesoro's

CSR contributions indicates that its partnerships are acknowledged. Conversely, a decrease may lead to a reassessment of strategy or tactics. Tesoro also measures the effect of sponsorship dollars. It asks, for example, Who is served by the nonprofit? What is the expense ratio? Is there a fit for both the nonprofit and the company? Moreover, are we improving the quality of life in our surrounding communities, ensuring a healthy economy and an educated workforce, balanced with social and sustainability concerns? Like PMI, Tesoro also assesses the contribution of its investment in a nonprofit to the well-being of the nonprofit's clients, as reported by the nonprofit through specific communications and in the nonprofit's annual report. Other for-profit partnership measures include the number of employee volunteer hours donated during a year to the nonprofit. For more information about measuring the value and contribution of corporate volunteers, the Points of Light Institute's website is a valuable resource.[17]

Measurement is an opportunity for the nonprofit to build the partnership. For example, the nonprofit can prepare and send media reports indicating the visibility they obtained within the community through press releases, news stories, and logo circulation with advertising posters displayed in storefronts. Furthermore, nonprofits can outline how monetary investments advance a specific program, for instance, showing how many pets are adopted or how many children attended summer camp. Identifying the long-term value of the nonprofit's contributions to the community is also important to include in the reports to the business partner. This type of long-term information reinforces the importance and value of the work the nonprofit does within a community. An example of qualitative and quantitative reporting is indicated in this research statement on early intervention: "After nearly 50 years of research, there is evidence—both qualitative (reports of parents and teachers) and quantitative—that early intervention increases the developmental and educational gains for a child, improves functioning of a family and reaps long-term benefits for society. Early intervention has been shown to result in a child: (a) needing fewer special education and other services later in life; (b) being retained in grade less often; and (c) in some cases being indistinguishable from non-handicapped classmates' years after intervention."[18]

CONCLUSION

Finally, I would like to mention what CSR partnerships have meant to We Care Services for Children's clients, to our community, and to me. When I think about the partnerships we have, I think about the many employees in corporations who have not only become personally involved in our work but also have become friends of We Care. Their involvement becomes more than a donation; they become invested in our work with children and families. Also, they recognize that our services make a difference to each client, as well as making our community a better place to live and work. This type of personal involvement creates lasting partnerships and friendships.

As indicated in my conversations with corporate leaders, many told me that although their CSR policies state a limited time frame for partnering with a nonprofit, once they became connected and recognized that the investment they were making was really working, they chose to continue the partnership. For smaller nonprofits like We Care with limited resources, this ongoing commitment from corporations means we know we have the funding needed for our children and their families. Because of our corporate partnerships, We Care has been able to provide additional services and expand existing programs to serve more children and families. Employee volunteers have provided annual maintenance on our school grounds and have painted classrooms. Business leaders are involved on our committees and board of directors, providing strategic direction for our agency. For We Care Services for Children, as with many nonprofits, corporate partnerships, including employee involvement, help us meet critical community needs. In our next chapter we will examine the role of government in sponsoring social responsibility by the business community.

5

Government as a Business Partner in the Pursuit of Social Responsibility

Andrew Domek

Given the community benefits of socially responsible business behavior, those in government at all levels have an interest in supporting these actions. This chapter examines existing strategies that governmental entities take to move businesses toward social responsibility, and offers perspectives on efforts to increase business participation in such behavior. Government is tasked with ensuring that the public good is protected and that the public's collective will is implemented as efficiently as possible. Therefore, it should be in the best interest of governments to promote or otherwise ensure socially responsible behavior by businesses in their jurisdictions. Included in this review are instances where the U.S. government has been successful in using strategies to encourage community-focused partnership with business. While the chapter focuses on efforts made by the federal government, these methods may also be used to varying degrees at the state and local levels. Also examined are some of the difficulties associated with government's role in promoting social responsibility, including possible solutions. The chapter concludes with suggestions for further government sponsorship of corporate social responsibility (CSR).

RELATIONSHIPS

The scope of the relationship between government and the business community regarding social responsibility, and whether any relationship at all should exist, is the subject of ongoing debate across the political spectrum. Some on the political left contend that socially responsible behavior is a veneer that can make a business appear to be concerned with community life, when in reality government is the institution best suited to protect the interests of society. Former Clinton administration secretary of labor, Robert Reich, argues that corporate social responsibility can "divert attention from the more difficult but more important job of establishing laws that protect and advance the common good."[1] Those on the political right who are followers of free-market economist Milton Friedman, however, might quote from his 1970 *New York Times Magazine* piece, where he argues that "the external forces that curb the market will not be the social consciences, however highly developed, of the pontificating executives; it will be the iron fist of Government bureaucrats."[2]

Still, many are supportive of efforts by business to address social responsibility. One perspective held by many is that of Christopher Holshek, a retired colonel in the civil affairs branch of the U.S. Army Reserve, who observes, "Public-private collaboration has long been trademark [*sic*] of the way America operates, when it operates best."[3] Holshek draws on examples from the country's history that illustrate government partnering effectively with the private sector in the pursuit of social responsibility—like the creation of the Internet, the Transcontinental Railroad, and, more recently and appropriately in these lean years, federal job training. Holshek's views on the subject echo many of the ideas found in this chapter, in that "the public-private debate shouldn't be about how much but how."[4] As mentioned in chapter 1, in practice, government plays a key role in CSR as part of an ongoing relationship with the for-profit and nonprofit sectors.

The specific aspect of this relationship that we focus on in this chapter is how governments can encourage social responsibility in corporations. Most efforts by government to encourage social responsibility fall into two categories—the carrot (positive reinforcement) and the stick (negative reinforcement). Examples include encouraging businesses to act in a certain way by providing financial incentives, such as favorable tax consideration (carrot) for investing in disadvantaged communities, or by levying additional fees (stick) to discourage certain behaviors, such as environmental emissions. Using the carrot refers to how governments can make the overall climate more favorable for businesses to engage in social responsibility. This method does not specifically require anything of the business community; it is merely an encouragement to action. Its use is persuasive, and there is no direct consequence if a business does not take advantage of what amounts to an enticement to action. The stick method has been used by the public sector to influence the private sector for many years and usually involves laws or regulations specifying certain business behavior. When introduced unilaterally, such steps can generate antagonism. We will look at the benefits and potential problems of this method later, along with an example of how it was used successfully.

COMMUNITY INTERESTS SHARED BY GOVERNMENT AND BUSINESS

One definition for the word *business* is "a usually commercial or mercantile activity engaged in as a means of livelihood."[5] Engaging in business necessarily places people within their communities, as this is both a means of engaging the community by providing a product or service that others need, and a means to afford the necessities of life that allow a person to live within their community. Businesses, then, by their nature, are not solitary endeavors; rather, they are community-based activities. As the act of engaging in business is a community action, so too is government a community action. A quote attributed to Congressman Barney Frank from Massachusetts provides a complement to the livelihood definition of business. Frank observes that government is "the name we give to the things we choose to do together."[6] So, while the actions of government and business are different, they are interconnected through communities. Businesses provide the livelihood for community members, and government ensures that the public's collective will is implemented.

One common goal is the need to invest in human capital, defined by the Organisation for Economic Co-operation and Development as "the knowledge, skills, competencies and attributes embodied in individuals that facilitate the creation of personal, social and economic well-being."[7] Supporting development of human capital can be viewed broadly as, for example, providing better healthcare for more people, making college affordable so as to create a larger group of well-educated people ready to participate in the economy and contribute to their communities, or ensuring that parents with children have access to nutritious food for their families regardless of their economic circumstances. Investments in human capital reinforce each other: A hungry, low-income child who is fed is able to do better in school, get into an affordable college, and secure a good job. She can then pay taxes and be a productive member of society, giving back to the community that invested in her future. Increasing human capital can help create a more prosperous economy and harmonious society. A more prosperous economy means a better climate for those in the businesses community to engage in their livelihood; so an investment by government in human capital benefits business.

Why is it necessary for government to partner with corporations to invest in human capital? Why can't government simply invest tax dollars independently? One reason is that tax dollars are sometimes constrained by political ideology. As reported by *The Hill* in 2011, "Most Republicans have signed a pledge not to raise taxes. . . ."[8] So, without any new revenue coming in, where is the human capital investment going to come from? Further, is it even possible for government to unilaterally invest the funds to create needed development of human capital without the assistance of other sectors?

Shannon Murphy of the Harvard Kennedy School of Government answers this question: "The public sector cannot successfully develop a nation's human capital alone. To maximize the opportunities and benefits of developing human capital, the private and philanthropic sectors are necessary partners."[9] Sound familiar? This reinforces the notion of the interdependence of the for-profit, nonprofit, and public sectors mentioned earlier in this book. Because of the interdependence, the investment in human capital by a corporation is a socially responsible action. Providing incentives for such investment is an opportunity for government to sponsor socially responsible corporate behavior. So, what can government do to encourage socially responsible corporate behavior?

ENCOURAGING THE BUSINESS COMMUNITY WITH CARROTS

The first type of encouragement for the business community involves creating an environment that makes it easier for corporate social responsibility to occur. This means either resolving potential problems or creating a set of incentives that make desired actions more attractive to business. Let us examine the case of a company engaging in a socially responsible action on a specific issue. Wal-Mart is now donating still-usable food, with a recently expired end-use date, to groups that provide it to people in need. A 2011 National Public Radio story outlined Wal-Mart's partnership with Feeding America, the country's network of food banks, to donate $2 billion in food aid over five years.[10] Food items are delivered from Wal-Mart stores to various food banks and soup kitchens to feed those in need. A 2010 *New York Times* article further explains, "Wal-Mart began taking on hunger as a cause in 2005, when it distributed 9.9 million pounds of food to food banks; last year [2009] it provided 116.1 million pounds of food. The company also has donated the services of its staff to help food banks improve lighting and refrigeration and develop ways to increase the amount of fresh food on their shelves."[11]

Relevant to this example is the federal government's passage in 1996 of the Bill Emerson Good Samaritan Food Donation Act.[12] According to the U.S. Department of Agriculture (USDA), the act "promotes food recovery" by limiting the liability of donors to instances of gross negligence or intentional misconduct. The Act further states that—absent gross negligence or intentional misconduct—volunteers, nonprofit organizations, and businesses shall not be subject to civil or criminal liability arising from the nature, age, packaging, or condition of apparently wholesome food or apparently fit grocery products received as donations."[13] This means that a company can donate food without fear of legal reprisals if someone unexpectedly becomes sick, provided the food was apparently wholesome. The act goes further by establishing basic "nationwide uniform definitions pertaining to donation and distribution of nutritious foods" that "helps assure that donated foods meet all quality and labeling standards of federal, State, and local laws and regulations." If Wal-Mart or other retailers want to donate, they will not be sued. There is little room for lawsuits here, as long as someone is not actively trying to offload spoiled food or engage in knowingly unlawful practices. After the Emerson law, the legal hurdle that might have prevented a company like Wal-Mart from donating was gone.[14]

So now Wal-Mart could donate—but would it? What could government do that might make the expenditure worthwhile? One direct incentive is a reduction of federal taxes. According to the U.S. Environmental Protection Agency, which provides information to potential donors of food, since 1969 "a taxpayer who contributes appreciated inventory or certain other ordinary income property is permitted a charitable deduction for an amount equal to the taxpayer's basis in the contributed property."[15] This incentive was sweetened by the 1976 Tax Reform Act (Section 2135), which "made inventory donation to charities more advantageous for business taxpayers by increasing the allowable income tax deduction and allowing the donor to determine the fair market value of their donation, not to exceed two times the cost."[16] Based on these tax laws, Wal-Mart could donate food to a charity or other nonprofit organization and for tax purposes could legally claim a value twice that of the cost to acquire the food. Keep in mind also that an unspecified amount of this food could not have been legally sold anyway because it had passed the expiration date. The government has created a situation where Wal-Mart benefits by donating food that might otherwise have been discarded, and the community also benefits. Al Norman, a well-known critic of Wal-Mart, estimates that "Wal-Mart's donated food is valued at $1.75 billion, and their enhanced deduction is equal to half the donated food's retail value, or $875 million; at a 35 percent tax rate, Wal-Mart could net a tax deduction of $306 million off their taxable income."[17] Again, this is tax money reclaimed by Wal-Mart from a donation of food that would have been discarded. The benefits to Wal-Mart from this donation are not just related to taxes; the organization was given effectively free advertising by two respected news organizations in the instance cited above. For a controversial company like Wal-Mart, beset by public outcries over its negative record on treatment of employees and other business practices, this coverage is invaluable.[18]

The extra publicity brings to mind my time as a fledgling communications professional when a mentor of mine observed that, when speaking with reporters, there is no off the record. If a spokesperson says something interesting enough, the informal agreement not to publish a fact or a name may be breached in favor of an exclusive story. As a journalist and former aide to late Speaker of the House Thomas "Tip" O'Neill, Chris Matthews wrote about reporters: "Like policemen, they are always on duty."[19] While dealing with reporters can be hazardous to a careless political communications professional, the converse is also true: media "always on duty" can benefit in a different setting. For Wal-Mart, its support of the community generates favorable publicity and credibility in the communities that hear the stories. Its policy of food donation has contributed to the communities where they are located, and to hungry people in those communities. We could debate whether the estimated $306 million in reduced taxes for Wal-Mart was a justifiable expenditure of taxpayer dollars. Regardless, the U.S. government, for $306 million dollars, secured nearly $2 billion worth of food in recent years for those who did not have enough to eat.

Thus in this one area, food donation, Wal-Mart has engaged in socially responsible behavior and has also profited handsomely. Although it would be difficult to claim that the actions of the federal government led directly to Wal-Mart's involvement, the donations from the corporation began in earnest after a multiyear effort to encourage food donation in the public sector. It does not appear that government action here was directly targeting Wal-Mart. The government simply created an environment where it was more profitable for this company to engage in socially responsible behavior. Were it not for the actions of the federal government, Wal-Mart would have had to take additional, more costly steps to provide the service it currently does for the food-insecure. The corporation has made, and is continuing to make, use of the incentives and protections offered by the government.

EFFECTIVELY WIELDING THE STICK

In addition to rewards and incentives to move the business community toward social responsibility, there is another direct way that the government can encourage corporations to engage in social responsibility—the stick method. It is not as complex as the carrot scenario but is still worthy of mention because it is relatively easy for the government to use and does not cost taxpayers money. The government does not force charitable giving; rather, it preferentially contracts with corporations that conform to standards related to social responsibility. Sometimes, as the arbiters of the people's collective will, those in government realize that a socially responsible action is needed, but there is limited willpower within the business community to embrace it. The government can encourage community-oriented behavior by establishing conditions that organizations must meet to secure government contracts. We will now examine food donation from another perspective to show how the stick technique can be effective.

The Federal Food Donation Act of 2008 "requires Federal contracts above $25,000 for the provision, service, or sale of food in the United States, to include a clause that encourages, but does not require, the donation of excess food to nonprofit organizations."[20] It further extends the Emerson law provisions to protect those businesses from legal liabilities that partner with agencies to provide food. The text of this law does not require the donation of excess food; it merely requires that all contracts with the federal government to provide food include a clause that encourages donation. How is this a stick example if there are no actual donation requirements? The answer is in the way that government agencies pick their contractors. Government agencies are under no obligation to work with any given food provider. And these contracts can be very lucrative. For instance, the military contracts out for its food services, and Sodexo alone prepares more than 80,000 meals daily for the U.S. Marine Corps. Therefore, providers that want to keep the government as a client have a large incentive to donate excess food.[21] While the government is not requiring food donation, it is strongly encouraging it. Sodexo's website publicizes the fact that "surplus perishable and non-perishable food is collected and donated through programs such as Caring Cans and Sodexo Cans Across America."[22] The government in this situation is using a vendor that has adopted its values. Other vendors hoping to secure similar contracts would be wise to do the same.

ADDRESSING CRITICISMS AND PROBLEMS

Both Sodexo and Wal-Mart engage in socially responsible behavior with regard to surplus food. The U.S. government actively encourages this behavior utilizing both the carrot and stick approaches, but in both cases it is not possible to quantify the extent of the government's influence. With this in mind, is it worth it for governments to attempt to partner with businesses? Former secretary Reich's anti-CSR arguments would seem to indicate that these efforts are not really how government should allocate its resources. Still, Reich seems caught up in a need for purity of motives. He is correct that a government encouraging corporate social responsibility cannot be a substitute for effective regulations and just laws. Further, the government cannot be expected to meet the needs of all people unilaterally. In a response to Reich's anti-CSR position, the *Economist* editorializes that the "real task is to get them [corporations] to act in their enlightened long-term self-interest, rather than narrowly and in the short term. Mr. Reich dismisses this as mere 'smart management' rather than social responsibility. But done well, CSR can motivate employees and strengthen brands, while also providing benefits to society."[23] And—even if it cannot be ascertained for certain that one policy or another led to a specific action—the simple fact that Wal-Mart and Sodexo behaved in the way that the federal government wanted them to behave indicates a positive connection. Given the relatively small cost of encouraging CSR and the fact that it benefits all stakeholders—the government, business, and the community, this is a worthy investment.

Another critique of government's role in promoting CSR has to do with the cautious, sometimes risk-averse way that the government operates as compared with the more streamlined approach taken by many businesses to decision making. While there are benefits to society and businesses to engaging in CSR, barriers presented by government policies need to be addressed to remove roadblocks. Businesses may be reluctant to trust that laws will not change and may question whether government policies will create desired results. Furthermore, enacting change in the public sector can be more challenging than in the private sector because of the many perspectives that need to be included. On most decisions, a government's constituency—the voters in the particular jurisdiction—must be consulted.

An example cited in the Doing What Works series from the Center for American Progress illustrates the fear of many in the business community about partnering with government—that is, it is unresponsive to the needs of business. "Consider the new federal home visiting program. This grant program, which pays for nurse and social worker home visits to low-income mothers, was enacted in 2010—thirty-three years after the first randomized controlled trial demonstrated the benefits of such visits. Among the benefits we put off for more than three decades: healthier children and families, and lower Medicaid costs for taxpayers."[24]

Why should businesses trust that the government will be an equal partner, given such lack of responsiveness to opportunities identified even in government studies? The answer is that while governments can be cumbersome to deal with, they are the most direct representative of the people. In democratic societies they are answerable to those who elected them, and business needs the legitimacy of this partnership to effectively navigate the waters of social responsibility.

While this chapter focuses on corporate social responsibility applied domestically, the U.S. government also encourages socially responsible behavior in the business community on a global scale—and receives positive feedback, as outlined in a report issued by the U.S. Government Accountability Office (GAO). This study found that "key private sector players in CSR, meanwhile, indicate that they generally found current U.S. government activities helpful in their voluntary CSR efforts. More generally, it appears that CSR—even if not a substitute for regulation—has resulted in the commitment of U.S. multinational resources and a focus on issues of importance to the U.S. and to host countries."[25]

LOOKING TO THE FUTURE

The public good is enhanced when businesses are active participants in community life through socially responsible actions. Businesses benefit and society benefits when profit is not the only motivator. As shown, the government can encourage business to engage in socially responsible behavior by using both the carrot and stick approaches. This chapter focused mostly on U.S. government approaches to partnering with business for the betterment of society. Regional and local governments are also in an excellent position to promote CSR through public/private/nonprofit sector collaboration at the local level. Collaboration could include establishing local regulations or state laws more tailored to local communities and local small businesses—something that the federal government cannot readily do. Like CSR at the national level, this strategy could take many forms—for example, a city government making it easier for a small business to sponsor an athletic team for at-risk youth or a county offering incentives for those who carpool. Local CSR initiatives offer much potential for future exploration to complement those at the national level. In an era of financial challenge and high unemployment, many can benefit from partnerships between government at all levels and the business community. We can conclude that the wisdom of public sector promotion of community engagement by business, through corporate social responsibility, is evident in the many benefits to all participants. Part II of our book explores examples of social responsibility, beginning with pro bono service in chapter 6.

PART II

EXPLORING EXAMPLES

The call comes from a place that we do not know, that the demands placed on us will be more than we ever expected, and that if we knew what was in store, we never would have said yes. These are excellent tests for the pursuit of what matters.

—Peter Block (quoting Sister Joyce DeShano)[*]

When people were hungry, Jesus didn't say,
"Now is that political or social?"
He said, "I feed you."
Because the good news
to a hungry person is bread.

—Desmond Tutu[**]

[*] Peter Block, *The Answer to How Is Yes* (San Francisco: Berrett-Koehler, 2002), 29.
[**] Accessed November 30, 2011, http://www.tutufoundation-usa.org/exhibitions.html.

6

Pro Bono Service: Driving Social Impact with Professional Skills

Aaron Hurst

St. Joseph's Villa is the oldest and largest continually operating children's nonprofit in the Richmond, Virginia, metropolitan area. Established by the Daughters of Charity as a children's home and school in 1834, St. Joseph's Villa is now a nonsectarian 501(c)(3) organization supporting more than six hundred children and families each day. More than 250 volunteers serve St. Joseph's to provide educational, residential, and day services to children and families experiencing autism, homelessness, and physical and cognitive disabilities.[1] In 2005 St. Joseph's Villa recognized a need to increase its funding support in order to continue to provide high-quality services for children and families. Because its internal capacity to secure additional funds was limited, the nonprofit sought out the resources of the financial services corporation Capital One to help expand its funding streams. In response to St. Joseph's request, Capital One donated the professional skills and expertise of its employees through its volunteer program, Brand Corps. Leveraging the company's extensive experience in direct mail marketing, the Capital One Brand Corps assisted St. Joseph's in creating more engaging promotional material and a more efficient process to secure donations.

After one year, Capital One's marketing efforts on behalf of St. Joseph's Villa resulted in a 41 percent increase in donations for the nonprofit and a 51 percent increase in overall responses to direct mailings.[2] With 245 new donors, 257 additional contributions from existing donors, and heightened visibility in the community, St. Joseph's was able to significantly widen its pool of support for the organization's programs and services. Capital One's leadership helped to spur the pro bono movement that has swept through the business community in recent years. By giving employees opportunities to use their professional skills for serving their communities, Capital One has applied the core competencies of its business to achieve social impact. The Brand Corps was only the first of several pro bono programs that Capital One developed; it was founded when two employees formalized a process for managing growing community requests for pro bono marketing support. Since the inception of the Brand Corps Program in 1998, Brand associates have contributed more than 12,000 volunteer hours and more than $2 million in branding and marketing services to community partners.[3]

Encouraged by the success of Brand Corps, Capital One went on to establish pro bono corps across its finance, information technology (IT), legal, and human resources (HR) functions. In 2008, the company's community affairs department created the Pro Bono Roundtable, convening the different pro bono corps and providing Capital One employees with opportunities to connect and share successes, ideas, and challenges related to pro bono service.

Employee volunteer programs such as those established at Capital One indicate that pro bono service has extended far beyond the legal profession. As the business community continues to engage in pro bono work, professionals are helping to expand the resources available to tackle society's most pressing issues. While the primary focus of the pro bono movement is to achieve social impact, pro bono service also holds business value—in enhanced corporate citizenship or increased employee retention, for example. From several vantage points, the growing prevalence of pro bono service among business professionals has redefined volunteerism for the benefit of our communities.

AN EMERGING PRACTICE IN COMPANIES
Corporations are increasingly adopting and formalizing pro bono programs to realize and maximize the benefits of pro bono service. While a select number of companies have built and scaled formal programs, there is a growing overall understanding as to what pro bono service means and how it can be implemented by business professionals.

Definition of Pro Bono Service

Pro bono service is professional expertise made accessible to organizations serving the public good.[4] Companies, professional services firms, intermediaries, associations, and individual professionals all can deliver pro bono services, but in order to qualify as pro bono, these services must leverage the core competencies and expertise of the professional(s) to meet client needs. Pro bono services are typically provided without the expectation of a fee or at such a nominal fee as to make them accessible to the client. The client in a pro bono engagement is an organization serving the public good—a charitable, religious, community, government, and/or civic organization, for example.

Pro bono contributions are professional services that client organizations would otherwise have to purchase. While corporate social responsibility (CSR) has evolved to include a variety of community supports—from cash grants to park clean-ups to student mentoring—the critical distinction between these resources and pro bono service is the use of professional skills to meet client needs. When corporations, firms, associations, and individuals are engaged in pro bono service, they are drawing upon the same skills and expertise that they use in their professional roles.

Examples of pro bono service are as follows:

- A team of human resource professionals from a corporation conducts an audit of a nonprofit's human resource systems.
- Finance executives from a university alumni association develop managerial accounting systems for a social service agency.
- Professionals from a real estate developers' association help their local government secure and design space for a cultural center.
- Graphic designers and copywriters from an advertising agency create an annual report for a women's health organization.

A key best practice in pro bono service delivery is making a formal commitment to the recipient organization for the final work product. Under this commitment, the pro bono provider manages responsibilities such as rendering the agreed-upon services, staffing the pro bono project, and ensuring the engagement's timely completion and overall quality. In short, the provider must apply professional standards to pro bono services, treating pro bono clients as if they were paying clients.

Trends in the Pro Bono Movement
As corporations continue to adopt the pro bono ethic, several trends have started to emerge in the field of pro bono service. For example:

- Companies are increasingly formalizing pro bono programs to best realize benefits. Examples include Capital One and Gap Inc., both of which offer employees a variety of pro bono service opportunities through structured systems and processes.
- Cross-functional pro bono programs are increasingly emerging in companies. Capital One, for example, created its Pro Bono Roundtable to build relationships between pro bono providers in its HR, IT, and marketing departments.
- Some advanced, formalized pro bono programs have created technology solutions that allow requests by nonprofits for pro bono service to be staffed and executed remotely. Through Cornerstone OnDemand's Strategic Partnership program, nonprofits can apply for free talent management software and outsourced pro bono consulting services that help the organizations best implement Cornerstone's HR platform.
- Graduating MBA students and highly qualified job applicants are increasingly pursuing careers that provide opportunities to engage in pro bono service. Northwestern University's Kellogg School of Management, University of Southern California's Marshall School of Business, and Yale University's School of Art are only a few professional schools that have developed pro bono programming for graduate students.

These examples are by no means exhaustive; rather, they briefly illustrate the ways in which the pro bono marketplace is evolving to meet growing community needs.

CRITICAL NEEDS IN THE NONPROFIT SECTOR
In a 2012 national survey conducted by the Nonprofit Finance Fund, 85 percent of nonprofit respondents reported that demand for their services

increased in 2011, and 57 percent reported that they have three months or less cash on hand for organizational expenses.[5] Nonprofits have limited means to deliver their programs and services, and much of their revenue carries restrictions that prohibit them from using funding to address infrastructural issues like branding, technology, strategic planning, and staff development. As philanthropic dollars become increasingly limited, pro bono service affords nonprofits the business resources they need to thrive. In a 2009 national study by Deloitte LLP, 95 percent of nonprofits surveyed agreed they were in need of additional pro bono or skilled volunteer support.[6]

To meet this demand from the nonprofit sector, corporations are leveraging pro bono expertise in design, marketing, strategy, human resources (HR), information technology (IT), and finance, helping community organizations magnify their impact.

Design

Few nonprofits have internal expertise in graphic, web, product, or interior design. Nonprofits are challenged to create websites, print collateral, and physical spaces that reflect the high caliber of their programs and services. In a competitive philanthropic environment, nonprofit organizations contend for visibility, support, and funds. Well-designed programs, products, offices, and marketing materials can set them apart. Forty-five percent of nonprofits report that increasing their visibility in the community is one of their organizations' top priorities.[7] Key areas of nonprofit need for design expertise include the creation of informational, event-based, and fundraising collateral; programs and campaigns; and branding guidance and implementation.

To help meet the design needs of elementary and public schools, Target Corp. contributes pro bono expertise through its Target School Library Makeovers program. Complementing hands-on volunteer opportunities that include food drives and disaster relief efforts, Target's Property Development team leads complete makeovers of K–12 school libraries across the country. Since this program was founded in 2007, Target has contributed pro bono design expertise to revamp nearly one hundred libraries in need of support. Leveraging their core competencies in design, construction, and project management, the Target Property Development team equips their nonprofit partners with new design elements, lighting, furniture, shelves, computers, fresh paint, and two thousand books per school.[8]

As a global design consultancy, IDEO hosts regular pro bono Social Impact Labs to provide product, business, and organizational design talent to organizations that cannot afford paid engagements with design firms. Convening about twenty employees to brainstorm design solutions, the labs have proven an effective forum for developing powerful collaborations. Social entrepreneurs leave the lab sessions with a host of usable design ideas they would not have access to otherwise. In 2010, IDEO's Palo Alto office hosted twenty-one labs with a range of organizational partners, among them an ambulance company in India seeking ways to promote business, a microfinance organization designing an innovative insurance project for the developing world, and a social investment firm in search of novel ideas for creating a conference that will inspire participants.[9]

Marketing

Nonprofits' needs for design expertise are often closely linked to those for broader marketing. Just as a polished website and engaging print collateral can help a nonprofit stand out, so too can strong messaging and brand positioning. As many nonprofits serve similar clientele—underprivileged populations with limited access to resources—it is critical for organizations to communicate clearly about who they are, what they do, and how they achieve social impact. When nonprofits have marketing strategies and tools that they can use to target their key audiences, they are better positioned to secure funds, engage volunteers, and support their communities.

Most nonprofit organizations have limited capacity to pursue dynamic marketing initiatives. The pro bono support of marketing professionals can help nonprofits in several areas: managing organizational reputation; clearly articulating a mission, vision, and values; establishing key messages for raising funds, recruiting volunteers, and connecting with clients; identifying strong brand attributes; and building creative media partnerships and social media strategies.

Since 2002, communications consultancy Hill & Knowlton has delivered pro bono marketing and public relations services to strengthen Ashoka, a nonprofit organization dedicated to advancing social entrepreneurship. Hill & Knowlton has leveraged pro bono marketing talent primarily to strengthen the Ashoka Fellows Program, which supports promising social innovators with financial and professional resources. Hill & Knowlton offices around the world provide ongoing counsel in strategic communications and media relations to help Ashoka Fellows share their visions for social change with key audiences. Through pro bono message development, speech and op-ed writing, media and presentation training, event strategy, award nomination support, and global stakeholder engagement, Hill & Knowlton employees help Ashoka position its Fellows for success.[10]

In 2008, Wells Fargo channeled pro bono resources in project management and marketing to create print collateral for Family Connections, an organization serving children and families in the Portola and Excelsior neighborhoods of San Francisco. Over the course of six months, a team of Wells Fargo employees identified Family Connections' target audiences, produced corresponding communications strategies, and developed a creative brief to inform the content and design of a four-panel brochure and one-page fact sheet. The new collateral created by the Wells Fargo team showcased clear, compelling, and concise information about Family Connections that the nonprofit could use to engage potential donors and clients, information that reflected both enhanced ability and professionalism.[11]

Strategy

Nonprofits operate in a competitive, ever-changing environment. A nonprofit's grant dollars are often contingent on its ability to produce measurable impact and are further limited by shifting government budgets and philanthropic priorities. Strategic planning is crucial to the growth and sustainability of nonprofit organizations, but many nonprofits lack the resources they need to develop informed organizational strategies. MAP for Nonprofits is an organization providing management consulting and board recruitment services to nonprofits in the Twin Cities. Executive Director of MAP for Nonprofits, Judy Alnes, explains the need for pro bono strategy resources: "We shortcut a lot of process planning in our sector simply because we're short of money. We plan by the seat of our pants rather than planning by thoughtful evaluation of strategy."[12]

Thirty-five percent of nonprofits report that developing or updating their strategic plan is one of their top organizational priorities.[13] Key areas of need include assessing and evaluating nonprofits' current and potential programs, markets, and competitors. Global consulting firm Booz Allen Hamilton has achieved significant impact by delivering pro bono strategy services to the Wolf Trap Foundation for the Performing Arts. In March 2007, the Wolf Trap Foundation announced ambitious goals to have the organization go green by becoming carbon neutral and generating zero waste. Booz Allen Hamilton was impressed by Wolf Trap's vision and established a pro bono partnership with the foundation to provide technical expertise and operational guidance in support of its greening goals. After developing a baseline and strategy and hosting Wolf Trap's National Summit on the Arts and Environment, the Booz Allen Hamilton pro bono team introduced a robust strategic plan to Wolf Trap's leadership, which included near- and long-term objectives, initiatives to achieve those objectives, resources, projected benefits, metrics to measure progress, and a communications plan.[14] At a February 2009 National Press Club luncheon in Washington, D.C., Booz Allen Hamilton and the Wolf Trap Foundation for the Performing Arts were honored with a PRNewswire Corporate Social Responsibility Award in the environmental stewardship category.[15]

Human Resources

In his monograph *Good to Great and the Social Sectors*, management consultant and innovative thinker Jim Collins states, "The number-one resource for a great social sector organization is having enough of the right people willing to commit themselves to the mission."[16] Nonprofits rely heavily on the dedication of their staff and volunteers to deliver their core programs and services. According to a 2008 survey, however, 37 percent of nonprofit executive directors see attracting and retaining skilled staff as one of their top five concerns.[17] Common HR challenges facing the nonprofit sector include managing, engaging, and growing internal talent. In a 2009 survey conducted by the Taproot Foundation, 86 percent of nonprofit respondents reported that they would seek out pro bono HR support if it were available to them.[18]

Through the Gap Inc. Leadership Initiative (GILI), Gap Inc. offered its youth-focused nonprofit partners the same level of intensive leadership training that its own executives receive. In partnership with the nonprofit, CompassPoint, Gap Inc.'s HR team designed tailored leadership development programs for selected nonprofit executives. From 2009 to 2011, Gap Inc. HR professionals provided pro bono coaching and mentoring to these executives on an ongoing basis, delivering support in areas such as strengths-based leadership, change management, and professional development.[19]

In 2008, American Express developed a pro bono program entitled the American Express Leadership Academy. In collaboration with the Center for Creative Leadership, American Express designed the academy to convene the nation's top emerging nonprofit leaders to help them develop the personal and business skills required for successful leadership in the nonprofit sector. After passing a competitive application process, academy members participate in a weeklong curriculum led by CCL trainers, nonprofit leaders, and top executives at American Express. To ensure that the Leadership Academy has a lasting impact, members set goals and action plans during the training and have access to follow-up support from CCL in the form of online networking tools, telephone coaching sessions, leadership goal checkpoints, and a one-year performance review.[20]

Information Technology

Like all businesses, nonprofits need strong IT capabilities to connect with their various stakeholders and audiences. A well-designed website and ample technology support can help organizations recruit volunteers, raise funds, and share mission-critical information with their constituents. In a 2008 survey conducted by Accenture, 31 percent of nonprofits reported that using IT to reduce costs and create value is one of their top organizational priorities.[21] With limited IT budgets and expertise, many nonprofits stand to benefit from pro bono IT support, especially in database implementation and website creation and development.

Through its pro bono program, "On Demand Community," IBM provides critical technology expertise to targeted community organizations and schools. In October 2007, IBM leveraged its On Demand Community program to expand the capacity of United Way's 2-1-1 call center in San Diego. A series of wildfires had been burning an estimated 515,000 acres in

Southern California, and the San Diego 2-1-1 center experienced a drastic increase in emergency calls—from 650 to 35,000 per day. The influx of calls caused United Way workers to exceed their building's capacity and take over an empty church next door to provide needed supplemental call capacity and physical space. The severity of the situation was apparent, and IBM sent employee and On Demand volunteer Mike Mendez to help the 2-1-1 center manage the high need they were facing. Working nonstop for three days, Mike assessed the 2-1-1 line needs and developed vital capacity expansion. Discussing options and risk with the director of the 2-1-1 center, Mike was able to move forward quickly and automate United Way's paper intake process. With ongoing support from IBM, Mike built an infrastructure to significantly increase the 2-1-1 center's capability to field calls in a time of crisis.[22]

Finance
Financial planning, cost analysis, and auditing skills are vital for nonprofit organizations. Nonprofits must operate on thin margins, which make a comprehensive understanding of expected costs and revenue imperative for nonprofit leadership. In addition, grant dollars are often contingent on the financial health and stability of organizations, and grant makers depend on sound, transparent financial reports to make decisions on philanthropic giving. Specialized expertise in finance can be expensive, and many nonprofits cannot afford financial services. Pro bono support in financial modeling, strategic planning, auditing, and financial literacy training can provide nonprofits with needed access to resources that help them continue to thrive.

By engaging in a pro bono partnership with Women's World Banking—a global network of microfinance institutions serving more than twenty-nine countries—Citi leverages its core competencies to support small businesses and families in some of the world's most disadvantaged communities. Employees from Citi's Microfinance Group work with Women's World Banking to deliver training to microfinance institutions on basic governance, policies, asset liability reporting, and financial risk management. To date, Citi has conducted ten pro bono financial training sessions, reaching more than two hundred participants and more than one hundred microfinance institutions.[23]

As part of its Global Development Initiative, KPMG member firms provide pro bono support to help eradicate poverty and build sustainable enterprise in sub-Saharan Africa. Through the Millennium Cities Initiative— a project of the Earth Institute at Columbia University—KPMG delivers pro bono investment reports to encourage potential investors to pursue commercially viable business opportunities in developing sub-Saharan cities. Since KPMG launched its pro bono programming in 2007, the firm has completed investment reports for Blantyre, Malawi; Kisumu, Kenya; Kumasi, Ghana; and Ondo State, Nigeria.[24]

Corporations across industries are leveraging pro bono talent across functional areas to make significant social impact. Whether they are building pro bono teams to help local nonprofits create websites or providing one-on-one pro bono coaching to help global organizations plan for growth, major companies are helping to increase community access to vital business resources.

BUSINESS VALUE

Pro bono service produces substantial benefits for recipient organizations. With access to support in design, marketing, strategy, HR, IT, finance, and more, nonprofits are better equipped to sustain and grow their critical programs. Pro bono also delivers value for the providers of community support. By channeling company expertise to tackle social issues, corporations are using pro bono service to make headway on a variety of business goals.

Leveraged Impact: The Multiplier Effect

Because the value of pro bono service is significantly higher than traditional volunteer activities, and because its impact can be transformational for recipients, pro bono service can be viewed as a leveraged social investment. Based on research conducted by the Committee Encouraging Corporate Philanthropy and the Taproot Foundation, pro bono service is valued at an average rate of $120 per hour, whereas such hands-on volunteer activities as park clean-ups are valued at a rate of approximately $20 per hour.[25] When corporations contribute the valuable time and talents of their professional employees to their community partners, they help recipient organizations become more effective in serving their constituents. Using business expertise to help organizations expand their capacity, lower their operating costs, and increase service delivery, pro bono providers help ensure that more people are supported by their service. As such, pro bono service produces the multiplier effect—a high social return on a valuable resource investment.

Enhanced Corporate Citizenship

Corporate citizenship is increasingly recognized as a vital component of sustainable business. Pro bono service is a particularly efficient and effective way to improve corporate reputation through visible, high-impact, low-cost engagements. By providing employees with opportunities to serve nonprofit partners, corporations ensure that the pro bono service of those individuals reflects positively not only on themselves but also on their company. In addition, the high value of pro bono service enables corporations to significantly increase their annual community giving, further improving their socially responsible reputations.

Human Resources Benefits

According to a 2007 national survey, 66 percent of the Generation Y workforce reported that they would prefer to work at a company that provides them with opportunities to apply their skills to benefit nonprofit organizations. In this same survey, 90 percent of corporate HR professionals agreed that contributing business expertise to nonprofits in a volunteer capacity would be an effective way to develop leadership skills.[26] Based on research conducted by LBG Associates in 2009, a majority of employees surveyed reported that they felt better about working at their company as a result of their experiences with pro bono service.[27] Corporations that develop pro bono programming for employees can realize HR benefits in recruitment, professional development, and staff retention. By providing staff with opportunities to use their skills to make social impact, companies can attract bright, motivated individuals to join their ranks. In addition, pro bono service helps employees learn and grow by applying their skills and expertise to new clients and challenges, which can foster strong relationships between companies and their staff members.

Improved Communication and Collaboration

Pro bono engagements create opportunities for collaboration among employees who may not otherwise work with each other. On pro bono projects, employees can work with team members from across business units, departments, and offices, facilitating understanding and opening lines of communication. As Sylvia Reynolds, chief marketing officer at Wells Fargo, explains, "One of the key benefits I see coming out of our employees' participation on pro bono projects is the opportunity to foster strong internal communication."[28] Through pro bono service, individuals are able to build and strengthen their relationships with colleagues and gain exposure to different aspects of their companies that they may not see in their daily job responsibilities. This type of cross-functional collaboration helps break down work silos and sharpens communications across company divisions and geographies. In addition, pro bono service allows employees to improve their skills in client management, oral presentation, and networking, which they can apply to their professional roles.

Opportunity for Innovation

Pro bono service often builds relationships between partners with very different core competencies. For example, pro bono engagements may pair a global financial services firm with a neighborhood tutoring center or a local advertising agency with a national environmental organization. Such unique partnerships create opportunities for innovation, as they challenge pro bono providers to apply skills they use every day in different contexts for different clients. By bringing fresh perspectives from one sector to focus on issues in another, pro bono service fosters inventive solutions that are applicable to both nonprofit and for-profit environments. Through corporate pro bono programming, employees are able to practice entrepreneurship and learn new lessons on market risks and opportunities, business models, and leadership styles. Employees can then take these valuable lessons back to their companies to drive innovation and build competitive advantage.[29] Many corporations have implemented pro bono programming because it holds business value in addition to creating social impact. Successful programs often focus on one or two business benefits, but the various goals that pro bono can achieve—from enhanced corporate reputation to increased employee development—make a convincing case for adoption.

CONCLUSION

While cash grants, in-kind donations, and hands-on volunteer opportunities continue to play an important role in corporate social responsibility, the pro bono movement is gaining momentum across the business community. Recognizing that community organizations have limited resources at their disposal, an increasing number of corporations are delivering pro bono support to help nonprofits sustain their programs and services. From financial modeling to logo design, nonprofits can position themselves to significantly advance with access to pro bono support. As the examples in this chapter illustrate, many organizations have been able to expand their services, cultivate new donors, and build their leaders as a result of pro bono partnerships with corporations.

By engaging in pro bono service, business professionals help nonprofit organizations operate more efficiently and effectively. In turn, nonprofits are better equipped to drive social change. The pro bono IT support that IBM delivered to a San Diego 2-1-1 center ensured the safety of victims of a devastating fire. Finance skills that KPMG provides pro bono to communities in sub-Saharan Africa ensure the development of strong, healthy urban centers. The pro bono design expertise that Target offers to school libraries across the United States ensures that children can learn in bright, welcoming environments. Pro bono service achieves an impact for recipient organizations, but its reach is much broader than final deliverables. Pro bono expands the capacity of communities, helping people grow. In our next chapter, we examine development and growth coming from public/private sector partnership.

7

Public/Private Sector Collaboration

Linda Williams

After graduating from college in 1972, I was one of the few social workers at the university who wanted to return to my hometown of Memphis, Tennessee, to work in public welfare, despite that it was a low-paying job. I wanted to be a part of the solution rather than standing on the sideline complaining about the problems of families supported by welfare. After returning home, I worked for four months in a program providing food stamps to those in need; in the Tennessee Department of Human Services (DHS), this was the first available spot for a paraprofessional (a worker without a master's in social work). It was a draining experience because, at the end of each workday, people still needed to be seen and were still in need of food for their families. However, when I was called to be a work incentive counselor, which involved collaborative work with the Department of Employment Security, my response was, "God has validated my calling!"

I still remember my first client; we'll call her Sarah, a short, stout, African American woman, clean in appearance but sloppy in her attire. My first thought before talking with Sarah was that a great deal of work on training/employability skills would be needed before she could go on a job interview. On our first encounter Sarah was not eager to share the information I needed to prepare a social history and assessment. As I learned later, she saw me as another young case worker, fresh out of college, who was going to put her into another training course that wouldn't improve her life or the lives of her children. However, after I asked her about her children, she warmed up considerably. She was willing to tell me all that I needed to know about her plight and her struggle to leave the welfare system with a job, as well as her desire that her children not grow up and depend on welfare. Sarah was thirty years old and had six children. She had her first child at sixteen and was only able to complete tenth grade. She wanted to finish her high school diploma but knew that since her youngest child was now seven, she had to be involved in training that would lead to work—and she wanted to work, based on the work requirements for welfare recipients to enroll in Work Incentive Program (WIN). Sarah had attempted to go back to school after her first child was born but had no family to care for her baby. And the rule then was that no matter how young you were, once you were a parent, you were no longer considered a child and could only attend night school with other adults. At that time the prevailing view was that if teenage mothers were around other youth, it would send the wrong message or somehow cause more teenage girls to get pregnant before marriage.

During the interview, Sarah shared with me that she had completed several training courses: cosmetology (which had come in handy with her four girls), upholstery, tailoring (helpful because she could make a few items for her children; however, they hated to wear them because she had not mastered this skill), and welding (she enjoyed and was extremely good at this, but since it was a male-dominated field, she could not secure employment). As Sarah related her history, I could see that she was only sent to various training programs to meet basic eligibility requirements, with no consideration of her talent, aptitude, personal career goals, or the labor market. The system, in its effort to make public welfare uncomfortable for Sarah, had served instead to create a woman with feelings of hopelessness. As I looked at what was available for Sarah, all that I could do was authorize after-school services for her children and pass her on to a job placement counselor. That was not what she really needed. She had done everything that she was told to do over the past fourteen years, and all that she had to show for her efforts were six beautiful children who were doing extremely well academically in school. Although Sarah was not able to find paid employment, it was noted throughout her record that she was doing all she could to make sure that her children didn't make the same mistake she had by not finishing high school. The system had failed her, and I was just another welfare worker with few options to offer her and certainly no training or tools to lift her out of her pit of hopelessness. I was just an energetic college graduate who wanted to save the world but didn't have the experience, tools, or power to assist Sarah with what she needed to become gainfully employed.

Why is this story important? Too often Americans assume that parents who receive cash assistance through welfare programs have done so because of their unwillingness to work and an expectation that the government should support their children. Many people don't understand that in order to receive cash assistance, one must be willing to allow the government to enter into what most people would consider personal and private family matters. Thus welfare recipients receive little money compared with what they give up in return. If they could avoid the series of welfare case workers (who often require repeated answers to the same questions to determine the truthfulness of the client) and visits to the welfare office, they would gladly do so. Moreover, various programs over the years have been developed for welfare recipients aimed at creating work opportunities rather than continuing benefits, but they were planned and executed in silos, that is, not in cooperation with business. Sarah is a good example, because none of the programs that she participated in and completed resulted in employment for her. While this is not true for everyone served, at the time she enrolled, welfare departments in the United States were only required to report numbers served. Few evaluations of program effectiveness were made or asked, for example: How many participants were trained, and did the training lead to employment? What were the rates of recidivism of welfare recipients who became gainfully employed? Let us look now at the evolution of the welfare system and then at an example of how partnership of the public sector with the business community can make welfare service delivery much more effective in equipping people to become self-sufficient. Although our focus is on the United States, the benefits of public/private sector partnership will likely be applicable elsewhere.

PUBLIC WELFARE EMPLOYMENT PROGRAMS IN THE UNITED STATES

To provide a context for reviewing a public/private sector partnership example, we will first briefly describe the evolution of the welfare system in the United States and then summarize the situation in the state of Tennessee.

Evolution of the Welfare System

In 1935 President Franklin D. Roosevelt introduced the first federal welfare program.[1] At that time 88 percent of welfare families received assistance because the father of the children was deceased.[2] The nation also had a surplus of workers and a shortage of work, so keeping widows at home not only allowed mothers to care for their children but also prevented women from competing with men for available jobs. Several government programs were created to combat male unemployment, such as the Civilian Conservation Corps and Works Progress Administration (WPA).[3] The next major change occurred in 1962 with the creation of the Community Work and Training program (CWT).[4] This government-funded program allowed states to choose whether to enroll adult recipients of Aid to Families with Dependent Children (AFDC) in workfare programs (meaningful public service jobs that did not displace other workers). In 1964, Title V of the Economic Opportunity Act (EOA) allowed states to develop work experience demonstration projects that used EOA funds instead of welfare funds intended for AFDC recipients. This act expired in June 1969.[5]

In 1967 the Work Incentive Program was created through an amendment to the 1935 Social Security Act; its purpose was to make AFDC recipients less dependent on welfare. WIN was designed to provide training for women; that is exactly what it did for Sarah, whom we discussed earlier. However, most recipients who were involved in WIN did not find jobs, and that was also Sarah's experience. WIN was revamped several times, then finally phased out in 1990 when it was replaced by a new program, the Job Opportunities and Basic Skills (JOBS) training program. In parallel, the Comprehensive Employment and Training Act (CETA) was set up in 1973 and the Food Stamp Workfare Act in 1977. The latter was designed to require that all able-bodied food stamp recipients work or make efforts to look for employment. In 1982, the Job Training Partnership Act (JTPA) replaced CETA.[6]

Needless to say, many families were helped by these programs; however, since cost-benefit analyses were not undertaken, documentation of success was not clear. The programs apparently existed to make sure that taxpayer dollars were only used to temporarily support families until they could become gainfully employed. Yet without comprehensive tracking of families to determine if those who left the program were successful or if they were able to adequately support their families as a direct result of services provided, it is hard to know if the programs' goals were achieved. Informational reports consisted of aggregated activity numbers transmitted through the states to the federal government. The emphasis was not on evaluating outcomes or determining if the appropriate services were provided.[7]

Implementation of 1996 Welfare Reform Legislation in Tennessee

During the presidential campaigns in the mid-1990s, much of the focus was on the need for welfare reform. When Bill Clinton became president in 1993, it was clear that political leadership wanted to set time limits for the welfare cash assistance program, since it was thought that the system had created generations of dependency on public support.[8] In preparing for this change in public policy, Tennessee's Department of Human Services made a bold move, as did several other states, by developing a waiver request that would allow the state to receive funds devoted to the cash assistance program (AFDC) through a federal block grant. A block grant is a consolidated grant of federal funds, formerly allocated for specific programs, that a state or local government can use at its discretion to serve welfare recipients. The criteria for individuals to receive support would meet some of the basic requirements to be included in the federal legislation. In preparing for the waiver, the state solicited ideas and support from the business community, the religious community, and clients who were receiving services. As a result of this planning, a new program replaced AFDC in the state of Tennessee named Families First. Families First was created under a federal waiver prior to the federal Temporary Assistance for Needy Families legislation of 1996, which is now known as TANF.[9]

A critical piece of the Families First program involved the creation of state and local area Families First Councils. It required that 60 percent of the council be representatives from the business community, with the rest to include representatives from the faith community and clients receiving services. This was the first major effort in Tennessee to solicit the business community's input on training and other employment preparation activities for adult participants in the cash assistance programs. In Tennessee, the state's Families First Council, as well as the local Families First Councils, were appointed by the state commissioner of human services based on recommendations from each of the eight regional district administrators. Because of the size of Shelby County, which includes Memphis, and the concentration of families living in poverty and on cash assistance programs, it was designated as a separate district—District 8. As district administrator responsible for making recommendations for the District 8 Families First Council, I could now use the ideas and lessons learned over the years to make welfare reform in Shelby County truly help the families it was meant to assist. Working with employers to determine their employment needs and ensuring that program participants were adequately trained to fulfill those needs were now incorporated into the state of Tennessee's TANF program of Families First.

Securing recommendations for individuals to be included on the Families First Council in Shelby County was not difficult. Our local chamber of commerce president not only recommended participants for the council, he also wrote letters to the presidents and CEOs of local companies. His letters were a passionate call to action, asking for involvement and help in working with the 27,000 families receiving cash assistance in Shelby County. We were required to assess and assist these families in finding appropriate employment. As a result of reaching out to the chamber and to the suggested companies, we were able to secure recommendations that allowed District 8 (Shelby County) to exceed the 60 percent business representation required on the council. The chamber president also told me that several companies in Memphis had relocated some of their company divisions to other parts of the country because they were unable to find local people qualified to perform the jobs; but these were not high tech or high-skilled jobs. It seemed this was the right time and place for drastic changes to be made in our welfare system.

FEDERAL EXPRESS EXAMPLE

Even though Federal Express (FedEx) was not one of the first businesses represented on the Families First Council in 1997, FedEx recruitment staff reached out to see how we could work collaboratively. They heard about our need to find jobs for our welfare clients and had positions that needed to be filled. Our first meeting with the FedEx hub recruitment staff involved discussing with them the details of the Families First program, and they shared the basic requirements for their entry-level positions. I saw this as a great opportunity for our Families First clients because the available positions were part-time but paid more than full-time minimum-wage jobs. The FedEx positions also included health benefits and tuition reimbursement. This was an opportunity for Families First participants to work part-time for a successful Memphis-based company, which also supported employees in continuing their education to reach long-term career goals. This was not a dead-end job but a job with a company having national recognition. The relationship with FedEx was a win-win for everyone.

The Federal Express HR department handpicked the managers who would be responsible for supervising Families First participants. Because the company wanted the collaboration to be successful, they assigned managers who were passionate about their responsibilities, had excellent people skills, and related well with their employees. At the same time we made a decision to have just one contractor (of several available) to provide job readiness, career advancement, and support services. As a result, FedEx had only one contractor to work with, and that contractor had staff available to address support service needs any hour of the day. One contractor stood out because of its flexibility and passion for working toward successful outcomes with clients. This particular contractor was willing to think outside the box in anticipating the needs of participants and their families and was able to transfer this thought process in their job readiness training to help participants overcome barriers and succeed in their employment.

Prior to the hiring of the initial Families First participants, we met with the FedEx managers and the contractor. During that initial meeting we discussed details about services offered by the Families First program (for example, child care, transportation reimbursement, emergency dental care, and job readiness seminars) and learned about FedEx from the staff. We were given a tour of the FedEx hub operations at night so we had a clear idea of the nature of the work in the hub that could be shared with the clients selected to apply at FedEx. We were very impressed by the organized manner in which thousands of employees moved through security to their work sites and immediately began their task without any apparent directions. People were working methodically together for a common cause. We were also surprised by a question from one of the FedEx male managers: "Will child care be provided?" He later explained that he was divorced with two children, had planned visitation with them, and always had child care for them in order to work the night shift. However, one night his child care plan broke down, and he was faced with driving around town, trying to find a relative or family member to keep his children. He was able to locate someone, but the situation made him clearly understand the plight of some of his staff with children and the unforeseen challenges that can occur. After this discussion, we assigned a staff person from the contract agency to be available to the participants after hours to troubleshoot situations that interfered with individuals' reporting to work. FedEx also shared with us the availability of a child care center that was located next door to the FedEx hub facility, operated by the Federal Aviation Administration Office in Memphis for its employees. We brainstormed other possible challenges that could affect work attendance in our partnership. This was a true partnership; FedEx was just as interested as we were in making sure that Families First participants were able to succeed in their job placement. This was a company willing to commit time and resources to helping welfare recipients. Its actions demonstrated a commitment to the Memphis community in working with those families that would not ordinarily seek employment with the company.

Meetings between the Tennessee Department of Human Services staff, contract staff, and FedEx continued on a monthly basis. We looked not just at how Families First participants could qualify for entry-level positions but also at how they could qualify for higher-paying full-time jobs that were posted by FedEx. One strength of the partnership with FedEx was that the company wanted employees to move up. As we began talking to managers, we quickly realized that most managers at FedEx began by working in the FedEx hub operations.

FedEx also wanted their employees in the Memphis area to be aware of the company's efforts to reach out to Families First participants, through the partnership with the Tennessee Department of Human Services. To share this information with staff, the company produced a video that included an interview with the manager of FedEx hub recruitment and me, as administrative district director and representative of the local human services agency. Employees watched the video on monitors placed along the paths staff use to get to their work site each night (the company used this media method to make sure that all employees were aware of important company information). The video demonstrated the importance of this public/private partnership not only to the management staff but also to everyone in the company.

The relationship with FedEx worked so well that the company was given the first State Employer of the Year Award in 1998. It was based on the company's commitment and partnership to assist the Shelby County/District 8 DHS staff in making sure Families First recipients were given proper training leading to employment. While FedEx received the benefit of tax incentives for hiring TANF and food stamp recipients, it was clear that a primary motivating factor for the company was making a difference in the community. The contractor also played an important role by preparing program participants for the expectations of the job. By 1998 FedEx had hired over 2,000 Families First participants, including one client who moved from the hub and became a secretary in the office of the director of human resources in the hub operations.

The federal Department of Health and Human Services, through its Urban Partnership for Welfare Reform, also took note of the success of this project. The Urban Partnership for Welfare Reform Initiative (UPI) was announced by Secretary of Health and Human Services Tommy Thompson as a project designed to improve outcomes for low-income families by facilitating peer exchanges among TANF stakeholders across the county.[10] In 2006 we were invited to participate in the initiative based on our outcome data and ability to engage employers locally to hire welfare recipients. As a result, we presented the FedEx story to other urban areas and a subsequent UPI event was held in Memphis. FedEx participated in a panel discussion to explain why it seized the opportunity to work with the local DHS staff and the benefits that the company received as a result of the relationship. As part of the two-day event, a tour of the FedEx hub was arranged so that our peers from other cities could see what we had observed prior to sending the initial Families First participant to FedEx. As a result of the work done in Memphis, FedEx began discussions with other hub operations around the United States so that similar partnerships could be forged with other TANF programs.

LESSONS LEARNED

During the UPI event we were asked to share what we had learned from our partnership with Fed Ex. Even though our participants benefited greatly from the relationship, we acknowledged some challenges and identified some lessons learned:

- *The importance of maintaining a successful process when contractual arrangements change and of staying connected to the employer (never abdicate this responsibility to a contractor)*

    DHS on a statewide basis decided to change arrangements with contractors, permitting only one in each district. This resulted in a new contractor for the FedEx project. This new contractor stated a willingness to continue the FedEx partnership but was not able to maintain the engagement of management staff at FedEx. The contractor also ended the monthly meetings that were critical to the success of the process. Continued involvement of local DHS staff would have helped overcome this problem.

- *Continuing job retention and career advancement support for individuals after initial employment*

    Even part-time employment at FedEx resulted in the closure of the DHS case. Our efforts to help program participants earn a living wage often left them without the services they needed to successfully complete a probationary period at FedEx. For many participants, support services were needed to guide them through difficulties that are often faced when moving from a period of unemployment to employment. Such services include emergency transportation, emergency child care, and availability of a job retention counselor; these were no longer available after participants were on the job for a short time.

- *The importance of staying attuned to changing company workforce needs*

    One example is that employment needs at FedEx are seasonal, so it is important to stay in close communication with the company to identify and meet workforce needs as they change.

- *Constantly reviewing employment and retention data*

Why have some participants remained employed while others have left or lost their jobs? Being able to answer this question is vital to guiding the process of identifying both the right candidates for a given position in a company and their appropriate training needs. Effectively matching people to opportunities is crucial to ensure successful employment relationships that benefit individuals and companies.

LOOKING FORWARD

As I started this chapter with a client, I would like to end with another one, in this case someone who demonstrates the results of a successful public/private partnership. We'll call her Julie. Julie had to drop out of college after the early death of her husband. Her husband had been the breadwinner. Julie had planned to have a career in healthcare after graduation from a local surgical technology program. The death of her husband set the family back, and since he was self-employed, Julie had no financial resources that would allow her to continue her education. She needed healthcare insurance for herself and her child and financial support for her child. Julie's perceived last hope was to apply for welfare and delay completing her education. This was a trying time for her in many ways, partly because the family had always been self-sufficient. It was difficult for Julie to come into the office because she felt a loss of self-worth at having to ask the government for help. However, the needs of her child made her put away her pride, move through the line, and apply for healthcare and cash benefits.

After her interview with the eligibility counselor, she was immediately identified as a candidate for FedEx employment as a way for her to earn money and continue her education. Julie was hired in a night-sorting role and, after completing her three-month probationary period, was able to receive tuition reimbursement so she could reenroll in school to continue her education. She continued to work part-time on the night sort while attending school during the day. Julie was only eligible for cash assistance for a few months because of her earnings from FedEx. However, with transitional child care services, transportation support, and tuition reimbursement, she was able to successfully complete her surgical technology training and move into a full-time job with a local hospital. Julie struggled for a while and had to make drastic changes in her lifestyle, but employment with FedEx was the prescription for a lifestyle of self-support rather than welfare dependency. Had the FedEx partnership not existed, she would likely have remained on welfare for a longer period of time and perhaps ended up as Sarah did, seeking help to get a job that never materialized. The availability of Families First (TANF) for Julie was a form of insurance available to her when she needed it in the short term until she was able to become gainfully employed and support her family. Her example is proof that the system can work and help families become self-sufficient. It involves public agencies, businesses, and the entire community working together to remove barriers and create access to employment opportunities that lead to independence. In the next chapter, we will explore another important dimension of social responsibility and social justice, healthcare, from a system level.

8

Healthcare as Social Responsibility: Implications for Business

Deborah LeVeen

The United States' system of healthcare is out of control. Our failure to create an integrated and comprehensive national health system has allowed the development of a medical industry that absorbs an ever-increasing share of personal income, business profits, and government revenues. Our fragmented system of insurance has responded by reducing coverage: we now have almost 50 million people without health insurance, causing great suffering and even resulting in deaths.[1] This approach to healthcare is morally intolerable and financially unsustainable. For business, change is imperative. Business cannot function without a healthy workforce; nor can it sustain continued double-digit increases in the cost of providing health coverage. Business has a critical role to play in advocating for the changes needed to create a more cost-effective healthcare system.

Despite the desperate need for change, it was not until March 2010 that the United States finally adopted legislation aimed at comprehensive reform, the Affordable Care Act (ACA).[2] Winning passage required a herculean effort and significant compromises. Yet even with those compromises, the new law constitutes a historic victory for those who believe that ensuring affordable access to comprehensive and high-quality healthcare is one of the basic responsibilities of a civilized society. For the first time, we have enshrined in law the principle that government must play a central role in both ensuring access and controlling costs. However, this new commitment is far from securely established. Its opponents, drawing upon the longstanding conservative tradition of laissez-faire government, attack the new law as "a government takeover of health care" and advocate instead a market-based approach.[3] The U.S. House of Representatives, won by Republicans in the 2010 election, has voted both to repeal the ACA and to replace Medicare's guaranteed access to basic services, for those aged 65 and older, with vouchers to purchase private insurance.[4] The business community has been divided in its approach to healthcare reform. The U.S. Chamber of Commerce and the National Federation of Independent Business, echoing the views of the conservative movement, are fighting to repeal or weaken the new law.[5] Others, such as the Business Roundtable and the National Business Group on Health, believe that effective reform is impossible without a stronger government role.[6]

Healthcare is a fundamental issue of social responsibility and social justice. Therefore, in this chapter we will analyze the underlying dynamics of our healthcare system to show why a strong government role is essential if we want reform that can control healthcare spending without reducing access or jeopardizing quality. In addition, we will identify the implications for business in addressing this key area of social responsibility. The term *healthcare system* is a misnomer, for even with the ACA, the United States has no overarching policy framework capable of both ensuring access to care and controlling overall spending. However, in keeping with conventional usage, we will use this terminology, recognizing that a true healthcare system is a critical future need.

The chapter is organized as follows. Section I analyzes the dynamics of our system of healthcare to show how it has given rise to both soaring costs and diminishing access; this analysis allows us to identify the critical forces that must be addressed if reform is to be effective. Section II looks at the policy implications of this analysis, critiquing the conservative proposal for more market-oriented reforms, reviewing the gains brought by the ACA, and suggesting some of the most important ways in which it should be strengthened. We conclude with a discussion of the implications for business.

The Imperative of Reform: Access, Costs, and Outcomes

Before beginning this examination, we need to remind ourselves why the status quo is morally unacceptable and economically unsustainable. The number of people without health insurance in the United States has increased steadily over the last two decades, with devastating consequences. As mentioned above, the total now stands at almost 50 million people, or 18.5 percent of the nonelderly population.[7] Since those without health insurance cannot pay for healthcare, they receive less care or receive it later than people with insurance, they get sicker, and they are more likely to die. A team of Harvard researchers estimates preventable mortality related to lack of insurance is as high as 45,000 people a year.[8] The majority of the uninsured are low-income working people: 76 percent are in working families; 78 percent have incomes below 250 percent of the federal poverty level, or about $55,000 a year in 2010 for a family of four.[9] In addition, a growing number of people are underinsured; they have insurance with such high cost-sharing or low coverage limits that they end up forgoing necessary care or being pursued by creditors seeking to collect unpaid bills.[10] Almost two-thirds of personal bankruptcies are related to medical costs.[11]

The problem of access cannot be solved without dealing with the problem of costs, as rising costs are a major cause of the growing number of uninsured. Healthcare spending has increased more than twice as fast as gross domestic product (GDP) over the last fifty years—about 2.5 percentage points more per year—thus absorbing an increasing share of GDP: from 5.2 percent in 1960 to 17.3 percent in 2009.[12] Between 2001 and 2011, the rate of increase in healthcare costs greatly exceeded that in wages and general inflation. Healthcare insurance premiums went up 113 percent, wages rose 34 percent, and general inflation was only 27 percent.[13] Thus individuals, families, businesses, and governments are all being forced to spend an ever-increasing share of their income on healthcare costs. And because medical spending is the major long-term driver of increased government spending, our deficit problem cannot be solved unless we find ways to contain healthcare costs.[14]

Finally, international comparisons make clear that we are not getting our money's worth. We spend far more than any other country in the world but get less, in terms of both utilization of care and outcomes. In 2008, the United States spent 16 percent of GDP on healthcare while the median among the thirty industrialized countries in the Organization for Economic Cooperation and Development (OECD) was 8.7 percent.[15] Per capita healthcare spending in the United States was $7,538, more than twice the

OECD median of $2,995. Yet Americans actually have fewer doctor visits, shorter hospital stays, and lower life expectancy. Most striking, the United States has the highest rate of preventable mortality—"deaths that might have been prevented with timely and effective care"—of sixteen OECD countries.[16]

Business should be alarmed not simply by their own rising costs but also by the manifest inefficiency of the American approach to healthcare. American business is at a competitive disadvantage relative to foreign businesses in other industrialized countries; the latter's costs are lower because their healthcare systems are more cost-effective. Indeed, the Business Roundtable, recognizing this problem, has begun an annual "value comparability study" to track the performance of the U.S. healthcare system relative to our major trading partners and to help identify and promote potential improvements.[17] Developing effective improvements requires accurate analysis of the underlying causes of the problems. That is the central task of the following section.

SECTION I. THE DYNAMICS OF THE U.S. HEALTHCARE SYSTEM

To begin our analysis, we will look further at international comparisons, which help identify the major factors associated with differences in health system performance. Next we will examine the role of the major players in the system as they have shaped its evolution, allowing an ever-increasing share of economic resources to be devoted to healthcare while leaving an ever-increasing number of people without access to that care.

U.S. Spending in Comparative Context:
Technology, Prices, and Administration

Within the growing body of international comparative analysis, there is broad agreement that the most important factors associated with much higher healthcare spending in the United States are the greater availability and use of advanced technology, higher prices, and higher administrative costs.[18]

Our healthcare financing system, and the much larger role of private insurance in our system, are also frequently mentioned. U.S. healthcare is more technologically intensive than that in other countries. For example, although hospital stays in the United States are shorter, they cost nearly three times as much as the OECD median, and our use of high-technology inpatient procedures is much higher.[19] We have a far higher level of technological capacity: for example, 26.5 magnetic resonance imaging (MRI) units per million people, versus the 7.7 OECD median; 33.9 computed tomography (CT) scanners per million people, versus the OECD median of 14.8.[20] The kind of care we provide is inherently more expensive.

In addition, our prices are higher, as captured in the title of one of the first detailed cross-national studies, "It's the Prices, Stupid: Why the United States Is So Different from Other Countries."[21] We pay more for hospital staffing and supplies, prescription drugs, and the other resources used in the provision of care. In its 2007 analysis of U.S. healthcare spending, the McKinsey Global Institute detailed the role of higher prices; for example, prescription drug costs were 50–70 percent higher in the United States than in peer countries.[22] Administrative spending is another major cause of higher costs. The McKinsey analysis found that the United States spent six times as much as the OECD average on healthcare administration. Two-thirds of private insurance administrative spending is for "product design, underwriting, and marketing—expenses that typically do not exist with public systems."[23] Moreover, the McKinsey analysis recognized the additional administrative costs imposed on providers by the need to manage the enormous array of product designs. One recent study found that U.S. physician practices spent almost four times as much as those in Canada on interactions with payers.[24]

In sum, all of these studies point to the same major drivers of excess spending in the United States: higher use of technologically intensive treatment, higher prices, higher administrative costs. But what accounts for these differences? Technology is probably the biggest factor regarding increasing healthcare costs in all industrialized countries. Why does the United States have and use so much more? To address these questions, we must examine the dynamics of our system of healthcare, in particular our financing system. And we must start by looking at its historical roots, for they continue to influence the system today.

The Evolution of the U.S. System of Healthcare: Blank-Check Financing
In the first two decades of the twentieth century, physicians were the dominant players as the system of hospital-based care developed.[25] They controlled

not only the provision of care but also hospital admissions, hence the flow of patient fees that were the major source of hospital financing. Hospitals competed for physicians by trying to offer them the best possible "physician's workshop," or the best technology and other support.[26] Providers—hospitals and physicians—were also the dominant players in the establishment of private insurance. Hospitals began to sell hospital insurance to employer groups during the 1930s to help counteract the steep declines in hospital utilization caused by the Depression. Physicians followed suit. The reimbursement system they adopted ensured that providers' needs were met: hospitals were paid based on costs or charges; physicians were paid on a fee-for-service (FFS) basis, or a separate fee for each service provided, with the amount essentially determined by local physicians. Insurance premiums were set to ensure sufficient revenues to cover these costs.

Employers became the primary purchasers of health insurance for several reasons. They had opposed efforts to enact national health insurance, arguing instead for voluntary, employer-sponsored private insurance. Their interest increased during World War II, when health benefits were exempted from wartime price controls and could be used to help recruit workers in the tight wartime labor market. The decision in the early 1950s to exempt premium contributions from taxable income, allowing health benefits to be tax-free income, further solidified the employer-based system. Employers generally accepted insurers' premiums because the postwar global economy offered little international competition to American businesses; thus employers could raise prices to cover the costs of increased insurance premiums. And when Medicare was established in 1965, Congress agreed to accept the private insurance model of reimbursement: charges or fees were essentially set by providers in order to overcome provider opposition.

Thus what came to be called a system of blank-check financing emerged. Physicians determined the care to be provided and its price. Hospitals engaged in a continual "medical arms race" to attract physicians and patients, seeking to build the best facilities and obtain the most up-to-date technologies.[27] Insurers "passively paid claims" and set premiums to cover their costs.[28] Employers paid the premiums. This system was not only inherently inflationary; it effectively allowed supply to determine demand. Physicians

and existing capacity (for example, hospital beds, new technology) domi-
nated the decisions about what kind of care to obtain as well as its price.
The pattern was summarized in 1961 by Dr. Milton Roemer, in what has
since become known as Roemer's Law: "A bed built is a bed filled is a bed
billed."[29] At the same time, the system of access to care remained incomplete: fragmented, primarily private, and voluntary. Employers provided
the major source of coverage, but whether and how much to offer was left
up to them. Public insurance was limited to the elderly and specific categories of low-income people: primarily women, children, and the disabled.
Once costs became a central concern, efforts to expand access came to a halt.

The Shift to a Dynamic of Cost Containment

A confluence of forces began to generate cost concerns during the 1970s.
Medical technology was advancing rapidly, and the provider-driven system
of financing allowed increases in capacity, utilization, and prices. Healthcare spending was rising dramatically, averaging 10.6 percent a year during
the 1960s and 13.1 percent a year during the 1970s.[30] At the same time,
global economic competition grew, making it more difficult for U.S. employers to absorb the continuing premium increases. Thus the pattern of
blank-check financing began to unravel.

The first step was what Arnold Relman, former editor of the *New England Journal of Medicine*, termed "the revolt of the payers."[31] Employers and
government began looking for ways to limit premium increases. Many larger employers turned to self-insurance, believing that "eliminating the insurers' cut would be an immediate cost-savings device."[32] By 2000, roughly half
of insured workers were in self-insured plans.[33] Although many employers
contracted with insurers to administer their plans, this arrangement was
worth far less to insurance companies than full insurance; thus the move to
self-insurance put significant price pressure on insurers.[34]

However, it was the federal government that established the first truly
effective cost-containment mechanism. In 1983, Congress adopted a prospective payment system (PPS) for Medicare to use in reimbursing hospitals. No longer would hospitals simply bill Medicare for their costs; rather,
they would be paid based on the average cost of treatment for the patient's
medical condition—its diagnosis-related group (DRG)—regardless of a

hospital's actual costs. Thus financial risk—the responsibility for paying actual costs—was shifted from insurers to providers; providers had to absorb costs above the preestablished rate.[35] In 1992, Medicare physician reimbursement was also transformed: although still fee-for-service, fees were no longer based on so-called usual, customary, and reasonable fees; submitted retrospectively; and simply paid by Medicare. Rather, fees were based on the estimated costs of resources used in treatment, relative value units (RVUs).

Private insurers followed Medicare's lead and turned to managed care, a set of arrangements that includes prospective payment agreements, mechanisms to manage use of care—such as utilization review and prior authorization—and selective contracting with providers willing to accept these conditions. Health maintenance organizations (HMOs) were the more tightly managed forms of managed care. They used smaller provider networks and often included measures to shift financial risk to providers, such as capitation, a fixed reimbursement per enrollee regardless of actual costs. Preferred provider organizations (PPOs) were a looser form of managed care. PPOs contracted with a broader network of providers who continued to use fee-for-service reimbursement but agreed to accept discounted rates and utilization review by insurers.[36] Employers responded enthusiastically to these new managed care plans, and enrollment soared: enrollment in HMOs alone increased from 2 million in 1970 to 51 million in 1995.[37] By 2001, only 7 percent of enrollees were in traditional indemnity plans—plans without provider networks or utilization review; in 2011 only 1 percent were in such plans.[38] The rapid shift of managed care plans to for-profit status provides further evidence of the expected cost-effectiveness of managed care: in 1982, only 18 percent were for-profit; by 1988, 67 percent were for-profit.[39]

Insurers further strengthened their leverage with providers by engaging in a wave of mergers and acquisitions, setting in motion the process of consolidation that has produced today's highly concentrated industry.[40] Providers, who had long opposed managed care for the very reason that purchasers and payers liked it—namely, its mechanisms for limiting both the provision of care and its reimbursement—were finally forced by the changing market dynamics to accept managed care contracts. The threat of exclusion from managed care networks, hence loss of patients, was real:

in some areas, in the late 1980s and early 1990s, insurers contracted with fewer than half of the area hospitals.[41]

Managed Care Backlash

The more tightly managed forms of managed care were effective in restraining both reimbursement and utilization, and the annual rate of increase in healthcare spending declined from more than 10 percent a year between 1960 and 1990 down to 5.5 percent between 1993 and 1997.[42] But its highly visible limits on care and restrictions on choice of providers provoked a backlash from both consumers and providers. This reaction led to a series of state regulations to limit some of its key cost-saving mechanisms, such as limiting provider choice. And in the tight labor market of the late 1990s, employers were more responsive to employee demands for greater choice and fewer restrictions.[43]

The backlash benefited providers and increased their leverage with insurers. Equally important, providers began their own process of consolidation. As early as 2000, the Community Tracking Survey (CTS)—an ongoing biennial survey of twelve representative healthcare markets initiated in 1996 by the Center for Studying Health System Change—reported finding extensive hospital mergers and growing "hospital pushback," that is, hospitals' rejecting unfavorable insurance contracts, especially those with risk-sharing requirements.[44] As a 2006 CTS analysis explains, "With the decline of risk contracting and a return to fee-for-service (FFS) payment, hospitals were relieved of the need to manage costs for defined populations. They returned to the traditional business model of filling beds with well-insured patients."[45] The medical arms race resumed.[46]

The Current System: An Expanded Medical Arms Race

The new medical arms race is much more complex and costlier. Competition is increasingly focused on specialty services, those that use the most advanced technology and that offer, because of prevailing reimbursement patterns, the highest profit margins.[47] Furthermore, physicians have joined the race, investing in specialty hospitals and outpatient facilities, which have become the most rapidly growing area of care and the area where the United States differs most dramatically from other OECD countries.[48]

The use of fee-for-service reimbursement, which continues to be the dominant form of physician reimbursement, has always offered financial rewards for more services. However, profit margins are the central focus of today's competition, and these are determined by the relationship of actual costs to reimbursement rates. To understand this relationship, we must look at Medicare, as it is the only source of publicly accessible information on reimbursement practices, and it plays a large role in shaping private insurance practices.[49] Medicare's system of predetermined payment rates has two components. The first is the base payment schedule, which consists of units of relative value assigned to different kinds of care—for example, diagnostic-related group for hospitals and relative value units for physicians. The second is the monetary conversion factor, or the price assigned per unit of value. The Medicare Payment Advisory Commission (MedPAC), the agency established by Congress to provide advice regarding Medicare reimbursement, reviews the payment schedules regularly and recommends changes. Private insurers make use of the Medicare payment schedules but set their own prices per unit of value.

While the base payment schedules are developed according to cost estimates, actual costs often diverge over time, thus allowing different profit margins on different types of service. There is clear evidence that some services are systematically overpaid relative to actual costs, while others are underpaid; for example, surgical procedures are overpaid relative to medical (nonsurgical) treatment. In general, the most technologically intensive, specialized treatments offer the highest profit margins.[50] MedPAC has identified these overpayments and recommended changes; however, pressure from affected providers has frequently blocked their recommendations.[51] This problem has ramifications throughout the system, as explained by Urban Institute researcher Bob Berenson: "The distortions in the current Medicare fee schedule . . . get compounded even more in private fee schedules. . . . We've got the prices really wrong."[52]

The drive to offer more profitable services is amplified by the growth of physician ownership in these services. Further, because physicians control the decisions about what care to provide and where, they are able to self-refer—that is, to refer patients to facilities in which they have an ownership interest. Specialty hospitals, owned largely by physicians, have sprung up to offer the most high-margin services—for example, cardiac care and orthopedic surgery.[53] They are likely to be located in affluent areas with well-insured patients, and profits may be further increased by treating a healthier, less costly mix of patients.[54] Competition in outpatient services has been even more intense. Ambulatory surgery centers (ASCs), almost all involving physicians as owners or investors, and office-based ancillary services (such as lab work and imaging) have proliferated.[55] The growth has been highest in the most profitable services, such as the more advanced forms of imaging like MRIs and CT scans: use of these services increased five times faster than the general rate of medical inflation between 2000 and 2006.[56] And this increase is concentrated among physicians who can self-refer and whose use of imaging has been significantly higher than those without an ownership stake in the imaging equipment.[57]

Thus the growth of capacity—for example, specialty hospitals and office-based diagnostic equipment—made possible by reimbursement practices has led to the increased utilization of higher-cost care. Roemer's Law still holds, and it helps explain why the U.S. system of healthcare provides so much more technologically intensive care than our OECD partners, where governments play a much stronger role in limiting both capacity and price.[58] And the fact that this growth is concentrated among self-referring physicians in the most profitable services has led to growing concern about financially motivated overtreatment.

Regional Variations in Healthcare Spending

Concerns about excess capacity and overtreatment are reinforced by evidence of dramatic regional variations in rates of utilization of specialized equipment, utilization that is associated with variations in spending but not in outcomes. For example, spending on in-office imaging varies as much as eight-fold.[59] If lower-spending regions can achieve as good or better outcomes as higher-spending ones, we must question the value of the more technologically intensive and expensive care. The Dartmouth Institute of Health Policy and Clinical Practice is the preeminent source of research on regional variations in U.S. medical spending. Using Medicare data, Dartmouth researchers have developed the Dartmouth Atlas of Health Care to track variations in Medicare spending and identify the factors that are associated with those variations.[60] Overall, Dartmouth researchers have found more than a two-fold variation in per capita Medicare spending among different regions.[61] These variations are not explained by health status, as the research adjusts for underlying health condition, age, race, and local prices. Nor is there any conclusive evidence of better outcomes.[62]

So what explains these variations? According to the Dartmouth researchers, the most important factors are capacity—the supply of resources—and the absence of clear evidence-based treatment guidelines. The type of care most affected is chronic care for ongoing medical conditions; it is also the area where Medicare spending is concentrated.[63] In these situations, the amount of care provided is linked to the per capita supply of medical resources such as hospital beds and specialists. As Elliott Fisher, a leading Dartmouth researcher, explains, "Patients in high-spending regions are hospitalized more frequently, spend more time in the ICU, see physicians more frequently, and get more diagnostic tests than identical patients in lower-spending regions."[64] There is also evidence that a local decision-making culture develops and reinforces the relationship between capacity and decision making. Dartmouth researchers surveyed eight hundred doctors from high- and low-spending areas, asking them to respond to a set of hypothetical cases. When the scientific guidelines were clear, doctors from high- and low-spending areas made the same recommendations, but when the science was ambiguous and discretionary decisions were required, the doctors from the high-spending areas recommended high-cost procedures, while those from the low-spending areas chose a more conservative, lower-cost approach.[65] The Dartmouth research also identified the importance of reimbursement and delivery systems. High-quality but lower-spending regions include organized delivery systems that have moved away from fee-for-service reimbursement and that emphasize teamwork, coordination, and accountability for overall costs and quality of care.[66]

In sum, the research on regional spending variations reinforces the importance of excess capacity and utilization, and the reimbursement practices that allow them, as major drivers of our excessive healthcare spending. The Dartmouth research has led to estimates that we could obtain at least 30 percent savings in overall national health spending if we could achieve the level of efficiency demonstrated in the low-cost regions; other studies generate similar estimates.[67] However, until we can restructure our system to encourage such efficiency on a broader scale, healthcare costs will continue to rise.

The Role of Private Insurance: Higher Prices, Higher Administrative Costs, Less Access

How has the insurance industry responded to this inexorable increase in medical costs? Clearly it has failed to hold down health spending. While it may use Medicare's payment schedules, its actual rates are invariably higher than those paid by Medicare.[68] Private insurers claim that their higher rates are owing to cost-shifting from Medicare and Medicaid and that they must charge private insurers higher rates in order to compensate for lower payment from public insurers.[69] Business has usually accepted this reasoning.[70] However, we need to examine it more closely. In a recent analysis of hospital reimbursement, James Robinson found that Medicare payment provided "positive contribution margins" (the difference between revenue obtained from the insurer and hospital costs) for the Medicare patients, "but the margins on privately insured patients were higher by a factor of ten or more."[71] Thus Medicare payments covered provider costs but offered far lower margins. Is cost-shifting necessary to cover costs or simply to generate profits?

Moreover, there is enormous variation in the prices paid by private insurers to different providers. For example, payments by a large New Jersey insurer for colonoscopies ranged from $178 to $431 for doctors and $716 to $3,717 for hospitals.[72] Why is there such variation in providers' ability to shift costs—if this is indeed what is happening—to private insurers? Most analysts believe that market power is the critical factor in private sector price variation; providers with greater market power are able to charge higher rates than weaker providers.[73] This, too, is documented in Robinson's analysis, which shows that higher margins are earned by hospitals in concentrated markets, "where private insurers cannot credibly threaten the hospitals with network exclusion."[74]

And recent research suggests this market power may also be a major factor in the payment differential between Medicare and private insurers.

MedPAC's recommendations regarding Medicare reimbursement levels are based on the costs of operating efficiently, defined in terms of both costs and quality, not on payments made by private insurers.[75] Hospitals with higher reimbursement from private insurers have higher profit margins, and thus less pressure to keep costs down, which may lead to higher costs; these hospitals then earn lower margins from Medicare than more efficient hospitals. As MedPAC stated in its 2011 report, "If private payers do not exert pressure, providers' costs will increase and, all other things being equal, margins on Medicare patients will decrease."[76] Even more important is the broader impact on healthcare costs. To quote Robinson again, "Costs are directly affected by prices, in that higher revenues permit hospitals to finance cost-increasing investments."[77] In other words, higher prices not only increase immediate spending, they also permit an increase in capacity, which is one of the most fundamental drivers of U.S. healthcare costs.

Insurers have certainly tried other approaches for reducing costs. Limiting utilization has been an important strategy, for instance, by requiring prior authorization for expensive treatments. While such methods have certainly antagonized providers and patients, they have not changed the fact that the United States still has far more technologically intensive, and expensive, care than other industrialized countries. Yet remarkably, despite the steady increase in payments to providers, insurers have managed to increase their profits. From 2000 to 2008, premiums increased faster than payments to providers.[78] Insurers have been able to limit their medical loss ratios (MLRs)—the percentage of premium revenue spent on actual medical claims—thus leaving sufficient revenue for overhead and profits; indeed, average MLRs for investor-owned insurers declined from 95 percent in 1993 to 81 percent in 2007.[79] Stock prices for the insurance industry increased 500 percent from 1997 through 2005, while the Standard and Poor's index increased only 100 percent.[80]

How has the insurance industry managed to do this? The industry's most important strategy has been consolidation to increase market power. And while this may not have curtailed provider rates, it has allowed increases in rates charged to employers sufficient to both cover increased provider costs and increase profits. By 2003, the top three insurance companies were dominant in all states, controlling over 50 percent of the market in all but three states and more than 65 percent of the market in all but fourteen states.[81] And in 2011, the American Medical Association's annual review of the insurance market found that 99 percent of markets met the federal definition of highly concentrated.[82] Purchaser pressure is largely ineffective in the face of such concentration. Indeed, one could argue that private insurers do not really need to hold down provider reimbursements as long as they can simply raise premiums: they can allow the supposed cost shifting from providers because they in turn can simply shift costs to employers.

The insurance industry does make heavy use of risk selection as a means of holding down costs. Healthcare spending is highly concentrated: 80 percent of spending goes to the sickest 20 percent of people; this trend provides a great incentive for insurers to find ways to avoid the sickest 20 percent and enroll the lower-spending 80 percent.[83] As former Medicare chief Bruce Vladeck and Professor Thomas Rice point out, "Because health risk is so widely—but predictably—distributed in the population, sophisticated risk selection is a far more potent economic strategy for insurers than even the greatest of administrative efficiencies."[84] This strategy may increase profits for insurance companies, but it lies at the heart of many of the most significant problems in our system of healthcare. It denies or limits coverage to those with the greatest need for care. And it generates significant administrative costs for both insurers and providers. Underwriting and marketing are the major administrative costs for insurers.[85] And for providers, the "tens of thousands" of different benefit packages cited recently by a spokesperson for the Association of Health Insurance Plans create an enormous administrative burden.[86] One recent study found that each full-time physician required two-thirds of a nonclinical staff position just for handling billing and insurance.[87] One of the most comprehensive studies of administrative costs estimated that administrative costs consume about 30 percent of overall healthcare spending in the United States.[88]

Thus private insurance has maintained its profitability at the expense of both consumers and employers while reducing coverage for the sick and increasing premiums for employers. As we see below, public insurance programs in the United States have been significantly more cost-effective in terms of both coverage and costs.

The Cost-Effectiveness of Public Insurance

Both Medicaid and Medicare provide benefits at a much lower cost than private insurance (Medicaid provides coverage to those qualifying based on financial need; Medicare provides coverage to those aged sixty-five years and older). The Congressional Budget Office (CBO), in its analysis of the Republican proposal to shift Medicare recipients into private insurance, estimated that by 2030, it would cost 40 percent more to provide Medicare benefits through private insurance rather than through the current Medicare program.[89] Medicare spending has also increased more slowly than private insurance: the most recent analysis from the Centers for Medicare and Medicaid Services (CMS), the agency that administers those programs, found that the average annual increase in per capita costs for a common benefits package from 1970 to 2009 was 9.3 percent in private insurance and 8.3 percent in Medicare. More recently, from 2002 to 2009, Medicare's costs increased only 4.6 percent annually, while private insurance increased 6.7 percent.[90]

These lower costs have not come at the expense of quality, and in fact some research suggests that Medicare outperforms private insurance in key areas of quality. Medicare beneficiaries have fewer problems obtaining medical care and express higher overall satisfaction with their coverage.[91] The major reasons for Medicare's lower costs stem from its status as a large and public program. Its administrative costs are lower because it does not need to generate profits, pay high executive salaries, or spend heavily on underwriting and marketing; it spends around 3 percent on administrative expenses, compared with about 12 percent for private insurance.[92] And as the largest national purchaser of healthcare, Medicare has significant potential leverage with providers, allowing it to be more effective in limiting reimbursement to them than private insurers. It has also pioneered quality improvement and delivery system reforms, as well as the changes in reimbursement methods noted earlier.[93]

Despite its effectiveness, however, Medicare remains embedded within and in significant ways limited by the dynamics of the larger system of healthcare. Medicare cannot allow its reimbursements to fall too far below private payer prices without losing provider participation and reducing beneficiary access. Furthermore, the higher costs in hospitals earning higher margins from private payer reimbursement may even produce negative margins from Medicare reimbursement, threatening Medicare's ability to limit reimbursements. As MedPAC stated in 2011, "This process could lead to pressure for Medicare to keep up with the prices that market power can generate in the private sector."[94] Thus preserving and increasing Medicare's cost-effectiveness requires us to address the broader forces in our system of healthcare.

The Role of Business
What role has business played in the dynamics of our healthcare system? Certainly business is concerned with costs. It should be even more concerned with the flagrant lack of cost-effectiveness in our current system, so dramatically illustrated by the international comparisons reviewed earlier. However, the business community includes both buyers and sellers of healthcare, and the costs that buyers want to reduce represent income to sellers. Moreover, buyers have generally had less power than sellers. As University of Chicago professor Harold Pollack wryly noted, "The supply side of a $2.6 trillion dollar industry does not lack for political resources."[95]

As the international comparisons make clear, sellers in the U.S. healthcare market have demanded considerably higher prices than their counterparts in other countries. We have already seen the power of providers and insurers. The pharmaceutical industry has grown increasingly powerful over the past two decades, not only because of the increasing role of prescription drugs in healthcare, but also because of its direct-to-consumer advertising.[96] Both the pharmaceutical industry and the medical device industry have invested heavily in efforts to influence healthcare provider recommendations regarding the use of their products.[97] For example, a central element in the initial business model of imaging manufacturers was including physicians as investors in order to ensure a steady flow of referrals. It was so effective that Congress soon took note and enacted restrictions on certain kinds of self-referrals.[98]

Employers are the major buyers in the healthcare system, and they have generally been the weakest player. Premiums for health insurance have increased much faster than economic growth or the general rate of inflation: average premiums for employer-sponsored coverage in 2011 were $5,429 for single coverage and $15,073 for family coverage.[99] Employers who offer insurance are also forced to cover some of the costs created by the growing number of uninsured, as providers incorporate the costs of uncompensated care in the premiums charged to private insurers. So how have employers responded to these continual premium increases? Their predominant strategy has been to reduce coverage and shift costs to employees.

Employer-sponsored insurance has declined steadily throughout the past decade. From 2000 to 2011, the percentage of firms offering coverage dropped from 68 to 60 percent, and the percentage of the nonelderly population with employer-sponsored coverage dropped from 69 to 59 percent.[100] Meanwhile employee cost sharing has increased: the percentage of employees enrolled in plans requiring a general annual deductible of at least $1,000 for single coverage increased from 10 percent in 2006 to 31 percent in 2011.[101]

However, there are significant differences in cost increases between larger employers and smaller ones. Larger employers have been better able than smaller employers to resist raising costs. As a result, the distribution of employment-sponsored insurance varies dramatically by company size. The 2011 Henry J. Kaiser Family Foundation survey found that while the overall percentage of employers offering coverage in 2011 was 60 percent, 99 percent of larger employers (200 or more employees) offer coverage, compared with only 59 percent of smaller firms.[102] Decline in coverage, as well as the increase in cost sharing with employees, has been concentrated in firms with fewer than 200 employees. Between 2006 and 2011, the percentage of workers enrolled in plans with deductibles of $1,000 or more increased from 16 to 50 percent in small firms and from 6 to 22 percent in large firms.[103] Nevertheless, despite greater market power, larger employers, not smaller ones, have come to the realization that they cannot deal with rising health costs alone; a stronger government role is essential.

Summary and Challenges Ahead

Business—the largest purchaser in our healthcare system—has been unable to control costs without reducing access. Clearly business does not have the power needed to challenge the dominant players in the system and change the underlying dynamics that continue to produce declining access and increasing costs. Shifting costs to individuals has become today's major cost-containment strategy, with grim results. Employee costs are absorbing an increasing share of family income.[104] And according to the Commonwealth Fund, the number of people defined as underinsured (spending at least 10% of income on out-of-pocket medical expenses) doubled between 2003 and 2010, from 16 million to 29 million people. Almost half went without needed or recommended care, and almost a fifth were pursued by collection agencies.[105] Yet costs continue to rise.

Effective reform—controlling costs and ensuring access—requires that we address the underlying causes of both declining access and uncontrolled costs. We must change the structures through which access is provided, the perverse provider incentives in our financing system, the lack of sufficient comparative effectiveness research regarding the care we provide, the wasteful administrative costs in our insurance system, and the market concentration that allows dominant players to continue to claim a disproportionate share of business profits, government revenues, and family income. These are huge challenges. The ACA is a foundation for beginning to meet these challenges. While it needs significant strengthening, it first needs to survive the attacks it is facing. And those calling the ACA a government takeover need to show how they would change the dynamics that are generating our spiraling costs without further reducing access to care.

SECTION II. TOWARD EFFECTIVE REFORM: THE ACA AND BEYOND

Effective healthcare reform must achieve the following goals:

- *Access:* Universal, affordable, comprehensive, and equitably and efficiently provided;
- *Financing:* Fair financing—if everyone is to be covered, everyone must contribute;
- *Cost controls:* Measures to limit healthcare spending so as to ensure long-term sustainability and affordability; and
- *Quality:* High-quality and cost-effective delivery, with outcomes that meet benchmarks set by the highest-performing regions and nations.[106]

Achieving these goals requires changing the underlying dynamics of our system of healthcare and disrupting the patterns of power and profits that have given rise to the problems we face today. Enacting and implementing effective healthcare reform in the United States, therefore, requires an enormous effort. While the landmark legislation passed in 2010 is attacked by its opponents as a government takeover of healthcare, in fact it represents a series of significant compromises that, while still unfortunately protecting key interests of the major players in the healthcare system, does significantly improve access and quality and takes important steps toward limiting spiraling healthcare costs.[107]

In this section, we will review the ACA and the conservative proposals for more market-based solutions, and we will show that not only are market-based measures inadequate, the ACA, while bringing major gains, needs substantial improvements if it is to be truly effective. We will conclude by discussing the importance for business of effective healthcare reform.

The Conservative Approach: Consumer-Driven Healthcare
The current version of a market-based approach to healthcare reform has been termed consumer-driven healthcare (CDHC).[108] It emerged during the 1980s and 1990s and has become the basis of Republican proposals for both Medicare and the general population. CDHC holds that market distortions, caused by such government interventions as the tax exemption given to employer health benefits and state mandates for insurance benefits, are the major cause of uncontrolled healthcare spending. The CDHC argument contends that, by encouraging or requiring excessive insurance coverage, these interventions have allowed excessive utilization of healthcare, thus generating excess spending.[109] The CDHC solution is to put consumers in charge of their own healthcare spending and deregulate the insurance market.[110] Rather than providing insurance coverage, give consumers vouchers to purchase their own insurance, and allow insurers to offer more low-cost plans with fewer benefits. Individuals would then be free "to choose a lower cost option that best meets their needs," which conservatives claim will result in competition to reduce prices and improve quality.[111] The 2012 budget resolution, passed by the House in April 2011, restructures Medicare according to these principles. As Republican House Budget Committee chair Paul Ryan explains, "That's how markets work: the customer is the ultimate guarantor of value."[112] But is this really how the healthcare market works?

The Limited Role of Consumers in the Healthcare Market

In fact, the role of consumers in the healthcare market is profoundly limited, both by the inherent nature of healthcare itself and by the more powerful forces shaping our system. Healthcare involves specialized knowledge, and while patients may be increasingly well informed, they usually must rely upon their provider both for a thorough diagnosis and for recommendations regarding treatment. This "asymmetry of information," first analyzed by Kenneth Arrow in 1963, is widely regarded as an inherent limit on the ability of patients to act as informed consumers in the healthcare market and thus an inherent limit on the use of markets to allocate healthcare resources.[113] The role of patients as informed consumers is further limited by our current financing system. With payment handled largely by insurers, and prices determined by the market power of insurers relative to providers, it is extremely difficult for patients to find out what alternative treatments will cost. As Princeton economist Uwe Reinhardt states, "Yet without major changes in the present chaos, forcing sick and anxious people to shop around blindfolded for cost-effective care mocks the very idea of consumer-directed care."[114]

Nor do individual consumers have much bargaining power in the insurance market. Those without employer coverage are forced into the individual market, where they encounter denials, exclusions, and exorbitant premiums. Recent research by the Commonwealth Fund found that almost three-fourths of those who inquire about individual coverage never get it.[115] Reducing regulations on benefits will simply increase the number of underinsured, and without reform of rating practices, premiums for those most in need of healthcare will continue to soar.

The highly concentrated nature of healthcare spending raises additional questions. Since 80 percent of healthcare spending is generated by 20 percent of patients, the vast majority of patients spend relatively little on healthcare.[116] It is not clear how higher patient cost sharing is supposed to affect decisions about the truly expensive care that constitutes the bulk of our spending.

The most conclusive evidence is from the international comparisons. The United States already has higher cost sharing than other countries— almost twice as much as the OECD median—and we already use fewer health services while spending twice as much per capita.[117] Patients who pay higher out-of-pocket costs do use less care, but services forgone include cost-effective preventive care, and savings from reduced outpatient care may be outweighed by the higher costs of increased hospitalization.[118] CDHC will not only worsen the problem of access, it fails to address the underlying dynamics of our healthcare system. Individual consumers simply do not have the power to challenge the provider decisions and insurer practices that drive our increasing costs and decreasing access.

The Affordable Care Act (ACA): Moving toward Effective Reform
Despite significant compromises, the ACA brings major gains—indeed, for some, lifesaving gains—and offers a strong foundation for further reform. Here we will review the legislation briefly, focusing on the most important provisions that address the underlying dynamics of our healthcare system. We will then look at some of the most important improvements needed and at how the ACA offers the basis for stronger reforms.[119] The primary attributes of the ACA are as follows:

Access: Nearly universal, comprehensive, affordable

- *Nearly universal:* All legal residents have access to coverage through one of three new or expanded sources:
  - ✔ *Employers,* with new coverage requirements.
  - ✔ *Medicaid,* with expanded eligibility.
  - ✔ State-based *health insurance exchanges,* offering approved insurance plans to small employers (no more than 100 employees initially, with the possibility of expansion later to larger employers) and individuals without an alternative source of coverage. (Medicare eligibility remains the same.) In addition, *insurance* reforms require that all applicants be accepted, preexisting conditions be covered, and premium rates exclude consideration of health status, gender, and other discriminatory factors.
- *Comprehensive:* A national *essential benefits standard* must be met by all qualified health plans, including those offered by employers.
- *Affordable: Subsidies* to increase affordability are available for the purchase of insurance through a state exchange for everyone with

income below 400 percent of the federal poverty line (about $88,000 per year for a family of four in 2010). Employer plans must meet affordability requirements. Patient cost sharing must be limited, and annual and lifetime caps on insurance coverage are eliminated.

Financing: Fair

- *Employer contribution:* Employers who do not offer comprehensive and affordable coverage and whose employees qualify for subsidies through the exchange must pay a penalty. Small employers (fewer than 50 employees) are exempt.
- *Individual contribution:* Individuals are required to carry qualified health insurance—insurance that meets the new essential benefits standard—or pay a penalty.
- *New taxes:* Medicare taxes are made more progressive through an increase in the wage base subject to the Medicare tax and the taxation of unearned income, both applied only to higher-income earners.[120]

Cost controls and quality improvements

- *Price reductions for providers and insurers:*
  - ✔ Medicare payment formulas for most providers are reduced.
  - ✔ Medicare is given more authority to reduce overvalued payment rates—those in areas of treatment that have generated the highest profit margins and shown the greatest increase in utilization.
  - ✔ Subsidies to the private Medicare Advantage plans are phased out.
  - ✔ Private insurance premium increases deemed unreasonable (more than 10%) must be justified and may be used to exclude insurers from offering plans in the new exchanges.
- *Payment and delivery system reforms to encourage quality and efficiency:*
  - ✔ New payment methods replace the volume-increasing incentives of fee-for-service payment, with incentives that reward quality and efficiency. For example, global budgets and capitation-based payment (fixed payment per person covered), pay linked to performance (bonuses and penalties tied to quality and outcomes), and bundled payments for episodes of treatment.

   ✔ Primary care and care coordination receive additional support.
   ✔ Quality reporting is required for Medicare providers and private insurers.
   ✔ Comparative effectiveness and outcomes research is increased.
  • *Administrative savings:*
   ✔ Private insurer spending on overhead and profits is capped at 15 percent for large group plans and 20 percent for small group plans.
   ✔ New insurance requirements such as guaranteed issue (requiring acceptance of all applicants, regardless of health status) and standardized benefits packages will reduce underwriting and marketing costs.
   ✔ Information technology will be used to streamline administrative procedures such as applications for coverage and claims submissions.
  • *A global budget for Medicare:* A new Independent Payment Advisory Board is charged with ensuring that Medicare spending does not exceed a specified target; its recommendations are fast-tracked through Congress and cannot include reduced benefits or increased costs for beneficiaries.

The ACA thus brings major benefits as well as measures to address the underlying dynamics of both deteriorating access and excessive costs. Everyone will have access to a source of insurance, and all plans must provide decent coverage. The unemployed will no longer have to bear the additional burden of losing their health coverage. Insurers can no longer use risk selection and denial of coverage as a means of increasing profits. The sick will no longer have to pay higher premiums than the healthy. Individuals and small businesses will no longer be priced out of coverage, the new exchanges will have market leverage and the authority to set standards of quality and cost-effectiveness as a condition of plan certification, and subsidies will increase affordability. The CBO estimates that by 2021, 34 million people will gain new coverage as a result of the ACA.[121]

The most important cost-containment mechanisms are the payment and delivery system reforms, which seek to reduce the incentives for excess capacity, utilization, and price and to create new incentives for quality and efficiency. The new exchanges will be able to reinforce these efforts by requiring or supporting similar efforts for plans seeking to participate in the exchange.[122] The CBO estimates that the ACA will reduce the deficit by $210 billion between 2012 and 2021 and by $1.2 trillion by 2029.[123] The cost-containment provisions are expected to become increasingly effective over time.

Strengthening Reform: The Next Steps

The ACA also has major limitations. Undocumented immigrants are not allowed to purchase coverage in the exchanges. Premium costs and patient cost sharing are still too high. Premium increases must be justified but cannot be prevented. Medicare cannot negotiate prescription drug prices. Reducing excess capacity depends on changing cost incentives rather than using more direct measures. The use of comparative effectiveness research to inform coverage and reimbursement decisions is prohibited. Most fundamentally, the decision to offer access on the basis of the current system—maintaining its fragmented categories of coverage and sources of payment and preserving the participation of for-profit insurance—is very costly, requiring an elaborate regulatory apparatus. We have already seen the greater cost-effectiveness of public insurance; so why didn't we simply expand Medicare? Why allow administrative costs and profits to absorb 15–20 percent of premium revenues when Medicare operates with only 3 percent of revenues spent on administration?

The Advantages of a Single-Payer Approach

A single-payer system, such as Medicare, would be far more cost-effective and more equitable. In a single-payer system, one agency collects all of the funding and disburses all of the payments. There is a single system of reimbursement for all providers; cost shifting is eliminated. Overall spending is limited by a global budget. A single program and a single benefits package offer major administrative savings, eligibility is automatic, and billing is greatly simplified. There is no need for profits or exorbitant executive compensation, and the costs of marketing and underwriting are eliminated. Using the tax system to provide financing is more cost-effective than collecting a variety of particular fees. A single-payer system also has much greater authority to limit excess capacity and utilization and to implement quality improvements. Capital investments—hence major increases in capacity—require public approval. Comparative effectiveness research can be used not only to develop clinical guidelines but also to inform decisions about benefit coverage.

The potential savings are enormous. The financial analysis of California's single-payer legislation done in 2005 by the Lewin Group, a consulting firm that has provided analyses for many state and national health reform proposals, estimated that, even with substantially expanded benefits provided to all California residents, total healthcare spending in California in 2015 would be $278.7 billion, as opposed to $345.6 billion without the legislation.[124] The legislation was passed twice by the California legislature but vetoed both times by Governor Arnold Schwarzenegger.

A Robust Public Option
And if not the single-payer system, why not at least a public option? "A robust public health insurance plan, with the authority to use Medicare payment rates and implement innovative payment methods," was included in the original House bill.[125] It would combine both regulatory and competitive mechanisms, with the former limiting reimbursement while implementing new payment methods and the latter forcing private insurers to compete based on price and quality. Both the Commonwealth Fund and the Lewin Group estimated substantial savings from the inclusion of a public option in healthcare reform.[126] Unfortunately, private insurers recognized the cost-effectiveness of this option—and thus the threat to their industry—and the public option was ultimately defeated. Major business organizations also opposed it.[127] But shouldn't they have recognized that the threat posed to private insurance would have represented a major gain to businesses that purchase private insurance?

Stronger Use of Government Purchasing Power: All-Payer Reimbursement
The use of concentrated government purchasing power is seen by many as the central factor in keeping healthcare spending in the OECD countries

so much lower than spending in the United States.[128] The greatest strength of the ACA exchanges will come from their ability to aggregate purchasing power, which can be used to drive both price reductions and quality improvements. But stronger government authority is needed, especially regarding prices. Given the continuation of our fragmented private system, the most effective measure would be an all-payer reimbursement system in which all payers use, and all providers accept, the same reimbursement methods and rates. As Uwe Reinhardt points out, the failure of private insurance to limit provider price increases should raise questions about using private insurance to control costs.[129] In an all-payer system, providers would have to accept one set of prices, and cost shifting would be eliminated. In addition, billing would be enormously simplified, reducing administrative costs. New payment mechanisms could be implemented system-wide. Comparative effectiveness research could be used to inform both coverage and reimbursement decisions. The state of Maryland has used an all-payer system in hospital reimbursement for several decades, and its hospital costs have increased more slowly than the national average.[130] A growing number of analysts and business leaders recognize the value of an all-payer system.[131]

Using the ACA to Move toward Single Payer: Vermont's Leadership

Legislation passed in 2011 by the state of Vermont shows clearly the possibility of using the ACA as the foundation for building a "unified and universal health care system."[132] The Vermont legislation calls for the creation of a single-payer system called Green Mountain Care (GMC). It will be open to all residents and will be launched once the state obtains the waiver offered by the ACA, which allows states to use their ACA funding to support their own system of coverage as long as it provides as much coverage as the ACA would provide. The law also establishes the Green Mountain Care Board as the policymaking body and charges it to develop payment reforms to reward quality and efficiency and implement an all-payer reimbursement system. The GMC also has final approval authority regarding premium increases greater than 5 percent, hospital budgets, and large capital investments. The new program is estimated to offer savings of between $553 million and $1.83 billion a year by 2020 (5.5–13.3% of total spending).[133] The Vermont health benefit exchange will be used to establish the infrastructure for the GMC. Insurers will be certified to offer plans in the exchange only if they agree to participate in the state's health reform efforts, including its payment reforms.

The Business Response

Business desperately needs a more rational healthcare system, one in which quality and efficiency are rewarded; costs are predictable, manageable, and competitive with our global trading partners; and access to healthcare—an essential condition of a productive workforce and a decent society—is both adequate and fairly financed. Those selling the healthcare goods and services that generate $2.6 trillion in annual revenue will hardly welcome cost reduction measures. However, discussions by business leaders of healthcare reform generally identify controlling costs as the overriding concern. And business as buyer—most importantly, employers—should be in the forefront of the effort to protect the gains brought by the Affordable Care Act and to establish the even stronger measures that are needed.

However, as already noted, employers are divided in their approach to reform. Ironically, smaller businesses, those with the least power in the healthcare market and the most to gain from the ACA, are also the most intensely opposed to an expanded government role. Small businesses will benefit from the insurance reforms prohibiting discriminatory coverage and premiums and from the new exchanges, which will offer much more cost-effective coverage than the small group insurance market. Yet their primary organizational representatives, such as the National Federation of Independent Businesses (NFIB) and the U.S. Chamber of Commerce, are fighting to repeal and/or weaken the law.[134] As the president of the Chamber of Commerce said recently, "The government should not dictate what the coverage must be and how costs are set. Instead, businesses must continue to freely negotiate with insurers."[135] The fact that such negotiations have not reduced costs but only shifted them to employees is apparently not important.

Yet organizations representing the large business community, such as the National Business Group on Health and the Business Roundtable, believe that effective reform is possible only with a stronger government role, and some would like stronger cost-containment mechanisms than those in the ACA. What is most striking is their call for public-private collaboration to ensure system-wide changes, without which, they believe, costs cannot be controlled. Fearing further cost shifting, some argue that payment must be aligned across the public and private sectors so that government price reductions will not simply increase prices for the private sector.[136] There is also support for all-payer reimbursement.[137] And in a sign of the growing recognition of the relative inefficiency of the U.S. healthcare system compared with its international competitors, all of these business leaders call for a comparative effectiveness review that is much stronger and whose results are reflected in decisions about coverage and payment.[138]

The imperative of government leadership and private sector cooperation is clearly stated in a Business Roundtable report: "Such changes in the private system would seem completely revolutionary were it not for Medicare leading the way. . . . Medicare has proven that it can demand payment reform and quality-of-care reporting from its provider base. However, if trends in the employer system are going to be reduced, these initiatives need to be implemented in the private insurance market as well."[139]

Nevertheless, even large businesses oppose the creation of a public option, arguing that it will necessitate increased cost shifting to the private sector. Again we must raise the question, why not welcome the greater cost-effectiveness of public insurance? Why not support the creation of a public option, which would help force private insurers to provide coverage more cost-effectively? Why not push for an all-payer system? Indeed, given the evidence that higher prices paid by private insurers reflect providers' market power, isn't it clear that we cannot limit costs without increasing the power of government to challenge that private market power? Higher premiums are the result not of too much but rather too little government intervention.

CONCLUSION

Our current system of healthcare is both intolerable and unsustainable. It is intolerable that we are the only industrialized nation in the world without comprehensive health coverage, that we have the highest rate of preventable deaths and bankruptcy from medical costs, that we allow private insurance to profit by discriminating against the sick, and that we compound the terrible pain of joblessness with the loss of access to healthcare. Our system is also unsustainable, as uncontrolled costs have led to continually declining coverage, while at the same time threatening family financial health, business competitiveness, and our nation's fiscal solvency.

Business must demand healthcare spending that maximizes efficiency, defined by Dartmouth researchers as producing "the best outcomes and highest quality for the lowest utilization and cost."[140] And if employers have been unable to limit their own costs without reducing coverage, and if private insurers have been unable, or unwilling, to hold down provider reimbursements, not to mention their own administrative costs and profits, how can we expect the private market alone to produce an efficient and high-quality healthcare system? Calling for consumers to drive the necessary changes in a deregulated market is cynical rhetoric. Not only does it fail to address the underlying dynamics of the system, it protects the rich and powerful from lower profits or higher taxes. In the words of Vladeck and Rice, "It deflects attention from the real issue: who has economic power in the system, and who doesn't."[141]

We are fortunate that there are business leaders who do recognize the issue of economic power and understand that it cannot be addressed without stronger government power to shape the system as a whole. We need them to recognize that government power must be used to establish a more rational payment system for all payers, including those in the private sector. Neither employers nor insurers have been able to do this, and the resulting cost increases threaten to limit the government's ability to restrain costs. Payment-and-delivery-system reforms to reward quality and efficiency are essential, and the ACA supports the development of these reforms. But only when all payers use the same payment methods and the same rates will we be able to control cost increases and work toward greater efficiency— better quality and outcomes—in our spending.

To say we are at a critical point is an understatement. The progress we have made toward effective reform is severely threatened by the conservative attack. Those who benefit from lower taxes and reduced regulation are playing an increasingly powerful, if not always visible, role in our political process.[142] The alternative argument must be heard much more clearly. Business carries enormous weight in American politics, both rhetorically and financially. Those in the business community who understand that effective healthcare reform is impossible without strengthening the role of government in the healthcare system must do more. They must speak more loudly and help educate the larger community. And they must dedicate the resources and help generate the political pressure that will be imperative if we want to preserve the gains provided by the ACA and build on the foundation it offers for even more effective change. This will be real social responsibility in action by the business community for the benefit of all. In our next chapter, we will look at how one healthcare organization honors social responsibility through culturally competent care.

9

Social Responsibility, Healthcare Equity, and Workforce Planning

Allyne Beach, Laura Long, and Bob Redlo

Martin Luther King Jr., once stated, "Of all forms of inequality, injustice in health care is the most shocking and inhumane."[1] He was speaking of health equity and well-being for all people, regardless of race/ethnicity, socioeconomic status, or spoken language. Achieving health equity means focusing societal efforts to eliminate inequality in access to healthcare for all groups, especially for those who have experienced socioeconomic disadvantage or historical injustice.[2] As such, health equity is an important facet of social responsibility. In this chapter we will focus on health equity in the United States, recognizing that some of the perspectives may also apply elsewhere. We will use Kaiser Permanente, one of the largest U.S. healthcare providers, as an example to illustrate the issues, challenges, and approaches throughout the chapter.[3] In addition, we will describe why cultural competence is important in the context of health equity, define the term, and review the links between workforce planning and development and delivering culturally competent care. Finally, we will explore approaches to workforce planning and development that provide a foundation for culturally competent care.

The U.S. Affordable Care Act (ACA) of 2010, also known as Health Care Reform (HCR), includes significant changes that move toward equitable provision of healthcare. We will use the terminology HCR in this chapter given that our focus here is on healthcare delivery, whereas in the last chapter our focus was on healthcare policy and its implications. HCR and ACA are synonymous. By 2014, 32 million Americans who currently lack health insurance will have new options to obtain healthcare. This incoming patient population, which is currently uninsured, is more likely to be low income, belonging to a minority, and in worse health than those currently insured.[4] The demographic trends resulting from implementation of HCR will increase the racial, ethnic, and socioeconomic diversity of the member population of Kaiser Permanente (KP). Culturally competent care is one element of KP's strategy, which will be even more important in the future. Providing culturally competent care is integral to KP's value of benefitting surrounding communities. Doing this will mean further developing the capacity to hear, learn, suspend assumptions, and respond in real time to meet members' particular needs.[5]

WHAT IS CULTURALLY COMPETENT CARE?

Culturally competent care is healthcare that is sensitive to the varying needs and health status of different populations. Studies now show that ethnicity is as important as age or gender in understanding healthcare utilization and the cost of delivering care.[6] Providing culturally competent care leads to:

- Decreased rates of hospitalization for preventable conditions that affect individuals in at-risk groups,
- Increased patient satisfaction,
- Increased employee satisfaction from better communication with patients, and
- Containment of rising healthcare costs.[7]

KP prides itself on providing culturally competent care, and many of its initiatives address this. One small but significant example is the creation of manuals for caregivers outlining cultural beliefs of different ethnic groups about the efficacy of traditional medicine. These manuals also discuss communication barriers and the health profiles of different ethnic groups. The health profiles include analysis of risk factors (for example, obesity) and research findings regarding population-specific attributes of various diseases. As another example, KP offers interpreters in several languages to help in communicating with patients. These languages include

Spanish, Cantonese, Mandarin, Vietnamese, and Russian. Furthermore, KP develops language capability in current employees by offering certification as Qualified Bilingual Staff (QBS) to meet language competency standards.

Language is just one component of culturally competent care. Healthcare providers also need to understand how the culture and beliefs of their patients affect healthcare utilization and shape health-related behavior. For instance, many of Latino background find involvement of significant others critical to successful treatment and healing. This requires that others, usually family members, be included in decision making. Enlisting strong family support systems is important in the care of Latino patients.[8] Providing culturally competent care, which is of growing importance with HCR, depends on a having a skilled, diverse workforce that is equipped to understand cultural differences. Let's look at how this is addressed in KP.

WORKFORCE IMPLICATIONS OF HCR

KP has a long-standing commitment to building a diverse work environment. In the 1940s, KP was the first healthcare organization to have a racially integrated hospital. In 2011, KP's strong commitment to diversity was recognized by the organization's top ranking on the 2011 DiversityInc Top 50 Companies for Diversity list, having previously maintained a top-50 spot from 2006 to 2010.[9] Other diversity accolades have come from external organizations such as *Diversity MBA Magazine, Latina Style Magazine, Black EOE Journal,* Filipina Women's Network, and the Association of Diversity Councils.

Nevertheless, to meet future demographic changes, KP will need to deepen this commitment. To sponsor movement and promotion within the company, this initiative must include providing career mobility training and resources to an increasingly diverse entry-level workforce. Workforce planning and development strategies are central to managing an undertaking of this scope. Workforce planning is a systematic approach to understanding future needs in order to ensure that steps taken now, through workforce development, mean that future capabilities are there when needed.[10]

Workforce planning and development are therefore important assets in KP's focus on cultural competence. The healthcare workforce is affected by supply, demand, development, and environmental factors. Included are the advent of new technology creating needs for new skills, emerging novel medical practice, changing public policy, and the availability of requisite training programs. Effective workforce planning incorporates a demand component that addresses needed workforce capabilities, recognizing the health attributes of demographic subgroups. Workforce professionals can integrate this information, with knowledge of current workforce capabilities and the needs of projected patients, to plan effectively. Relevant patient attributes comprise health status, language needs, racial/ethnic makeup, and the trends of chronic disease in cohort demographic groups.

With KP as an example, in 2011 its infrastructure and workforce break down as follows:

- Delivers services in eight regions in the United States,
- Provides services through thirty-six hospitals and 533 medical offices for more than 8.6 million members,
- Employs over 183,000 people, of whom 47,000 are nurses and almost 16,000 are physicians, and
- Had the following race/ethnicity and gender workforce composition in 2011:
  - ✔ 42 percent white, 26 percent Asian, 17 percent Latino, 13 percent African American, and 2 percent unidentified;
  - ✔ 73 percent women and 27 percent men.[11]

The incoming patient population resulting from HCR is anticipated to have the following attributes, which are representative of those who are uninsured:

- Nine in ten of the uninsured are in low- or moderate-income families, meaning their family income is below 400 percent of the federal poverty limit.
- More than three-quarters of the uninsured are in working families, 61 percent are from families with one or more full-time workers, and 16 percent are from families with part-time workers.
- Young adults ages 19 to 29 make up more than 32 percent of the incoming group.

- Approximately 64 percent have no education beyond high school.
- Minorities are much more likely to be uninsured than whites. About one-third of Hispanics and twenty-three percent of African Americans are uninsured compared with 14 percent of whites.
- Not surprising, the uninsured tend to be in worse health than those with private insurance.
- More than 70 percent of the uninsured have gone without health coverage for more than a year.[12]

This information is critical to ensuring that the increased demand for services is addressed appropriately with a well-trained workforce. While the demographic changes resulting from HCR are unfolding, federal health-care reimbursement for services will decline. Thus healthcare organizations like KP will need to do more with less. In an effort to keep healthcare costs down and maintain needed operating margins, alternative models of delivering care will need to be developed to ensure that patient care workflows are efficient and streamlined.

How can the current workforce be used more efficiently to care for more patients, taking into account the scope of practice, staffing ratios, length of visit, and types of services needed? Key considerations include:

- Providing culturally competent care;
- Moving to a preventive approach;
- Increasing the served population's level of health literacy to encourage healthy behaviors;
- Affording access not only to electronic health resources, such as online health information and telehealth, but to healthcare professionals by e-mail; and
- Increasing team-based, coordinated care to maximize the effectiveness of each patient encounter

For a socially responsible healthcare organization, this means creating a skilled and flexible workforce to provide high-quality and efficient health-care to members of diverse populations who may not be accustomed to obtaining preventative care or managing a chronic disease. George Halvorson, CEO of Kaiser Permanente, frames it this way, "Changing demographics dictate that diversity considerations should play a significant role in how we deliver care. Being culturally competent as caregivers helps us serve existing members and attract new ones. . . . It would be impossible to improve the health of communities we serve if we didn't recognize and support the diversity of those communities."[13]

Under HCR, primary care providers will be held accountable to standards of care that include recommended health screenings, vaccinations, and management of chronic diseases. Team-based, patient-centered delivery of services will require that healthcare workers collaborate effectively in service delivery during each patient encounter while identifying gaps in care.[14] Workforce planning and development are central to ensuring that needed skill sets are in place, which will then result in better patient health outcomes. Enhanced workforce skill sets that will be called upon once HCR is fully implemented include:

- Cultural competency and agility,
- Interpretative skills,
- The ability to work at the leading edge of medical practice,
- The ability to work well in a team environment,
- Critical thinking and judgment skills, and
- Computer and technology skills to effectively use electronic health records and emerging medical technology.

Let's now look at how workforce planning is used to address these issues, again, using KP as an example, while also suggesting broader implications.

KP'S WORKFORCE PLANNING IN AN ERA OF HEALTHCARE REFORM

Workforce planning in an era of healthcare reform extends beyond the internal organization to include collaborative relationships with labor partners, academic institutions, economic development and trade associations, and other industry partners. A primary goal of workforce planning is aligning workforce supply and demand while considering external forces that can affect that balance. The career lifecycle of a healthcare worker begins with career awareness, continues through academic training, and extends into a life of professional practice. Accordingly, workforce planning at KP includes the following elements:

- A needs assessment of critical position requirements based on estimated vacancy rates, incorporating expert judgment,
- A gap analysis to identify supply and demand imbalances by job classification,
- An analysis of workforce recruitment and retention metrics, including workforce demographics,
- Job forecasting that incorporates financial and business planning scenarios at the facility level, and
- Gathering input from exit and new-hire interviews to understand critical employee issues.

These workforce planning fundamentals are then integrated with community health, race/ethnicity, and socioeconomic demographics to estimate future workforce needs. Aligning provider demographics more closely with patient demographics leads to improved patient outcomes.[15] For example, patient-physician communication, trust, and understanding increase when patients and physicians share the same ethnic, racial, cultural, or primary language background.[16] This alignment improves the accuracy of diagnosis. It is a particular challenge in healthcare, as national statistics show a relative lack of diversity in healthcare occupations requiring advanced education, such as nursing, pharmacy, physical therapy, and behavioral health. KP's current workforce has much greater racial/ethnic diversity in entry-level positions than in more senior positions requiring advanced education.

It is important to acknowledge challenges with the educational infrastructure that provides a flow of recruits for healthcare organizations. A major impediment to greater diversity in the healthcare professions is the state of primary education in the United States, particularly in meeting the educational needs of minority and low-income students in kindergarten through grade 12.[17] By high school, more than one in five Latinos and one in ten African Americans have dropped out, compared with one in seventeen Caucasian students.[18]

Most training programs for healthcare professions require the same basic course prerequisites—for example, math, English, and selected science courses. In addition, many healthcare professions require degree completion as part of the educational process. As an illustration, by January 2015, the American Registry of Radiologic Technologists (ARRT) will require that all candidates for primary certification by ARRT in radiography, nuclear medicine technology, radiation therapy, sonography, and magnetic resonance imaging have an associate degree.[19] Unfortunately, the current levels of educational attainment for Latinos, African Americans, and some Asian subpopulations are a barrier to increasing the ethnic diversity of the healthcare workforce.

In spite of these challenges, there are steps that healthcare organizations can take to increase workforce diversity. In addition to sponsoring increases in the educational pipeline of students from diverse and underrepresented populations into healthcare, healthcare organizations can focus on career mobility within their incumbent workforce. Current employees in less technical positions are a good source for candidates who can provide culturally competent care.[20] Entry-level classifications comprise rich ethnic/racial diversity. Using workforce development programs to sponsor technical training for those in entry-level positions will both provide options for career mobility into technical disciplines and increase workforce diversity in those disciplines.

To do this effectively employers in the healthcare sector must continue strengthening partnerships with academic institutions to ensure that the curriculum and training provided is consistent with the needs of the sector. Meeting the skill and workforce composition needs will depend on raising the completion rates of a diverse student body. Key findings from a recent report, which examined educational completion in California community colleges, showed that after six years of enrollment, 70 percent of degree-seeking students had not completed a certificate or degree and had not transferred to a university. Rates of failure to complete were higher for ethnic minority students: about 85 percent for African American students and 80 percent for Latinos. Most had dropped out; only 15 percent of those who had not completed the program were still enrolled.[21] Studies show that, not surprisingly, increased support such as academic advising, case management, and financial resources can improve educational achievement, retention, and completion.[22] Furthermore, the provision of remote-learning options can strengthen the engagement of working professionals.

Recent interactions with middle and high school students indicate that their knowledge of healthcare professions is centered on physician and nursing careers.[23] Allied health occupations such as imaging, laboratory, pharmacy, and rehabilitation positions, where there is high demand for qualified staff, are not as familiar to the students. Thus workforce planning outreach needs to involve building awareness and understanding of all healthcare positions, including those in allied health, so that students know about the broad range of available career choices in the healthcare field.

Since clinical positions are central to healthcare service delivery, workforce planning efforts must also include increasing and sustaining the capacity within healthcare organizations for clinical training. Most licensed and degree healthcare education programs require clinical rotations or internships that include supervision by a preceptor. Building a cadre of preceptors by training seasoned staff is a starting point. Educational training capacity is directly linked to the number of clinical rotations available through healthcare providers. For example, KP has a strong presence in the training community in providing clinical rotations for affiliated academic programs. However, to meet the impending need of additional healthcare workers, the number of available clinical rotations for many classifications will have to increase. In KP the workforce planning and development group is exploring how to increase preceptor/internship capacity by implementing train-the-trainer courses for preceptors. Since the coordination of students/interns can be a barrier, KP's workforce planning and development group is also exploring how to streamline the process. Now we will look at what this means for workforce development, the process of ensuring that future capabilities are there when needed, with KP as an example.

WORKFORCE DEVELOPMENT IN KP INFORMED BY WORKFORCE PLANNING

KP is well positioned to translate workforce planning into the commitment of resources for workforce development. Four key components of workforce development in KP are:

1. Career counseling services,
2. Defined career paths,

3. Communication through a career planning website, and
4. Alignment with workforce planning and recruitment.

The following list illustrates workforce development resources offered at KP that will be critical to ensuring that the workforce is positioned for HCR. Many of these resources are a direct result of KP's partnerships with labor unions and the work of education trusts resulting from those partnerships.[24] Workforce development resources include:

- Tuition reimbursement
  - ✔ Employees are reimbursed for tuition, books, and continuing education activities that support their professional development.
- Education leave
  - ✔ Most union members at KP have education leave that may be up to four weeks per year. This can be used in daily or weekly increments.
- Student financial aid
  - ✔ Student financial aid from external sources, whether from government or other sources such as loans and aid from educational institutions, is integrated with employees' benefits.
- Scholarships
  - ✔ Scholarships to support career mobility are offered by unions and by individual programs within KP. In addition, some KP affinity groups offer scholarships for education and training—for example, KP Latino Association, KP Asian Business Resource Group, and KP African American Business Resource Group.
- Stipends for individual wage replacement
  - ✔ Stipends are available to union employees to replace wages while undergoing training. Stipends cover up to eight hours of supplemental wages per week.
- Stipends for wage replacement of cohort groups
  - ✔ Stipends are available to provide wage replacement for cohort groups undergoing training—for example, from medical assistant to licensed vocational nurse or radiology technician.

Over a ten-year period, KP's workforce planning and development function, in partnership with the education trusts, have created varying types of workforce development programs:

- Skill enhancement (for example, computer, language, and soft skills),
- Healthcare profession preparatory work (support for educational preparation),
- General education (English, math, science, and humanities), and
- Healthcare career pathway programs (such as nursing, imaging, laboratory, and other allied health professions).

Several emerging workforce development practices offer promise for replication and expansion. The following illustrate how identifying a problem through workforce planning led to solutions supported by organizational resources. Such efforts will be important in preparing for HCR.

Qualified Bilingual Staff Program
   Problem: Insufficient number of people able to pass KP's test for cultural and linguistic appropriate services standard (QBS certification) to meet demand.
   Solution: Additional training and time to participate.
   Outcome: Eleven cohorts, approximately 150 people, were trained in six months in a rapidly growing medical facility, yielding a 55 percent cost saving versus individual training.

Distance Learning
   Problem: Workers need to pass a medical terminology examination for a variety of classifications. Passing the examination also offers opportunities for career mobility. It is difficult for workers to attend classes in person because of work or personal commitments.
   Solution: Using distance learning, develop an introduction-to-medical-terminology class with an affiliated school to prepare participants for the regional KP medical terminology examination.
   Outcome: More than one hundred people enrolled in classes in 2011.

Success through Educational Preparation Program
   Problem: Lack of available college prerequisite classes—including chemistry, anatomy, physiology, microbiology, math, English, and medical terminology—keeps employees from being able to develop professional healthcare careers.

Solution: The success-through-educational-preparation program prepares students for entry into nursing and allied health programs by providing needed prerequisite courses at local community colleges. The program sequence begins with English and math and builds students' academic success before moving into science classes. The program pays for tuition, student fees, parking passes, mandatory textbooks, and materials. Tutoring and bridge classes are offered to help students improve their study skills and grasp challenging material.

Outcome: Classes are offered at forty community colleges in California. In 2010, 81 percent of enrolled students completed the courses. Of these students, 78 percent achieved the necessary grades to be able to move on to advanced courses.

As full implementation of HCR approaches, evaluation and measurement of workforce planning and development initiatives will continue. This will be integrated with additional information about healthcare differences within the overall KP system and in the broader community. A key aspect of KP's workforce planning and development efforts, and recruiting, will be to attract multicultural populations into the healthcare professions. The health of our communities will benefit from success in this area. KP's commitment to providing culturally competent care not only fulfills a social responsibility objective to provide equitable health care but also recognizes a commitment to the community to provide career development for an ethnically diverse workforce. In the next chapter, we will examine labor management partnership in KP, an example of a socially responsible workforce practice.

10

Labor-Management Partnerships: A Collaborative Path toward Improved Business Results and Employee Satisfaction

Zeth Ajemian

Creating a mutually supportive relationship with employees in an organization is an important aspect of business social responsibility. This chapter will examine one facet, namely, labor-management partnerships. Also reviewed is their capacity to move beyond traditionally adversarial relations between unions and management toward more productive partnerships, which yield improved business outcomes and provide support and respect for workers. As a framework for successful collaboration, we will use the example of Kaiser Permanente (KP) and its partnership with labor unions, as it may have applicability to other organizations and sectors.

The battle in early 2011 over public sector unions in Wisconsin and numerous other states illustrated the strained relations between labor and management in the United States that persist in both public and private sectors. Unions and management often take intractable positions, resorting to combative negotiating approaches rather than working collaboratively to improve organizational performance and worker satisfaction. Concurrently, however, one can find examples of labor-management partnerships at organizations like Kaiser Permanente that provide concrete evidence of an alternative way forward. These partnerships involve the active participation of unions in the strategic direction of the organization and engage frontline workers in teams to fully embrace innovation and improvements in productivity, quality, and service. By working together to focus on the customer, unions and management are able to transform their typically narrow relationship, focused on contract negotiations, into an innovative

model for business success. The partnerships rely on both parties rejecting outdated, antagonistic approaches to negotiations in favor of creating
a team-based, high-performance work organization dedicated not only to
the achievement of organizational results but also to key union interests
such as job security. When successful, partnerships rise above entrenched
ideology and partisanship of typical strained union-management relations
to embrace collaboration and teamwork for mutually beneficial outcomes.
This chapter will demonstrate how, in today's economy, conflict-based relations between unions and management are failing both American workers
and businesses, and how KP's labor-management partnership has evolved
into a viable alternative approach for management, unions, and employees. As background we will first look at the evolution of organized labor in
the United States.

THE CURRENT STATE OF ORGANIZED LABOR

Organized labor, once a powerful force in American society, is currently
on the defensive and in a fragile state after years of progressively declining
membership. In 2010 less than 7 percent of America's private workforce
were members of labor unions (11.9%, if public sector unions are count-
ed).[1] This is in stark contrast to the decades following World War II, where
unions represented as much as 35 percent of the private sector workforce.
After a long history of sometimes violent conflicts to secure worker rights,
unions gained power in the early part of the twentieth century. Their
struggles culminated in 1935 with the passage of the Wagner Act, or the
National Labor Relations Act (NLRA). The NLRA allowed workers to create and organize into unions, bargain collectively, and legally strike. Labor
contracts negotiated with employers resulted in wage increases, benefits,
and workplace safety legislation. Unions were also successful in securing
the forty-hour work week, overtime pay, work breaks, healthcare insurance,
sick days, vacations, retirement and pension benefits, laws banning child
labor, and increased job security.[2] Unions were able to organize in most
major manufacturing industries, including railroads, coal, steel, automo-
biles, telephones, tires, airlines, and trucking.

Following World War II, U.S. industrial strength grew dramatically: real
GDP increased by 41 percent from 1950 to 1960.[3] Wages rose steadily, by

over 2 percent per year, and union workers (from 1950 to 1975) earned a comfortable 20 percent more than nonunion workers of similar age, experience, and education.[4] As Hendrik Hertzberg notes, "Organized labor was powerful and, for the most part, respected. Its economic and political muscle had played an indispensable role in insuring that the benefits of postwar prosperity were widely shared, transforming much of what many had unironically called [*sic*] the proletariat into an important segment of the broad American middle class."[5] The rise of union power can be correlated with the rise of the middle class in America in the decades following World War II.

Then, with the rise of international economic competition in the 1960s and 1970s, American industrial might was suddenly challenged by foreign competitors that exported cheaper products manufactured by significantly cheaper, and often exploited, labor. In response, American companies began shifting capital and jobs offshore to cheaper areas of production and invested heavily in technology and automation to increase productivity. This movement, along with a variety of other factors, led to the closing of factories, the disappearance of many union jobs, and the deindustrialization of many American cities.[6] Moreover, the Taft-Hartley Act of 1947, which had limited the ability of unions to support each other during strikes and to organize, also led to the development of right-to-work statutes in twenty-two states that ended closed shops or union membership as a mandatory requirement for employment.[7] Further, business and labor market transformations resulted in a shift to a part-time, nonbenefited, and contingent workforce, further impeding American unions' ability to retain jobs and membership.[8] Finally, American companies led organized assaults on unions with campaigns to dissuade and intimidate workers attempting to organize. Thomas Kochan and his colleagues describe how the National Labor Relations Board (NLRB), whose job was to implement the NLRA law by developing an orderly process for reaching agreements over wages, hours, and working conditions, has been ineffective in its enforcement of these regulations. Indeed, studies show that workers face enormous obstacles when attempting to join unions or achieve collective bargaining contracts. Data indicates that only one in five organizing efforts is successful in reaching a first contract.[9]

As Berkeley labor professor Harley Shaiken notes, "Today, if workers try to organize, the NLRB generally sets a secret-ballot vote a month or more after the formal request. During this period, it is legal for the company to hire anti-union consultants, schedule an unlimited number of mandatory meetings with employees, and 'predict' that the workplace could be shuttered if the union wins and bar labor representatives from the premises."[10]

All of these factors have played a role in labor's continued decline over the past several decades. While unions have been somewhat successful in moving into service industries such as restaurants, retail, janitorial, and healthcare, as well as into the government public sector, their cumulative loss of membership has been devastating to their base.[11]

Public Perceptions of Unions and the Current Plight of the Middle Class

It is therefore not surprising, whether justified or not, that the American public's perception of unions has shifted and, in some cases, grown increasingly negative. Some view unions as outdated organizations that only had value in an earlier industrialized society where more labor-intensive, manufacturing jobs were equated with workplace safety concerns and wage and hour exploitation. Now, with numerous labor laws in place protecting workers and many nonunion businesses offering benefits that previously were only available in union jobs, some believe that unions have no relevance in today's modern workplace and provide few tangible benefits for workers. Many in management believe that unions exist simply to collect membership dues, file grievances, and resist change of any kind, even if change means company growth and profits. Others accuse unions of being unable or unwilling to adapt to the modern, global economy. Andy Stern, the former head of Service Employees International Union (SEIU), the largest union in America, put it this way: "(Unions) seem like a legacy institution and not an institution for the future."[12]

Conversely, some argue that unions are the last remaining cornerstones of middle-class existence in America. During periods of economic growth, unions are sometimes the sole force ensuring that corporate profits are shared with working and middle-class families in the form of higher wages and benefits. The fact that unions have lost half of their membership since 1983 certainly has had a direct impact on the middle class. As Hertzberg observes, "Organized labor's catastrophic decline has paralleled—and pre-cipitated—an equally dramatic rise in income inequality."[13] The plight of the American middle class is real and is confirmed by an examination of the data. Rising income inequality in America has affected the middle class for decades. Average hourly wages of American workers, when adjusted for inflation, have remained essentially stagnant since the 1970s, while wealth has been concentrated in the upper 1 percent of the nation's population.[14]

Robert Reich, former U.S. labor secretary under President Bill Clinton writes, "The richest 1 percent of Americans now takes home more than 20 percent of total income. That's the highest share going to the top 1 percent in almost 90 years."[15] And Mary deWolf adds, "The U.S. ranks 64th in income inequality, just behind Nigeria and just ahead of Rwanda. The income gap is at an 80-year high with the bottom 50 percent of our citizens sharing just 2.5% of the nation's wealth."[16]

If the upward trend of inequality over the past few decades isn't enough, the 2008 economic downturn decimated middle-class families' pensions, retirements, and savings. Massive layoffs, rampant unemployment, and the bursting of the credit bubble, which, for years, had held middle-class families afloat by creating artificial purchasing power, have crippled the purchasing power of the middle class. Again, Robert Reich posits, "Starting in the late 1970s, the middle class began to weaken. Although productivity continued to grow and the economy continued to expand, wages began flattening in the 1970s because new technologies . . . started to undermine any American job that could be automated or done more cheaply abroad. The same technologies bestowed ever larger rewards on people who could use them to innovate and solve problems. Some were product entrepre-neurs; a growing number were financial entrepreneurs. The pay of gradu-ates of prestigious colleges and M.B.A. programs—the 'talent' that reached the pinnacles of power in executive suites and on Wall Street—soared."[17]

A 2012 U.S. Census Bureau report documented that not only have middle-class wages remained essentially stagnant since the 1970s when ad-justed for inflation, but income fell to $50,054 in 2011, a level not seen since 1996. Between 1999 and 2011, median household income is actually down 9 percent.[18] According to Jared Bernstein, senior fellow at the Center on Budget and Policy Priorities, "Economists talk about the lost decade in

Japan. . . . Well, with these 2010 data, we can confirm the lost decade for the American middle class."[19] So, while labor unions are perceived by many to be increasingly obsolete, the middle- and working-class issues they have traditionally fought for, and continue to fight for, are more relevant than ever. Despite their dwindling membership numbers, unions may indeed be the last major force advocating for the rights of working- and middle-class workers. Paul Krugman commented, "You don't have to love unions, you don't have to believe that their policy positions are always right, to recognize that they're among the few influential players in our political system representing the interests of middle- and working-class Americans, as opposed to the wealthy. Indeed, if America has become more oligarchic and less democratic over the last 30 years—which it has—that's to an important extent due to the decline of private-sector unions."[20]

Polls suggest that members of the American public are split on their view of unions. For example, an August 2011 survey indicated that 52 percent of the American public have a positive view of unions.[21] Furthermore, in a survey taken during the 2011 Wisconsin struggle, a notably higher rate, 62 percent, indicated support for workers' right to collective bargaining.[22] And significant evidence exists to show that unions continue to generate concrete gains for working people. For example, a report by Lawrence Mishel and Matthew Walters points out that union wages are, on average, 20 percent higher when compared with similar nonunion jobs and 28 percent higher if benefits are included.[23] "Union employers are also significantly more likely to provide benefits to their employees. Union workers nationwide are 28.2 percent more likely to be covered by employer-provided health insurance and 53.9 percent more likely to have employer-provided pensions compared to workers with similar characteristics who were not in unions."[24]

When surveyed, workers indicate that they support representation and participation in the workplace and cooperative relations with management, and they generally support their unions and their ability to represent individuals. Polls over many years consistently indicate the majority of Americans disapprove of strikes, and a majority of workers want management and union leaders to create workplaces that are productive and relationships that are respectful.[25]

Current Labor Relations Environment

In light of the various factors and conflicting messages regarding how unions are viewed, what is the current outlook for relations between labor and management? Even in a worsening economy, with more than 14 million Americans unemployed in 2011, there was little evidence that labor and management intended to reform their adversarial approaches, let alone begin to work together in partnership. Similarly, political discourse in Washington on unions reflected traditional partisanship and was exemplified in early 2011 by the Obama administration's proposed Employee Free Choice Act. The act would have allowed unions to form by simple card check versus private ballot; the latter approach has been alleged to facilitate employers' antiunion campaigns. The Republicans quickly dismissed this proposal as antibusiness and antiworker.[26]

This familiar pattern is replayed frequently. For example, it occurred in the 2011 Wisconsin conflict where Republican governor Scott Walker not only demanded concessions from public employee unions to dramatically scale back pensions and pay raises in order to balance the state budget but also passed legislation that eliminated union rights to bargain collectively. While this particular conflict focused on public sector unions, some interpreted the action as an attempt to permanently cripple the union movement in America. Regardless of the real intent, rather than use this conflict as an opportunity to modernize and improve the way unions and management work together, both sides further entrenched their existing positions. This point is emphasized by Jim Newton: "The (Wisconsin) conflict began over the Republican governor's attempt to address the State budget shortfall of more than $3 billion, but it quickly morphed into an attack on the bargaining rights of unions. Highlighted by histrionics on both sides, the face-off dominated a few news cycles, produced an inconclusive set of recall elections and sharpened the hard feelings on both sides."[27]

With some exceptions—for example, Republican mayor Michael Bloomberg in New York City—many Republican politicians picked up the fight with their public sector unions in the name of fiscal responsibility.[28] While the attack spurred many to labor's defense, the ultimate outcome may be the further decline of union power. The dysfunctional relations between labor and management can be partly explained by the fact that U.S. labor laws are premised on the general framework that such relations are inherently adversarial. The NLRA is not structured in a manner that promotes or even anticipates cooperation between labor and management. In the view of Kochan and his colleagues, "The Act draws a clear line of demarcation between management responsibilities and rights to allocate resources and direct the workforce and labor's rights to negotiate over the impacts of management decisions on wages, hours, and working conditions."[29]

Peter diCicco, the leader of the KP Coalition of Unions and one of the original founders of the labor-management partnership at KP, illustrates this perspective with what he calls the NLRB "box."[30] Inside the box, he places the subjects of mandatory bargaining that the NLRB requires unions and employers to negotiate, such as wages, benefits, and grievance procedures. Outside the box is a long list of other issues—for instance, staffing levels, hiring practices, service methods, and business strategy—which is important to union members; one example would be a successful healthcare organization focusing on service and quality. However, these areas, which are of vital interest to both parties, are ignored by the NLRB's scope and vision for collaboration. The NLRB is essentially saying that the parties should only negotiate if there is a problem, rather than encouraging both parties to work together to improve organizational performance.

Richard Freeman and Joel Rogers provide survey data demonstrating that employees consistently express their desire for cooperation with management in the workplace.[31] In order to improve relations, the nation's labor laws need to be updated and modernized to promote cooperation between currently warring entities. Undoubtedly, extreme points of view will continue to exist on both sides, with some in management simply desiring the eradication of unions and some in unions focused solely on punishing management for alleged wrongdoings. The question is whether more moderate players from each side will step up and work for an alternative way forward. Can labor and management learn from both positive and negative experiences to shape a labor relations system that better fits a modern workforce and economy? Or will they continue to replay the combative and nonproductive labor relations epitomized by events in Wisconsin and elsewhere? It appears that most people wish for a better approach, one that allows employees to have a voice at work in cooperation with company management.

ANOTHER WAY FORWARD: LABOR-MANAGEMENT PARTNERSHIPS

An alternative direction is a labor-management partnership. Labor-management partnerships (LMPs) are cooperative agreements, primarily in unionized companies but also occasionally in nonunionized companies, that bring together management and the voices of frontline employees to create an environment of continual performance improvement built on the common interests of both parties. The success of such partnerships is built on their ability to combine employees, managers, and union representatives to capitalize on shared knowledge. LMPs focus on improving quality and service, cutting costs, eliminating waste, and increasing company profitability. Employees on the front line are encouraged to come up with innovative solutions to workplace issues, thus allowing managers to operate more in a coaching and mentoring role.[32] Gains for employees and their unions include job security, performance-sharing programs, increased union membership as the business grows, an improved workplace environment, and market-leading wages and benefits.

Prior to KP's implementation of its LMP, there were two other notable, large-scale attempts at labor-management partnerships in the United States. The first was at Harley-Davidson, formed in the 1980s–1990s, and credited with helping the company avoid bankruptcy. The other was at Saturn in the 1990s, a collaboration between General Motors (GM) and the United Auto Workers. While the latter partnership was successful in the early years, changes in local union leadership resulted in a move back to traditional collective bargaining. And because of the downturn in the U.S. auto industry by 2008, GM elected to discontinue the manufacture of the Saturn line to save costs.[33]

LMP at Kaiser Permanente

KP's example of labor-management partnership represents the largest and longest-lasting partnership of its kind in the United States. In 1997, following years of labor turmoil and competitive pressure within the healthcare industry, the partnership was formed at KP; the first national agreement between KP and the Coalition of Kaiser Permanente Unions was ultimately signed in 2000. Twenty-seven local unions representing KP workers across the country had joined together in the coalition to better coordinate bargaining strategy. As a way to change, not only how labor and management related, but also how to work together to transform the organization to be more successful in an increasingly competitive environment, KP and the coalition then created the LMP. In 2011 the KP LMP covered more than 92,000 union employees in thirty-eight local unions, and more than 20,000 managers and 16,000 physicians in nine states and Washington, D.C. It is the most comprehensive partnership of its kind. Despite frequent challenges and some criticism, the partnership continues to thrive after two national five-year agreements (2000 and 2005) and a two-year national agreement (2010).

A Short History of the LMP at KP

The viability of the partnership at KP is based on a long history of positive relations between KP and labor unions that dates back to the founding of the organization. In the late 1930s, in addition to his ambitious work building American ships for World War II, Henry J. Kaiser led a massive construction effort to build the Hoover, Bonneville, and Grand Coulee Dams. Working with his partner, Sydney Garfield, MD, Henry Kaiser offered to provide healthcare for the workers on the Grand Coulee Dam project. Rather than adhere to the traditional fee-for-service healthcare program, the steelworkers union representing the workers at that site successfully negotiated a prepaid medical plan to cover workers at a cost of 10 cents per day. The program was eventually expanded to include family dependents. While this arrangement was not the first prepaid medical plan in the United States, it was the first to provide a prepaid, integrated, health maintenance organization (HMO)–style plan on a large scale. From this beginning, KP would eventually grow into the largest nonprofit healthcare organization in the country, serving a wide range of members. But this early relationship with union employees laid the foundation for a long tradition of labor and management working together.[34] Speaking of Henry Kaiser, Garfield said, "It was his feeling that unions were absolutely necessary in the industrial world of today. He felt that the unions were a great contribution to that; he felt they were necessary and he was 100 percent for them."[35]

By the 1980s KP, a nonprofit, integrated healthcare system (doctors, health plan, and hospitals are all within one system), represented an affordable healthcare option for thousands of working families. However, beginning in the late 1980s and early 1990s, KP was confronted with growing competition from for-profit healthcare insurers who sought to capture some of KP's substantial market share. In response, KP employed an aggressive new business strategy involving lowering prices in an effort to attract new members. In addition, the company expanded into new regions, where they had less experience (New England, New York, North Carolina, and Texas), some of which were traditionally more antiunion. Quality and service problems ensued, and cost pressures forced the company to scale back these efforts. Simultaneously, KP management pursued a more aggressive labor relations strategy that led to layoffs, collective bargaining concessions, and, ultimately, to a demoralized workforce. Once known for its nonprofit, union-friendly, accessible healthcare, KP was now receiving consistently negative publicity.[36]

By the mid-1990s, KP, still the country's largest nonprofit health maintenance organization, faced annual losses of $250 million.[37] This business crisis led KP to consider breaking up its integrated model of care delivery to better compete with other HMOs. Unions, worried about employee job security, responded aggressively, and strikes followed. Having recently formed into a national coalition, the unions began to plan a full corporate campaign against KP, a move that, considering the competitive environment, could have permanently crippled the organization. The situation was deteriorating significantly. Both sides began to consider an alternative as they realized that their respective fates were interwoven. If the organization failed, thousands of union jobs would be lost.

In December 1995, representatives of KP and the Coalition of KP Unions met to discuss the development of the labor-management partnership, and in 1997 the LMP was officially launched. However, because of labor's distrust of management, the partnering unions agreed that traditional contract bargaining would continue as it had before. As 2000 approached, labor saw that trying to create a partnership with KP and, at the same time, continue a traditional approach to negotiations was not feasible. Thus the common-issues bargaining process was developed to negotiate a national contract reflecting the principles and goals of the LMP. The historic result was the first national agreement in 2000.

Kochan and colleagues frame it this way: "The partnership was thus not the product of an ideological conversion to labor-management cooperation on the part of either the union coalition or Kaiser Permanente management, but developed out of a pragmatic judgment that the parties would have more to lose separately and jointly by going further down the path of escalating conflict."[38]

Kaiser Permanente LMP Basics

So, what is a labor-management partnership and how does it work at KP? KP's version of partnership involves workers, managers, and physicians who use interest-based problem solving and consensus decision making, as a cooperative team, to provide the highest level of patient care.[39] The partnership was designed not as an alternative way to negotiate with labor but as a business strategy to create a high-performance work organization. It relies not only on the partnership of KP management and unions but perhaps, and more important, on the active participation of each employee and physician in a team-based approach to providing care. The partnership's work is depicted in a value compass, a pictorial representation that contains four business goals as compass points with the KP member (patient) in the center. The points are: best place to work, best service, best quality, and most affordable. This is achieved by unit-based teams, which include frontline managers, workers, and physicians, collaborating to ensure that each patient receives the best possible quality and service at an affordable price. This team-based approach to care is also intended to solve day-to-day problems together at the front line and ensure that KP is a great place to work.

Partnership represents a fundamentally different approach to how a company can be run. The way just-in-time and modular production models transformed shop floors of manufacturing plants, partnership attempts to transform how care is delivered in clinics and hospitals. Fundamental to successful delivery of care is a well-informed and well-coordinated team-based approach, where sharing of information is vital not only to patient care but also to innovating and eliminating inefficiencies. KP's approach to partnership brings together frontline managers, workers, and physicians to fully harness each individual's expertise in the overall delivery of care. Rather than segmenting these perspectives in a traditional hierarchical structure, the perspectives are integrated into a constantly changing and improving model of care. Roles evolve and expand. For example, union stewards and union team coleaders begin to manage work units. Rather than simply directing work, managers can coach and mentor employees. All staff support physicians in providing high-quality, compassionate, patient-centered care. This framework is crucial at a time of transformation in healthcare delivery. It is a transformation that reflects structural changes in the healthcare sector discussed elsewhere in our book, with increased demand for healthcare services driven by aging baby boomers and broader accessibility to healthcare, coupled with growing technological sophistication. KP's partnership structure provides a basis for healthcare delivery that enables the organization to better adapt to this dynamic environment.

Crucial to the success of KP in the face of new regulations, competitive pressures, and rapidly increasing demand is having labor and management work together rather than confront each other in an adversarial manner. By allowing the active and meaningful participation of every worker, manager, and physician in the delivery of care, the entire organization is focused on service delivery. While unions still play an important role in collective bargaining, that role now expands to include engaging every worker in the path forward. A significant change for labor leaders is that, through the partnership, unions are brought directly into making decisions about at least some aspects of company policy. This places much responsibility on the unions, which, through their partnering with management, have shared accountability for organizational goals. Instead of engaging solely in collective bargaining and employee disputes, they now engage in consensus decision making and interest-based problem solving regarding day-to-day operations of the organization. Interest-based problem solving involves identifying common interests, not focusing on antagonistic positions, as a means to create joint solutions. Consensus decision making ensures that all parties are heard and, as a result, tries to arrive at decisions that each participant can actively support.

Performance-Sharing Program

Another important aspect of the LMP is the performance-sharing program (PSP). This program engages union members in helping KP achieve strategic or operational goals that increase organizational performance and lower operational costs. Incentives for this program take the form of employee bonuses, thereby aligning worker interests with the overall success of KP. PSP goals are developed using consensus by LMP regional councils to target such areas as high attendance, workplace safety, quality, service, clinical goals, inpatient care experience, outpatient care experience, and measures of a healthy workforce. At the end of the year, provided that goals established by the LMP regional councils are met or exceeded based on KP performance in these areas, the PSP–variable pay program provides cash awards to program participants.

Unit-Based Teams
The partnership is implemented on the ground level via unit-based teams (UBT). These teams employ frontline workers to organize and make decisions about day-to-day operations. More than 90,000 KP employees now work in 3,444 unit-based teams, a major effort that began in 2008.[40] These teams involve all members of the department working together to continually improve departmental service and performance. The teams have been successful in improving patient care and boosting morale and engagement of the workforce.[41] Each team's members are engaged in planning and designing work processes, setting goals and metrics, and evaluating team performance, as well as in budgeting, staffing, and scheduling decisions. The UBTs use a rapid improvement model, which is defined by a four-step process: plan, do, study, act. This methodology allows teams to improve performance by implementing small changes, testing the results, and adjusting operations as needed. Each team's development and improvement in service and quality are measured and monitored by regional and local LMP staff to ensure that goals and targets are met.

As Ben Chu, president of the Kaiser Foundation Hospitals, Southern California, sums it up: "The UBTs unleash the knowledge of the workers."[42] Oliver Goldsmith, former executive medical director of the Southern California Permanente Medical Group and early national LMP committee member, commented in 2001:

To me it is very simple: the improvement in Kaiser Permanente's performance can only go so far unless everybody is engaged equally in trying to improve the organization. We've made some significant progress through a variety of initiatives, but in my opinion we're still performing at maybe 70% of our potential. Perhaps we can bump that percentage up a few points through efforts similar to the ones we have initiated in the past. But we can't reach our full potential unless our employees are participating much more energetically in these efforts. To accomplish that, we must involve them and bring their leadership and their unions on board. By working in a partnership model, we will more clearly understand their needs, and they will have a better understanding of our needs as physicians and managers. It is similar to the way that we in the medical groups work in collaborative partnership with our health plan and hospitals.[43]

In a relatively short time, KP has been successful in organizing most of its frontline workers into UBTs, launching a transformative process of providing service.

Attending a regional LMP council meeting provides a glimpse into how labor and management can work together collaboratively. As an example, in Southern California, the council trichairs include the regional union leader of the Coalition of Kaiser Permanente Unions (CKPU), the regional president of the Kaiser Foundation Hospital, and the leader of the Southern California Permanente Medical Group (SCPMG, the physicians' partnership). The council members, operating by consensus, include operational representatives from various hospitals, labor representatives, and regional representatives in various functional areas such as quality/service, human resources, nursing, organizational effectiveness, and labor relations. Routine agenda items include goal setting and tracking and monitoring of performance-sharing programs. Particularly noteworthy is the fact that labor and management are discussing and collaborating on issues outside the collective bargaining process. For instance, new technologies, such as computerized, walk-up kiosks that allow for quicker patient-member check-ins, are discussed and debated based on their potential both to save time and money and to displace current receptionists. The council meetings provide a forum for managers to discuss new ideas with unions well before implementation. This approach requires more time and effort for management initially but generally prevents significant conflict with labor during implementation, as early buy-in from all parties has been obtained.

Kaiser Permanente LMP Results

Has the partnership been successful? Has it achieved its goals and helped improve KP as an organization? While it is difficult to quantitatively correlate improvements in company performance with the LMP, it is clear that KP's performance has improved in multiple areas as a result of this endeavor. Kochan and his colleagues provide an insightful external evaluation of the partnership's progress and success.[44] Perhaps most significantly, they point out that the organization, which in the mid-1990s was on the brink of collapse, is now a leader within the healthcare sector, with significantly expanded membership and more than $45 billion in annual revenues. The partnership was successful in staving off a potentially crippling battle between labor and management during the tumult of that period and transforming the organization into a model for success within the sector. That the partnership has endured for so long, through fourteen years and three national agreements, is impressive.

As measured by significant declines in grievance rates and illustrated by many applications of interest-based problem solving and consensus decision making, labor relations have improved. Seventy percent of the workforce prefers the partnership over normal labor-management relations. The partnership has endured multiple challenges on both the labor and management sides, including changes in leaderships and tensions among many of the union partners. Examples of the beneficial effects of partnerships on clinical outcomes in healthcare have also been cited.[45] Here are some summary words from Kochan and colleagues about the value of the partnership in KP: "It turned around dangerously deteriorating labor-management relations; deepened the organizational capacity of Kaiser Permanente to meet challenges and crises as they arose; demonstrated that workers, unions, managers, and physicians could work together in delivering high-quality health care; and yielded significant benefits for managers, employees, and unions."[46]

FURTHER OPPORTUNITIES FOR PARTNERSHIPS

Is KP's experiment and success with partnership a framework for other companies to follow? Possibly. Despite LMP failures in other companies, KP's demonstrated successful approach, outlined in this chapter, could potentially be applied in other industries outside healthcare. Certainly KP has unique attributes, and LMP applicability may vary when applied in more traditional companies. KP's nonprofit status, coupled with a long history of working with labor, provided it with distinct advantages when approaching partnership. Management in publicly traded companies, responding to pressure from shareholders to focus on short-term quarterly earnings, might not have the patience for labor-management partnership processes. Also partnerships are expensive to implement, requiring extensive employee and management training and education. Further, KP unions and management entered into the partnership out of necessity, amid a fiscal crisis in the face of severe competition and plummeting revenues.

However, while KP's experience may be unique for these reasons, its venture into partnership represents success on a large scale in an organization with more than 175,000 employees, $45 billion in annual revenue, and almost 9 million patient-members. Indeed, KP management faced the same challenges many healthcare and other organizations face, including stiff competition within the sector, an ongoing need for quality and service improvements with minimal impact on costs, as well as rising costs and significant sector change and uncertainty. So KP's successful partnership is significant and relevant, one that deserves consideration as a possible template for management and labor partnerships at other organizations.

It is my hope that other organizations, both nonprofit and for-profit, will explore similar collaborative practices as a better way forward. Specifically, I believe that there is both an urgent need and a significant opportunity for labor-management partnership in the public education arena. Not only is there major conflict between teachers' unions and management in American public education, but there are tremendous challenges to reinvigorate a struggling educational system. At a time of high unemployment, particularly among those less skilled and educated, it appears that our schools do not have the capacity to prepare our children for the twenty-first-century global economy. Recently, much of the blame has targeted the teachers' unions, specifically their defense of teacher seniority. In a time of severe cuts to public education, many are exasperated with union contracts that result in higher-performing teachers being laid off while those more senior and less proficient are retained.[47] At the same time, teachers can point to ineffective and bloated school administration, massive cuts to education, and intense pressure to focus solely on test scores as a means of evaluating educational proficiency. As in the 1990s when KP and its unions faced similarly intense pressures and ultimately sought an alternative approach, public schools need an alternative. And, like the situation with KP, the fates of teachers, unions, and administrators are interwoven. Moreover, just as the patient must be the focus of the LMP partnership at KP, so must children and students be the focus of potential labor-management partnerships in the educational arena.

A 2011 report documents several LMP efforts focused on transforming public school education.[48] While the report indicates that teachers' unions and school administrators work together as equal partners, it still appears to take place in the context of traditional collective bargaining. Nevertheless, the report points to benefits of improved academic performance and parent and community engagement. I hope that we see more comprehensive partnership structures instituted in education, structures that allow labor and management to move beyond the confines of collective bargaining and focus broader efforts on the needs of students. Perhaps school versions of unit-based teams could engage the expertise of teachers, coaches, administrators, parents, and other stakeholders. Whatever the particular approach, I strongly believe that labor and management in the educational sector could learn from the LMP model at KP and transition from limited, conflict-based relations to a more collaborative approach focused on their customers, namely, our children and future leaders. Indeed, labor-management partnerships in general offer much hope as one means of engaging in socially responsible workforce practices. In the next chapter, we will move to the financial sector and explore social responsibility in that setting.

11

Financial Institutions and Social Responsibility

Jim Leatherberry

> Capitalism requires a structure and value system that people
> believe in and can depend on.
>
> —John Bogle (Founder, Vanguard Group of mutual funds)[1]

Social responsibility is especially important for the financial sector because this sector, directly or indirectly, touches the lives of most people in the developed world. In the United States and the rest of the industrialized nations, this may take the form of the nest eggs people have on deposit at banks and investment firms, the collective savings of many people through pension funds, or the accumulation of charitable gifts at endowments. The stewardship of these funds is a heavy responsibility since these monies represent the accumulated hard work of myriad individuals and institutions. All too often the trust placed in our financial institutions to safeguard these investments has been betrayed.[2] This betrayal has been in not only the form of well-publicized cases of fraud but also more insidious practices: unreasonable fees, excessive trading, and conflicts of interest.[3] Moreover, the products themselves have uncertain outcomes, and their true costs are often not easy to identify.

In exploring the implications for social responsibility, this chapter will briefly identify the principal participants in the investment markets and how they interact. It will outline what investors should reasonably expect from the financial institutions with which they deal. Cases of recent financial malfeasance will be explored with the intent of learning how these mistakes can be avoided in the future. After listing examples of good corporate behavior on the part of investment professionals, we will examine how this could be more widely practiced. The relative merits of government regulation and industry self-governance will be considered. Finally we will postulate whether current industry trends will result in more responsible conduct. While the focus will be on the U.S. financial markets, the increasing convergence and interconnectedness of global financial markets means that many of the principles and conclusions apply to other international markets as well.

THE INVESTMENT COMMUNITY: THE INVESTORS AND THE PROVIDERS

> If you believe you or anyone else has a system that can predict
> the future of the stock market, the joke is on you.
>
> —Ralph Wanger (Founder, Wanger Asset Management
> and Acorn mutual fund)[4]

The United States has one of the most well-developed and diversified investment communities in the world, one with a plethora of investment vehicles and a diverse group of participants. The public, that is, individuals, participates directly in the markets in the form of investment accounts with brokerage firms, insurance companies, banks, and mutual fund companies. People have indirect exposure to the investment industry through private and public pension funds and the charities and endowments that are the recipients of their donations. Individual investors are generally making long-term investments to secure their own financial future or that of their families. They want to preserve their capital and earn an acceptable return on products that are easily understood and have a reasonable cost.

There are a variety of approaches for people to invest their money, ranging from self-direction to delegating all decision making to professionals. The most basic, and in many cases cost-effective, way is for individuals to make their own investment decisions; however, the level of financial literacy among the public is fairly low. Annamaria Lusardi and Olivia Mitchell showed that only 30 percent of Americans could correctly answer three simple questions on interest rates, inflation, and risk diversification.[5] The rise of defined contribution pension plans rather than defined benefit plans has put even more decision-making responsibility in the hands of the public. This trend, which has been prevalent in the private sector for the last decade, is increasingly spreading to the public sector in the wake of state and local budget problems. From 1990 to 2009 the number of single-employer-defined benefit plans declined from 92,000 to 29,000. In 2008 only 20 percent of private sector workers were covered by defined benefit plans, compared with about 79 percent of public sector workers.[6]

Thanks to the Internet, individual investors have access to a wide range of investment research and financial information. Further, the cost of trading stocks has plummeted to as little as $5 per transaction, making trading affordable.[7] However, this type of investing presupposes a reasonable level of sophistication that many investors do not have. Most people invest their savings through mutual funds, company 401(k) plans, pension plans, variable annuities, or, for those with greater investable funds, wrap plans. A wrap plan charges a flat fee per year and doesn't give brokers any incentive to overtrade an account since commissions are included in the fee. Even though these methods entrust investment decisions to professionals, careful thought is still required in their selection.

A number of institutions provide investment services. They include banks, brokerage firms (sometimes referred to as wire houses), investment banks, insurance companies, credit-rating agencies, and mutual fund complexes. The level of service and expertise varies greatly from firm to firm. Generally, the highest level of service goes to the largest accounts. It is difficult to get much individual attention for an account under $50,000–$100,000. The test required for brokers (generally called the Series 7) has increasingly emphasized ethics and regulation, but it is no guarantee of investing competence. Firms are anxious to acquire and retain investment assets, while most investors infrequently change providers even in the face of poor performance.

WHAT DO INVESTORS HAVE THE RIGHT TO EXPECT FROM THEIR INVESTMENT PROVIDERS?

> Managers of other people's money [rarely] watch over it
> with the same anxious vigilance with which . . . they watch
> over their own."
>
> —Adam Smith, *Wealth of Nations*[8]

The most basic expectation that investors should have is that investment advisers always act in the best interests of their clients. Amazingly, according to James Green, only some investment professionals are currently covered by this so-called fiduciary standard: "Fiduciaries (which include registered investment advisers and mutual funds) must disclose all unavoidable conflicts and always be able to show regulators why their recommendations are in their clients' best interest; brokers need not disclose material conflicts, or control investment expenses, much less recommend what is best for clients."[9] Roy Diliberto, in *Financial Advisor* magazine, made an excellent analogy when he said, "One of the examples that is used by many as a non-fiduciary relationship is when a client calls and asks to buy a particular investment. If that investment is not in the best interest of the client, I believe the CFP (Certified Financial Planner) practitioner has an obligation to tell him that. The fiduciary hat must remain on at all times. Imagine a patient asking a doctor to prescribe a drug that is not in her best interest. The doctor cannot dispense with the Hippocratic Oath and prescribe the drug. So it should be with all CFP practitioners. If we are ever to become a profession, nothing less than that should be acceptable."[10] There is currently much discussion in the financial sector about extending the fiduciary standard to all investment professionals. Some in the sector are fighting this change quite vociferously. I find it extremely difficult to understand this position. It can't be that they fear increased litigation since most brokerage agreements only provide for arbitration, a practice that usually favors the sector. It seems indefensible that you could be permitted to do things that are not in your client's best interest.

Investment products should have a clear and accurate disclosure of risks. While many risk disclosure statements are required to open a brokerage account, there is not usually a clear, concise document that most people will read. Knut Rostad of the Institute for the Fiduciary Standard notes, "There is a substantial body of research showing the lack of effectiveness of financial disclosures to consumers. So when applied to a fiduciary standard, disclosure should be considered to be ineffective unless proven otherwise."[11] Most people know that investing is inherently risky, but investors encounter a broad spectrum of risk. Buying a broad-based stock index fund is not the same as buying a thinly traded mining stock, for example. Perhaps there should be a relative rating scheme of investment risks. Morningstar, the mutual fund–rating service provides such a risk measure for mutual funds. Another measure could be creating a broad categorization of potential risks for the investing public. Such an action would be a socially responsible project for the financial industry to consider sponsoring. It would allow investors the opportunity to match the relative risk of investment vehicles with their own investment goals.

A similar criticism could be leveled at the disclosure of investment costs. Most investments do have a description of fees and costs, but they are often buried in dense documentation. Costs should be prominently displayed and the total cost identified; according to John Turner and Sophie Korczyk: "More than 80 percent of 401(k) participants reported in a nationwide survey not knowing how much they pay in fees."[12] In addition, a table of what the impact of costs is over the life of an investment should be given. According to a 2009 U.S. Government Accountability Office report on 401(k) fees, paying an extra percentage point in annual fees would shave a sixth off one's total retirement savings after twenty years.[13] The investment community could demonstrate a higher level of social responsibility by taking the lead on implementing this disclosure; it would help investors make more informed choices about investments.

Even with mutual funds that have significant required disclosure, there are problems. A typical fund might have a front-end load, an early redemption penalty, management fees, operating expenses, and 12-B1 fees (the marketing expenses of the fund charged back to investors). Such funds might need as much as a 7 percent return just for the investor to break even. I doubt that most individual investors know what they are paying in their mutual funds. Those who do must wade through a thick prospectus document to ascertain the costs. A more effective approach would be to include a short, more accessible summary document that would highlight the costs and key attributes of the fund's strategy.

FINANCIERS BEHAVING BADLY

> Wall Street never changes. The pockets change, the suckers change, the stocks change, but Wall Street never changes because human nature never changes.
>
> —Jesse Livermore (early twentieth-century stock trader)[14]

Financial malfeasance has been with us for a long time. The book *Extraordinary Popular Delusions and the Madness of Crowds,* written in 1841 by Charles

Mackay, clearly documents financial bubbles that burst in the seventeenth and eighteenth centuries, such as the South Sea Company in England and the tulip bulb mania in Holland.[15] In many respects, these events bear an uncanny resemblance to more recent events—for example, the crisis of 2008. During such periods, some of the blame falls on investors who didn't question returns that were too consistent and too good to be true. Lax regulation was also at fault: existing laws were inadequate to police some of the worst misdeeds. However, there were also many other instances where financial institutions were the culprit.

The well-publicized frauds of Bernard Madoff and Allen Stanford were relatively easy to spot if regulators and investing institutions had been paying attention. Harry Markopolos brought the $65 billion Madoff fraud to the attention of the Securities and Exchange Commission (SEC) in 2000, nearly nine years before it unraveled in 2008.[16] The SEC never acted on Markopolos's detailed allegations. He described the crooked returns as "the equivalent of a major league baseball player batting .966 and no one suspecting a cheat."[17] These frauds could have been uncovered with routine due diligence.[18] Three simple checks would have disclosed the problems: third-party verification of investment positions, a third-party cosigner on all money movements, and no dealing with related entities such as Madoff's two-man accounting firm, which handled his billions from a tiny suburban storefront.[19]

Many products with a high degree of risk were improperly sold to institutions that were not equipped to understand the risks. These institutions were further disadvantaged when the credit-rating agencies conferred their top ratings on these instruments. The industry refers to such products as toxic waste. One such example was the sale of collateralized debt obligations (CDOs). These instruments are investment-grade securities backed by a pool of bonds, loans, or other assets. The riskiest ones were backed by pools of mortgages from subprime or less creditworthy borrowers. Many of the instruments bore the highest possible AAA credit ratings. One egregious case concerned the sale of these instruments to Wisconsin school districts. According to *Investment News*, security regulators said that Stifel, Nicolaus & Co. and a former executive at the brokerage defrauded five eastern Wisconsin school districts through the sale of $200 million in risky investments that turned out to be worthless.[20] In its civil complaint, the SEC said that the St. Louis–based company, along with former senior vice president David Noack, promised the districts it would take "15 Enrons," or "that 100 of the top 800 companies in the world would have to go under," before the school districts would lose their principal.[21] The SEC said in its suit, filed in U.S. district court in Milwaukee, that Stifel, Nicolaus, and Mr. Noack knew the school districts didn't have the sophistication or experience to evaluate the risks of the program they created to fund retiree benefits through investing in notes tied to the performance of synthetic collateralized debt obligations.[22]

A more difficult practice to detect is that of conflict of interest. For example, some mutual fund companies execute their trades in the market with their own brokerage firms. Often they charge commissions that are not competitive. Even harder to detect are the conflicts inherent in some over-the-counter or customized products sold to pension funds or corporations. Frequently, the financial firm selling the product trades the same item for their own account. For example, Citibank was recently fined $285 million by the SEC for selling securities backed by mortgages that it simultaneously bet against. The securities subsequently became worthless and resulted in $160 million in losses to customers.[23] To prevent this sort of abuse, firms are supposed to have walls between the sales divisions and the trading divisions to prevent information leaks. However, the walls often appear to be made of rice paper. In some markets there are no restrictions. Although front running, or trading ahead of customer orders, is strictly forbidden in equity markets, it is permissible and standard practice in other markets such as foreign exchange.

Perhaps one of the worst examples of a conflict of interest concerned the credit-rating agencies. They received their fees from the very firms that were anxious to issue bonds with as high a credit rating as possible. A recent study by Jess Cornaggia of Indiana University further confirmed this behavior. He and his two collaborators found a strong correlation between the asset classes that generated the most revenue and those that had the highest credit ratings.[24] The credit-rating agencies also relied heavily on the very firms they were rating for an analysis of these securities, as their own personnel were often not equipped to render judgment on the securities they were supposed to rate.

Insider information is another area of perennial abuse. This practice involves traders obtaining information that is not readily available to the public and using it for their own gain. One of the most publicized incidents of insider trading in the post-2008 period involved billionaire hedge fund manager, Raj Rajaratnam.[25] He and twenty-one other defendants were charged with trading on insider information. Rajaratnam was accused of reaping more than $60 million in illegal profits from his scheme of systematically amassing nonpublic data, with much of it coming from so-called expert networks. These networks are research firms often made up of former high-technology industry executives who provide information to Wall Street. Rajaratnam was convicted in May 2011 on fourteen counts of securities fraud and subsequently sentenced to eleven years in prison—a record for insider trading.[26] Rajaratnam "joins the pantheon of Ivan Boesky and Gordon Gekko," said Peter Henning, a professor at Wayne State University Law School in Detroit, citing the real-life stock trader who was jailed after pleading guilty to conspiracy in 1987 and the fictional *Wall Street* film character who came to symbolize the financial scandals of the 1980s, respectively. "It is a defining case," said Henning, a former federal prosecutor, before the verdict was handed down.[27]

Financial malfeasance has a variety of forms. Below we have identified four main varieties and possible preventive steps, or remedies, that represent socially responsible practices:

- Outright fraud/Ponzi schemes—preventive measures:
  - ✔ Third-party verification of positions,
  - ✔ Adequate controls on money movement,
  - ✔ No dealing with commonly controlled entities.
- Selling products that were known to be bad investments—preventive measures:
  - ✔ Better risk disclosure,
  - ✔ Vigorous enforcement and penalties.
- Conflicts of interest—preventive measures:
  - ✔ Enactment of Volcker Rule prohibiting banks from trading for their own account,
  - ✔ Oversight of credit-rating agencies.
- Insider trading—preventive measures:
  - ✔ Close monitoring of expert networks,
  - ✔ Vigorous enforcement and penalties.

FINANCIERS BEHAVING COMMENDABLY

> If we do well for the client, we'll be taken care of.
>
> —Thomas Rowe Price (founder, T. Rowe Price mutual
> fund and investment advisory firm)[28]

Discussion of commendable investment behavior begins with mention of John Bogle, who has been called the conscience of Wall Street.[29] Bogle is the founder of the Vanguard Group of Mutual Funds. His funds usually charge the lowest fees and expenses of funds in their categories. He was the first to eschew sales loads or front-end fees to purchase mutual funds. He was the first to create a mutual investment company that was owned by its clients. Bogle also believes strongly that most mutual funds don't outperform the major stock indexes and that purchasing an index fund is the best way for individuals to invest in the market. He created the world's first index mutual fund, the Vanguard 500, in 1976.

Some investment professionals have distinguished themselves by offering pro bono investment services to the public. Rick Fingerman of Financial Planning Solutions was one of the first advisers to sign up for the Dana-Farber Cancer Institute's pro bono program of matching financial planners with cancer patients and families: "Since 2008, [Fingerman] has been counseling patients, coaching other planners [sic] work with families stricken with cancer, and overseeing the daily operations of the program. To date, he has matched more than 200 patients with planners. . . ."[30] Joyce Frost of Riverside Risk Advisors provides pro bono consulting in the use of derivatives (investments where the investor does not own the underlying asset, but makes a bet on the direction of the price movement of the underlying asset via an agreement with another party).[31] She offers her services to nonprofits that are often no match for investment banks when it comes to pricing and evaluating these complex financial products.[32] Some industry professionals have created advocacy groups to champion more ethical conduct in the investment industry. The newest of these is the Institute for the Fiduciary Standard founded by Knut Rostad. This group aims "to help guide the regulations resulting from the Dodd-Frank legislation."[33] As noted elsewhere in this chapter, the fiduciary standard is an important step in improving the treatment of retail investors.

Successful investment managers have reaped large personal financial compensation for their efforts, but some have also been generous in their philanthropy. The most extraordinary gift is famed investor Warren Buffet's donation of $37 billion to the Bill and Melinda Gates Foundation and four other foundations.[34] The gift, phased in over a period of years, will result in a donation of 85 percent of Buffet's wealth, the balance to be given away on his death. It is the largest philanthropic gift ever. Other fund managers have taken a hands-on approach to their giving by using their business acumen to ensure their donations are used effectively in causes they are impassioned about from personal experience. Hedge fund manager James Simons, the founder of Renaissance Technologies and the father of an autistic child, has pledged more than $100 million for autism research.[35] Dinakar Singh of hedge fund TPG-Axon Capital Management has contributed more than $100 million to find a cure for his daughter's spinal muscular atrophy.[36] There are also industry groups that make collective donations to various causes. Hedge Funds Care is a group committed to gifts to help prevent and treat child abuse. Started by former fourth grade teacher Rob Davis, who became a hedge fund manager, the charity has raised more than $40 million and has enlisted the Columbia School of Social Work to help it select organizations for its grants.[37]

These cases illustrate that there are those in the financial sector who have made significant social contributions in terms of money, expertise, and time. Leading by example can have a powerful influence on others in the sector. Warren Buffet's call to fellow billionaires to give at least half of their wealth to philanthropy resulted in sixty-nine billionaires rising to the challenge.[38]

HOW BEST TO ENCOURAGE SOCIAL RESPONSIBILITY IN THE FINANCIAL SECTOR: GOVERNMENT REGULATION, INDUSTRY SELF-REGULATION, OR ENLIGHTENED SELF-INTEREST?

> Playing by the rules, one does the best he can, irrespective of the social consequences. Whereas in making the rules, people ought to be concerned with the social consequences and not with their personal interests.
>
> —George Soros (founder and chairman, Soros Fund Management)[39]

It seems that we cannot rely exclusively on enlightened self-interest to avert unethical and illegal behavior in the financial markets. Is government regulation required? And, if so, what form should it take to be effective? Existing regulations, in some cases weakened by prior administrations, did not prevent the crisis of 2008 and its various abuses. Is self-regulation by the industry a viable solution? This method has also failed to prevent the consequences of financial misdeeds.

The primary regulator of securities markets at the federal level is the Securities and Exchange Commission. The SEC was created in 1934 in the middle of the Great Depression "to restore investor confidence in our capital markets by providing investors and the markets with more reliable information and clear rules of honest dealing."[40] With broad judicial enforcement powers, the SEC is viewed by market participants as a much more effective and feared force than other regulators, such as state securities commissions. Indeed, the SEC uncovers many frauds and misdeeds and files hundreds of enforcement actions each year. Typical infractions include insider trading, accounting fraud, and providing false or misleading information about securities and the companies that issue them.[41] The primary self-regulatory body in the United States is the Financial Industry Regulatory Authority (FINRA). FINRA also has broad enforcement powers that pertain to investment firms and broker dealers and their representatives.

In fairness to both primary regulators, they do prevent and shut down many fraudulent and abusive practices in the securities industry. The SEC indicted eighty-one individuals and organizations since the 2008 financial crisis began until late 2011, and collected $2 billion in fines and restitution.[42] Where they are weakest is in preventing more systematic practices that are legal but possibly deceptive or misleading, and in uncovering fraud by industry leaders like Bernard Madoff.

The Dodd-Frank Wall Street Reform and Consumer Protection Act is a complex, far-reaching 2,319-page document that touches on a number of areas of finance. However, four sections are relevant to our discussion of social responsibility. The first is the implementation of the so-called Volcker Act, which, among other things, limits banks' ability to conduct proprietary trading or trading on their own behalf. This potentially eliminates an important source of conflict of interest, since the organizations are not permitted to recommend instruments that they also trade for their own account.

The second section requires most hedge funds and private equity funds to register with the SEC. This at least brings many large organizations under the oversight of regulators. However, it remains to be seen whether the SEC will have the resources and expertise to effectively oversee all these additional entities. The third section institutes regulation of the credit-rating agencies after their questionable behavior in the financial collapse of 2008. It puts them under the authority of the SEC and requires them to describe their rating methodology and the qualifications of their personnel; perhaps most important, it allows investors the ability to file lawsuits against them. The fourth section concerns investor protection and securities enforcement. It provides additional enforcement authority for the SEC, creates a new whistle-blower bounty program, and permits the SEC to impose a fiduciary duty on brokers dealing with the retail investing public.

Unfortunately, the implementation of these rules has been repeatedly delayed and is an administrative nightmare. According to ProPublica's Jesse Eisinger and Jake Bernstein, "Dodd-Frank requires 387 different rules from 20 different regulatory agencies. The Byzantine, tedious rulemaking process has occasionally pitted regulator against regulator and proved a bonanza for lobbyists." They go on to state, "Emerging roadblocks reinforce a fear that Dodd-Frank, which was intended to touch on almost every aspect of the American financial system, may never provide the sweeping reform it promised."[43] Given the complexity of our financial sector, detailed regulatory oversight will be challenging. Socially responsible behavior will require targeted legislation that is unencumbered by special interests and protects individual and community needs.

PROGNOSIS FOR THE FUTURE

> When it comes to the future, there are three kinds of people: those who let it happen, those who make it happen, and those who wonder what happened.
>
> —John M. Richardson, Jr. (professor, American University)[44]

There is much anger directed at Wall Street in the wake of the 2008 financial crisis. After all, few have been prosecuted for financial transgressions. The rapid growth of the Occupy Wall Street movement, with 900 sites worldwide in October 2011, is symptomatic of public discontent. Protests are about social and economic inequality; corporate greed; the power and influence of corporations, particularly from the financial sector; and the influence of lobbyists on government.[45] Because of the complexity and arcane nature of some of the questionable practices, it is difficult for the public (or, for that matter, Congress) to direct their desire for change in an effective and appropriate manner. Will the emerging sentiment translate into meaningful reforms that will make our investing institutions behave more responsibly? We do not know whether Jesse Livermore's cynical depiction of Wall Street, mentioned earlier, will prevail or whether real change can occur.[46]

There are financiers who do the right thing for their clients and for society. We'd like to think that their ranks would grow and that the admonition from John F. Kennedy, "To those whom much is given, much is expected," will be practiced.[47] Popular discontent led to the creation of the Dodd-Frank Act, which may contain some positive changes, but it is a large, unwieldy, and complex law. As of this writing, many of its regulations have yet to be put in to practice. Implementing some relatively simple disclosure rules and tightening up money transfer procedures and dealings with related companies would prevent many abuses. However, regulation can only go so far in redressing the problems of the financial sector. A business with a preponderance of the best and brightest minds will find ways to circumvent regulations. Yet meaningful change may have to come from within the industry, so there have to be more John Bogles who want to do the right thing. The creation of groups like the Institute for the Fiduciary Standard is an encouraging step in the right direction.[48] Industry groups like FINRA and others would be wise to address public anger by taking proactive steps to improve industry practices. These steps should include enthusiastically embracing the fiduciary standard, championing clear and understandable descriptions of investment fees and risks, and doing more to raise the level of investment literacy in the United States.

The most potent defense against financial chicanery is an informed public. We need not have a low level of financial literacy in our society. Basic financial concepts are not hard to teach, especially if they are integrated into our educational system from an early age. These concepts will be more easily applied if we have regulations that mandate concise and easily understood explanations of the risks and costs of financial products.

In this chapter we have discussed what an investor has a reasonable right to expect from an investment provider. In addressing social responsibility of the financial sector, we have looked at some of the more egregious examples of financial misconduct and suggested some possible preventive steps to avoid future problems. Many of these measures are those that industry can take proactively, both to demonstrate a commitment to social responsibility and to address some of the current public anger. We have highlighted examples of exemplary conduct on the part of various members of the financial sector and expressed the hope that others will follow their example. In addition, we have examined the prospects of successful government regulation, particularly in the form of legislation like the Dodd-Frank Act, and concluded that effective rules need to be clear and concise. Ultimately, we have expressed the hope that a more informed investing public is the best defense against an investment climate that penalizes the individual investor. The final chapter will present some concluding thoughts about our exploration of social responsibility.

CONCLUDING THOUGHTS

Ron Elsdon

A group of us were volunteering at Project Homeless Connect in the San Francisco Bay Area, a periodic, one-day event to help link those who are homeless with community resources. The day was well on track, and many people were receiving support. At midday, as a friend and I were helping point people to the resources they needed, suddenly a person headed in our direction, muttering to herself, disheveled, making strange noises. I held back, not knowing what to do, and my friend reached out with a kind word. The distressed woman came to us and began explaining her situation. She was fully present and completely lucid; it saddened me that she had to contend with a life of such hardship. The courage and compassion of my friend was just what was needed, in contrast to my own inappropriate reticence. May I behave differently should such a situation arise again.

I am struck by the parallel for those charged with business leadership when a need for advocacy about social responsibility is clear, but circumstances surrounding it might be difficult and uncomfortable. Similarities exist across sectors. For example, some would propose that individuals, without knowledge or training, make complex health or financial decisions while advised by specialists who have competing financial self-interests. Such approaches can lead to hardship and unnecessary medical procedures or financial transactions. This is why we need voices of advocacy to combat ill-advised proposals, voices that honor individuals, organizations, and communities.

The contributors to our book speak both of advocacy for social responsibility and practical implementation—whether related to policy or practice, such as in the healthcare or financial sectors; whether in the form of community service, such as in education or pro bono services; or whether in the form of partnership or operations in each of the business, nonprofit, and public sectors. It is heartening to see a foundation of ethical principles, tied to the common good, surface throughout. We will need such inclusive principles in the future to sustain the health and vitality of our society. Intimately interwoven and a consistent theme throughout our book is the importance of relationship and collaboration, collaboration first for each of us with others, then as institutions finding common goals. Embracing such interdependence, whether we are in a business, nonprofit, or public sector setting, is an important step in addressing social responsibility and social justice. It starts with our individual awakening. Dominique Browning describes hers: "I find room in my life again for love of the world, let the quiet of solitary moments steal over me, give myself over to joy. . . . These are moments of grace. . . . I connect with something I may have once encountered as a teenager and then lost in the frantic skim through adulthood—the desire to nourish my soul. I do not have the temerity to think I have found God; I think instead that I have stumbled into a conversation that I pray will last the rest of my life."[1]

It continues by recognizing the kind of society we are striving to create. As Louis Brandeis observed, "We can have a democracy or we can have great wealth concentrated in the hands of the few. We cannot have both."[2] Unfortunately our society has been evolving more toward William Sloane Coffin's observation that we have "a government of the wealthy, by the wealthy, and for the wealthy."[3] Reversing this trend—building on the kinds of examples and principles we have explored so that prosperity and social justice are there for all—is an essential aspect of a healthy society in which collaboration of businesses, nonprofits, and the public sector provides a foundation of social responsibility. We are confronted with a fundamental question of how to balance public good with organizational gain, similar to the question that surfaces about balancing individual aspirations and the common good.[4] Corporate after-tax profits in 2011 accounted for a record high percentage of GDP; wages and salaries were at a corresponding low.[5] Are we losing sight of the purpose of business? Pursuit of profit in situations where community service is the primary need, as has occurred in much of U.S. healthcare, fails our society. Conversely, overemphasis on centralized planning can be equally problematical, as we saw in our education example. At a time in the United States when our political system is gridlocked by extreme right-wing ideology, collaborative business practices that embrace social responsibility offer a path forward to regenerating and strengthening our social and economic base. These practices contribute to addressing serious societal issues. It is no coincidence that, when we look back over recessions in the United States since the early 1980s, employment recovery has become increasingly difficult.[6] As we saw in the introduction, inequality has grown over this time. We have gradually depleted the economic fuel needed to power recovery, and economic resources are increasingly concentrated in the hands of a few.

There are moments in our history where we have risen above personal greed, where there has been inspiring personal and political leadership. In 1944 President Roosevelt described a second Bill of Rights.[7] This instrument builds on fundamental political rights, the rights to life and liberty: the right of free speech, free press, free worship, trial by jury, and freedom from unreasonable searches and seizures. The second Bill of Rights recognizes that these alone are inadequate to ensure equality in the pursuit of happiness. This second bill extends rights to include economic truths, which President Roosevelt saw as having become accepted as self-evident. Among the rights he described are:

- The right to a useful and remunerative job in the industries or shops or farms or mines of the nation;
- The right to earn enough to provide adequate food and clothing and recreation;
- The right of every businessman, large and small, to trade in an atmosphere of freedom from unfair competition and domination by monopolies at home or abroad;
- The right of every family to a decent home;
- The right to adequate medical care and the opportunity to achieve and enjoy good health;

- The right to adequate protection from the economic fears of old age, sickness, accident, and unemployment; and
- The right to a good education.

It is perhaps one of our great national tragedies that all of these rights have yet to be achieved. Indeed, they are now under increased threat. And it is one of our great national opportunities to bring them into being: to recognize again that business is in service to our society, not the other way round; to recognize that social responsibility is central to the purpose of business; and to recognize that our economic system is sustainable only when it creates better lives for all of us. President Roosevelt's administration established a legacy of broad-based prosperity for future generations from which many of us benefitted. How different this has looked since the 1980s. The earlier foundation is being dismantled, threatening the economic and social fabric of our society. Our economy almost collapsed because of rising inequality and a move to take from the many, including future generations, in order to benefit a few wealthy individuals. There is a physics experiment that involves connecting two soap bubbles of different sizes by a tube and then opening a valve between them to see what happens. It turns out that the larger bubble grows at the expense of the smaller—the very thing that happens in our society if we allow special interests and those with economic power to define our economic path. That path leads only to greater inequality. The larger bubble gets bigger.

Why does inequality have such drastic social consequences? According to Richard Wilkinson and Kate Pickett, we are all affected by the stress and insecurity that go with big differences in status.[8] Inequality increases social distances and we worry how we are judged by others. This damages physical and mental health, increases the strain on family life, and can trigger violence. It damages community cohesion and fuels consumerism. People are less concerned with the well-being of others. And yet everyone benefits from equality. It is not just the poorest who benefit; the evidence shows that most people benefit. While the greatest improvements are experienced by those lower down the economic ladder, there are still significant benefits for those at the top. And it doesn't seem to matter how this greater equality is created, whether by more equitable compensation levels, as occur in

Japan, or by a redistribution of societal resources, as is the case in Scandinavian countries.[9]

Inequality also creates practical economic problems. As observed above, income and wealth are concentrated in the hands of a few, the economic fuel to power our economy is depleted, and the engine of our economy stalls. Using tools of mathematical modeling (see appendix B), we can see this by examining how discretionary spending, the fuel of our economy, changes with growing inequality. This modeling approach is intended to show directional trends rather than numerical precision. It is offered as an initial framework to help stimulate further analysis. In figure 6 we can see the estimated cumulative loss in discretionary spending in the United States from 1970 to 2010 arising from growing inequality and the growing concentration of income.

FIGURE 6. Estimated U.S. Cumulative Discretionary Spending Loss from Growing Income Inequality since 1970

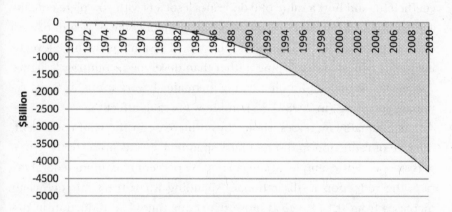

This estimated cumulative loss of discretionary spending since 1970 totals more than $4 trillion (in 2008 U.S.$); more than $3 trillion has been lost since the early 1990s. Greater concentration of wealth and income significantly hurts our economy; we need trickle up, not trickle down, approaches. Figure 7 illustrates, directionally, how we can address this issue by returning federal tax rates to more appropriate levels for high-earning individuals, levels that have generally been in place for much of the time since the Great Depression. Indeed, the detrimental outcomes of the George W. Bush–era tax cuts in 2001 are well documented.[10]

FIGURE 7. Annual Discretionary Spending Loss with Inequality (at Various Maximum Federal Tax Rates)

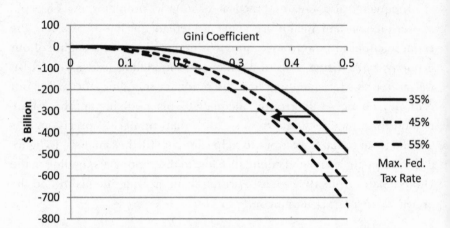

In the introduction, we mentioned an index of inequality, the Gini coefficient, and how a value of 0 describes a society with complete equality and a value of 1 means a single family has all the income or wealth of a society. The current U.S. Gini coefficient of 0.44 resembles the high level of inequality typical of developing, rather than developed, countries.[11] Figure 7 shows an estimate of how increasing inequality lowers annual U.S. discretionary spending (in 2008 U.S.$) and how tax rates affect this.

As inequality increases, shown by an increase in the Gini coefficient, the rate of reduction in discretionary spending speeds up since the curve gets steeper. For example, at the current 35 percent maximum federal tax rate, the reduction in discretionary spending when the Gini coefficient increases from 0.4 to 0.45 is more than four times the reduction in discretionary spending when the Gini coefficient increases from 0.2 to 0.25. Projecting a possible future, the arrow in Figure 7 indicates the estimated reduction in inequality when the maximum federal tax rate of 35 percent is increased to 55 percent for those in the highest tax bracket (incomes over $373,650 in 2010). We can see how increasing tax rates for high earners potentially lowers inequality, in this case returning the Gini coefficient to about 0.36 as shown by the arrow. This is closer to the level of inequality in other developed countries and similar to the level of inequality in the United States in the early 1970s.

Business has a significant role to play in advocating for policies that support community well-being, as we saw in healthcare and financial services. It can also be a major actor in reducing inequality, for example, with equitable internal compensation practices. This means supporting policies that benefit our society broadly. In the case of healthcare, this is a human rights issue.[12] With profit as a primary motive, we have created an approach to healthcare that places the United States thirty-seventh among countries in healthcare outcomes, behind Costa Rica.[13] Meanwhile, per capita healthcare costs are more than 50 percent higher than in any other country.[14] We have excellent options available, such as the single-payer approach that would use a single insurance entity, eliminating the unnecessary and costly private insurance bureaucracy, providing needed coverage for individuals, and strengthening the competitiveness of our business organizations that struggle with escalating healthcare insurance costs. These solutions require concerted societal action, an effective public sector, political courage, and collaborative support from our business community. Our chapter authors shine a light on these kinds of collaborative practices. The practices address many social issues, including healthcare, and, in so doing, address inequality and the abiding principles of the second Bill of Rights.

Fundamental to this second Bill of Rights is equality in the pursuit of happiness. Let's look at happiness and economic circumstances to further frame social responsibility practices. Ed Diener and Martin Seligman, looking at different countries, describe how life satisfaction typically increases significantly as gross domestic product (GDP) per capita rises to about $10,000; then life satisfaction levels off.[15] Once basic survival needs are met, income is not the primary determinant of life satisfaction. This observation is also supported by their noting that life satisfaction measures in the United States stayed about the same from the late 1940s through the 1990s, even though GDP per capita tripled over the same time frame. We see a similar pattern as self-reported happiness in the United States levels off with increasing family income; a much slower increase in happiness appears above the mean family income level.[16] Luxury is not a prerequisite for high life satisfaction. The African Masai, who live in huts made from dung with no electricity or running water, have about the same high level of life satisfaction as Forbes's richest Americans.[17] Meanwhile, homeless people in Fresno, California, and Calcutta pavement dwellers have about the same low level of life satisfaction; in both cases their basic physical needs are not met. Studies by Diener and others reporting a Gallup World Poll show a similar trend of the declining marginal effects of income on subjective well-being.[18] Diener and his colleagues also observe that income is not the major factor in psychological well-being (positive and negative feelings), since other aspects—such as learning, autonomy, using skills, respect, and the ability to count on others when needed—are more important.

Once basic survival needs are met, the pattern of happiness or life satisfaction rapidly leveling off as income increases can point us to a path that strengthens our society for the benefit of all. One question this raises is what would the optimum income distribution be if our goal is to create the greatest level of satisfaction or happiness for all. I looked at this using tools of mathematical optimization. This is a way of finding out how to create the largest amount of one thing, in this case happiness for a society, by varying something else that affects it, in this case income distribution. It turns out to be a rather obvious result: when happiness levels off with increasing income, as it does, then happiness for our society is greatest when income for everyone is roughly equal. Creating much greater income for some subtracts from the overall level of societal happiness when the curve linking happiness to income is shaped as it is (see figure 8).[19]

When we think about what happens when a society moves away from equality, we can see why this is so. Let's say our starting point is the mean family income, which is a value of 1.0 on the horizontal scale in figure 8. If now we introduce inequality, some people have greater income, which means moving to the right along the curve from this point, and some have lesser income, which means moving to the left of the same point on the curve. Then the loss in happiness for those with lower incomes on the left more than offsets the gain by those on the right, because the curve is steeper to the left than it is on the right. In other words, we lose as a society. If the curve were shaped differently, let's say rather than leveling off, it increased exponentially with income, then we would come to a different conclusion. In that case, the greatest societal happiness would result from giving all of our resources to one individual, just as bees do with the queen bee in a hive. But that is not how we are made. It is one reason why the

FIGURE 8. U.S. Happiness and Income

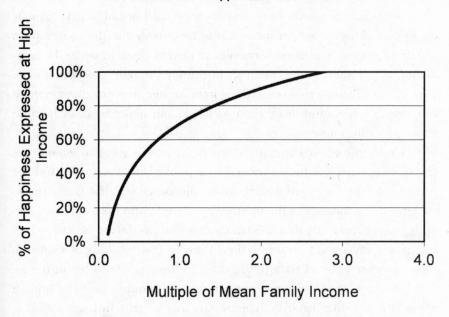

Multiple of Mean Family Income

world's major faith traditions speak to the importance of supporting all in our society. It is one reason why societies that are more equal are better places to live. We reach a similar conclusion about the negative effect of inequality when looking at a human development index, which combines the dimensions of standard of living (income), health, and education, where greater inequality lowers the value of the index.[20]

There are, of course, factors that support some degree of inequality and the associated incentives this provides, and in turn benefit individual happiness. However, as we saw in the comparison of different countries in the introduction, in general, greater equality is associated with greater economic prosperity. So it is not surprising that people in the United States say they would prefer much greater wealth equality.[21] Indeed, the current level of inequality in the United States creates reduced life circumstances for many and threatens economic and social stability. This is why David Shipler observes, "Being poor means being unprotected. . . . A poor man or woman gets sacked again and again—buffeted and bruised and defeated. When an exception breaks this cycle of failure, it is called the fulfillment of the American Dream."[22] It is therefore not surprising that Harold Pinter offered the following observation, "If to be a socialist is to be a person convinced that the words 'the common good' and 'social justice' actually mean something; if to be a socialist is to be outraged at the contempt in which millions and millions of people are held by those in power, by 'market forces', by international financial institutions; if to be a socialist is to be a person determined to do everything in his or her power to alleviate these unforgivably degrading lives, then socialism can never be dead because these aspirations never die."[23]

An example of real community, one not driven by greed or self-interest but by concern for others, surfaced in a public broadcasting episode of *Soundprint*.[24] The segment describes how the Dutch city of Amsterdam arranges for the funerals of the twenty or so people who die each year completely alone, ensuring that their funerals are respectful and accompanied by flowers and poetry honoring their lives. In this small act of kindness, with no expectation of reward, the city and those participating in the funerals bring a beautiful reverence for their community and the human spirit. It is just such a spirit of community that we seek through social responsibility. How disappointing that the radio host of this excellent piece, Lisa Simeone, was dismissed by her employer, Soundprint, for leading an Occupy camp in Washington.[25] We have a long path yet to travel to honor those such as Ms. Simeone, who are standing up for principles of social responsibility and social justice.

Business, nonprofits, and the public sector working together, honoring the principles of social responsibility and social justice, have the opportunity to make this society better for all of us. What are some action steps that can help in this regard? Let me suggest the following, starting at an organizational level:

- Establish effective corporate governance to ensure that the interests of all constituencies are honored.
- Address compensation practices to ensure greater equity and eliminate excessive compensation at senior levels.
- Reinforce leadership practices that create safe, secure, and supportive working environments that honor all.
- Choose to work with those suppliers and customers who have demonstrated a commitment to principles of social responsibility.

- Partner with other organizations, whether business, nonprofit, or public sector, to advance principles of social responsibility, for example, in healthcare or in addressing hunger.[26]
- Explore and support emerging approaches to financing social innovation. Social impact bonds are one example. In this case, service delivery is funded by private sector financing through a bond-issuing organization. This in turn is supported by government funding when service delivery meets performance targets.[27] Another example is the development of flexible-purpose corporations, which are part social benefit and part low-profit entities, now permitted under laws in more than a dozen U.S. states—for example, California and Michigan.[28]
- Support collaborative workforce practices such as the labor-management partnerships described in chapter 10, and encourage emerging forms of workforce organizing.[29]
- Support social and community causes that benefit all, such as full access to healthcare in the United States through a single-payer, Medicare-for-all system.
- Support strengthened education at all levels, recognizing that education offers a significant opportunity to break the bonds of poverty and that we have far to go in the United States today to provide equitable access.[30]
- Respect our environment with appropriate operating practices.
- Proactively sponsor regulation that benefits our community rather than special interests, for example, needed progressive taxation levels for individuals and organizations.
- Encourage participation in our political processes, and address the challenge of lower voting rates at lower income levels.[31]

Steps each of us as individuals can take are:

- Stay informed about emerging social, business, and workplace issues so we can decide where to best commit our time and energy.
- Become well informed about organizations and their approach to social responsibility so that, based on their performance, we can decide to engage or not, whether as employee, contractor, supplier, investor, or customer.

- Influence public policy by supporting candidates who speak to the needs of all in our society, not just the wealthy and powerful, and engage in legislative campaigns and direct action in this regard.

We have seen that there are growing economic inequities in our society that have led to reduced circumstances and constrained life choices for many. Businesses, nonprofits, and the public sector have an opportunity to embrace principles of social responsibility and address these inequities for the benefit of all. Action will require courage. In the words of Joan Chittister, "Courage is coming to realize that what does and does not happen in the world does so because of what you and I fail to say—not when silence is right, but when we fear the cost to ourselves of speaking out."[32] It is in embracing such courage, individually and collectively, that we can create a better world for all. I hope we can then say, "Compassionate at last, we are compassionate at last."

APPENDIX A
Income Inequality and Gross National Income per Capita
(123 Countries, GNI/Capita in U.S.$)
also TABLE 2

Countries listed from most equal to most unequal

Country	2009 GNI/ Capita[1]	Gini Coefficient[2]
Sweden	48,840	0.23
Norway	84,640	0.25
Austria	46,450	0.26
Czech Republic	17,310	0.26
Luxembourg	76,710	0.26
Serbia	6,000	0.26
Slovak Republic	16,130	0.26
Albania	4,000	0.267
Germany	42,450	0.27
Belarus	5,560	0.279
Belgium	45,270	0.28
Hungary	12,980	0.28
Iceland	43,430	0.28
Slovenia	23,520	0.284
Kazakhstan	6,920	0.288
Croatia	13,720	0.29
Denmark	59,060	0.29
Finland	45,940	0.295

Country	2009 GNI/ Capita[1]	Gini Coefficient[2]
Bulgaria	6,060	0.298
Ethiopia	330	0.3
Montenegro	6,650	0.3
Kyrgyz Republic	870	0.303
Australia	43,770	0.305
Pakistan	1,000	0.306
Ireland	44,280	0.307
Netherlands, The	48,460	0.309
Ukraine	2,800	0.31
Korea, Rep. of	19,830	0.313
Italy	35,110	0.32
Romania	8,330	0.32
Spain	32,120	0.32
Canada	41,980	0.321
Tajikistan	700	0.326
France	42,620	0.327
Mongolia	1,630	0.328
Greece	29,040	0.33
Bangladesh	580	0.332
Moldova	1,560	0.332
Switzerland	65,430	0.337
Estonia	14,060	0.34
United Kingdom	41,370	0.34
Egypt, Arab Rep.	2,070	0.344
Tanzania	500	0.346
Poland	12,260	0.349
Algeria	4,420	0.353
Latvia	12,390	0.36
Lithuania	11,410	0.36
Azerbaijan	4,840	0.365
Benin	750	0.365
India	1,180	0.368
Uzbekistan	1,100	0.368
Armenia	3,100	0.37

Country	2009 GNI/ Capita[1]	Gini Coefficient[2]
Vietnam	930	0.37
Yemen, Rep. of	1,060	0.377
Guinea	370	0.381
Japan	38,080	0.381
Portugal	21,910	0.385
Macedonia, FYR	4,400	0.39
Malawi	280	0.39
Mauritania	960	0.39
Mauritius	7,250	0.39
Israel	25,790	0.392
Ghana	1,190	0.394
Indonesia	2,050	0.394
Burkina Faso	510	0.395
Jordan	3,980	0.397
Tunisia	3,720	0.4
Mali	680	0.401
Georgia	2,530	0.408
Turkmenistan	3,420	0.408
Morocco	2,770	0.409
Turkey	8,720	0.41
Venezuela, R.B. de	10,090	0.41
Senegal	1,040	0.413
China	3,650	0.415
Russian Federation	9,340	0.423
Burundi	150	0.424
Kenya	760	0.425
Cambodia	610	0.43
Thailand	3,760	0.43
Nicaragua	1,000	0.431
Nigeria	1,190	0.437
Iran, Islamic Rep. of	4,530	0.445
Cameroon	1,190	0.446
Côte d'Ivoire	1,070	0.446
United States	46,360	0.45

Country	2009 GNI/Capita[1]	Gini Coefficient[2]
Uruguay	9,010	0.452
Jamaica	4,590	0.455
Argentina	7,550	0.457
Uganda	460	0.457
Philippines	2,050	0.458
Malaysia	7,350	0.461
Rwanda	460	0.468
Nepal	440	0.472
Mozambique	440	0.473
Ecuador	3,970	0.479
Costa Rica	6,260	0.48
Singapore	37,220	0.481
Mexico	8,960	0.482
Sri Lanka	1,990	0.49
Dominican Republic	4,550	0.499
Gambia, The	440	0.502
Swaziland	2,470	0.504
Niger	340	0.505
Zambia	970	0.508
Papua New Guinea	1,180	0.509

Country	2009 GNI/Capita[1]	Gini Coefficient[2]
Peru	4,200	0.52
El Salvador	3,370	0.524
Paraguay	2,250	0.532
Honduras	1,800	0.538
Chile	9,470	0.549
Guatemala	2,650	0.551
Panama	6,570	0.561
Bosnia and Herzegovina	4,700	0.562
Brazil	8,040	0.567
Colombia	4,990	0.585
Bolivia	1,630	0.592
Central African Republic	450	0.613
Sierra Leone	340	0.629
Botswana	6,260	0.63
Lesotho	980	0.632
South Africa	5,760	0.65
Namibia	4,270	0.707

Note: There can be slight differences in Gini coefficients according to the source and basis.

APPENDIX B
Modeling Income, Spending, and Inequality

This appendix outlines a mathematical modeling approach to link income, disposition of income, and inequality. We hope it provides insights into directional trends and interrelationships; it is not intended to offer numerical precision. We also hope this will stimulate further development and evaluation of modeling approaches. While the analysis is illustrated with U.S. data, the approach is equally applicable elsewhere.

The modeling approach incorporates the following stages sequentially. Details for each stage are covered after this summary. When the word "describe" is used in these stages, it refers to a mathematical description.

1. Establish the relationship of household income to survival spending, discretionary spending, savings, and tax payments.
2. Describe how the federal tax rate, and therefore household tax payments, vary with household income based on the tax code.
3. Describe how savings rates vary with household income based on prior studies.
4. Describe how discretionary spending varies with household income based on stages 1, 2, and 3.
5. Describe how household income is distributed across the population using published data.
6. Estimate overall population spending, savings, tax payments, and household income by integrating (mathematically) these individual characteristics across the entire population.

7. Estimate overall population spending, savings, and tax payments for complete equality and complete inequality, building on stage 6.

8. Describe how discretionary spending for the population is reduced as
inequality grows, based on stages 6 and 7.

9. Estimate the cumulative reduction in discretionary spending over time
attributable to growing inequality, from stage 8 and published inequality data.

Mathcad 15 software was used to develop the mathematical model. Details of each modeling stage are as follows:

1. Establish the relationship of household income to survival spending,
discretionary spending, savings, and tax payments.

The following relationship describes disposition of household income
(this applies for any time period; we use a calendar year here):

**Household income = Survival spending + Discretionary spending
+ Savings + Tax Payments**

Survival spending for modeling purposes is set at $14,500, the poverty
threshold for a householder younger than 65 based on the approximate
average of either having no children or one child.[1]

2. Describe how the federal tax rate, and therefore household tax payments, vary with household income based on the tax code.

Tax rates for head of a household from the 2010 Internal Revenue
Service tax tables were used.[2] The genfit module in Mathcad was then used
to create the following equation linking tax rate to household income (the
maximum tax rate is 35%; in the following equation, the tax rate is expressed
as a fraction [e.g., 0.35 for 35%], and household income is in $):

Tax Rate = 0.351 x (1 − exp(1 − 0.00001244 x household income))

The coefficient of determination (R^2) is 0.969, indicating that the
equation fits the data well (a value of 1 would indicate that the equation

exactly describes the data, and a value of 0 would indicate that the equation does not describe the variation in the data at all).

Further analyses examining how this would change for maximum tax rates of 45 percent and 55 percent led to the following equations, based on increasing only the maximum tax rates while keeping tax rates at lower incomes constant at the 2010 tax table levels:

Maximum tax rate 45 percent:

Tax Rate = 0.453 x (1 – exp(1 – 0.000007991 x household income))

Maximum tax rate 55 percent:

Tax Rate = 0.561 x (1 – exp(1 – 0.000005938 x household income))

We recognize that actual tax rates will vary because of the inclusion of state and local taxes, and the fact that wealthy individuals were being taxed at a lower rate as the maximum capital gains tax rate was only 15 percent in 2011 for most people.[3] The principles that follow apply regardless of the specific tax rates used.

3. Describe how savings rates vary with household income based on prior studies.

Several studies over more than fifty years support the observation that savings rates increase with increasing income.[4] To estimate the variation of savings rate with household income, we used the savings rate information from Karen Dynan and others, using the active savings rate from the panel study of income dynamics (PSID).[5] This provides savings rates by household income quintile. They were then coupled with 2008 household income quintile information from the 2011 Census Bureau Statistical Abstract, adjusted to an after-tax basis using the relationship between tax rates and household income from stage 2.[6]

The linfit module in Mathcad provided the following equation (where savings rate is expressed as a fraction and after-tax household income is in $):

Savings rate = 0.064 x ln(after-tax household income) – 0.625

The coefficient of determination (R^2) is 0.908, indicating that the equation fits the data well.

4. Describe how discretionary spending varies with household income based on stages 1, 2, and 3.

Discretionary spending can now be calculated using the equation in stage 1, knowing tax rates from stage 2 and savings rates from stage 3.

5. Describe how household income is distributed across the population using published data.

To calculate values across the entire population, it is now necessary to build a relationship between household income and the cumulative number of households with at least that income. Data for this is available in the U.S. Census Bureau Statistical Abstract.[7] Applying the expfit module in Mathcad to this data provides the following relationship (household income is expressed in $):

Household income = 2115 x exp(0.0000000399 x cumulative number of households) + 19770

The coefficient of determination (R^2) is 0.974, indicating that the equation fits the data well.

6. Estimate overall population spending, savings, tax payments, and household income by integrating (mathematically) these individual characteristics across the entire population.

The expression linking household income to the cumulative number of households from stage 5 is now substituted into the equations describing the relationship of tax rates (and therefore tax payments), savings rates (and therefore savings), and spending to household income from stages 2, 3, and 4. The resulting expressions, along with the expression for household income from stage 5, are integrated mathematically over the total number of households to generate values for the entire population (117,181,000

households in 2008). These integrations are carried out numerically in
Mathcad. Survival spending for the entire population is simply the multiple of single household survival spending and the number of households.
Each item is shown as a fraction of household income in figure 9 based on
the number of households. The number of households shows those having at least a given level of income as described by the equation in stage 5.
Consequently the level of income increases in moving to the right on the
horizontal axis in figure 9. Discretionary spending when all incomes are
equal, as a fraction of household income and calculated as described in
stage 7, is also shown.

FIGURE 9. Components of Household Income
(Based on Number of Households)

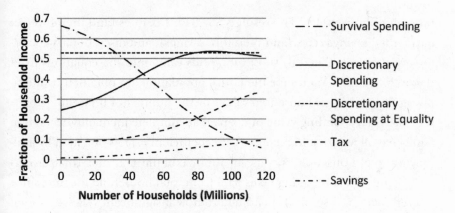

For comparison purposes, the results are also shown based on household income in figure 10 (the scale of the horizontal axis is in $10,000 in-
crements, so the chart maximum is $1,000,000 in household income [100
x $10,000]).

7. Estimate overall population spending, savings, and tax payments for com-
    plete equality and complete inequality, building on stage 6.

Household income when all are equal (Gini coefficient = 0) is now
calculated by dividing total household income from stage 6 by the total

FIGURE 10. Components of Household Income
(Based on Household Income)

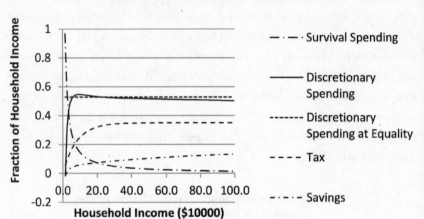

number of households. The result is $67,840. Tax rates (and therefore tax payments), savings rates (and therefore savings), and discretionary spending are then calculated by substituting this value into the equations from stages 2, 3, and 4. Values for the entire population are obtained by multiplying the individual household values by the number of households.

The corresponding value of tax paid at complete inequality, when one family has all wealth and income (Gini coefficient = 1), is obtained by multiplying total household income by the maximum tax rate. Total savings are obtained by subtracting taxes paid from total household income, since discretionary and survival spending are now insignificant relative to total household income.

8. Describe how discretionary spending for the population is reduced as inequality grows, based on stages 6 and 7.

The equation describing the reduction in discretionary spending for the entire population because of inequality is now calculated from stages 6 and 7, knowing discretionary spending at complete equality, complete inequality, and at current conditions with a Gini coefficient of 0.44. This equation linking the reduction in discretionary spending to the Gini coefficient was developed from the three data points using the linfit module in Mathcad for maximum tax rates of 35, 45, and 55 percent (as indicated earlier, the 45 and 55 percent tax rates were only applied to the highest tax bracket, of incomes over \$373,650 in 2010; the modeled tax rates for lower incomes were maintained constant save for slight variation from smoothing when applying the model equations). In each case, the coefficient of determination (R^2) is 1, indicating that the equations fit the data well.

When the maximum tax rate is 35 percent the equation is (discretionary spending is in \$billion):

Reduction in annual discretionary spending =
– 4517 x Gini^3 + 319.509 x Gini^2

When the maximum tax rate is 45 percent, the equation is:

Reduction in annual discretionary spending =
– 3440 x Gini^3 – 829.914 x Gini^2

When the maximum tax rate is 55 percent, the equation is:

Reduction in annual discretionary spending =
– 2725 x Gini^3 – 1569 x Gini^2

The estimated annual loss in discretionary spending at 35, 45, and 55 percent maximum tax rates because of increased inequality, calculated from these three equations (in 2008 \$), is shown in figure 7 in the chapter "Concluding Thoughts."

9. Estimate the cumulative reduction in discretionary spending over time because of growing inequality, from stage 8 and published inequality data.

The reduction in discretionary spending each year since 1970, based on the current maximum tax rate of 35 percent, from rising inequality is calculated knowing the rate of change of discretionary spending (in \$billion) per unit of Gini coefficient, obtained by differentiating (mathematically) the first equation of stage 8:

$billion reduction in discretionary spending per unit of Gini coefficient = – 3 x 4517 x Gini^2 + 2 x 319.509 x Gini

This equation is used to calculate the reduction in discretionary spending each year from 1970 from growing inequality, knowing the Gini coefficient each year from the data cited in the introduction, inserting this value into the equation, and multiplying the result by the increase in Gini coefficient for that year relative to the average value of 0.352 between 1965 and 1969.[8] The results are described in the chapter "Concluding Thoughts," where the cumulative loss in discretionary spending from 1970 to 2010 is shown in figure 6 (in 2008 $).

NOTES

Introduction

1. David Miller, *Principles of Social Justice* (Cambridge, MA: Harvard University Press, 1999), 1.
2. Ibid., 265.
3. Daniel Schraad-Tischler, "Social Justice in the OECD—How Do the Member States Compare?"(Gutersloh, Germany: Bertelsmann Stiftung, 2011), accessed August 18, 2012, http://www.sgi-network.org/pdf/SGI11_Social_Justice_OECD .pdf.
4. Lawrence Mishel and Josh Bivens, "Occupy Wall Streeters Are Right about Skewed Economic Rewards in the United States" (Washington, DC: Economic Policy Institute, October 26, 2011), accessed November 22, 2011, http://www.epi .org/publication/bp331-occupy-wall-street/.
5. Richard Wilkinson and Kate Pickett, *The Spirit Level: Why Greater Equality Makes Societies Stronger* (New York: Bloomsbury Press, 2009).
6. Ibid.
7. Ibid., 20; UNICEF, "The Children Left Behind: A League Table of Inequality in Child Well-Being in the World's Richest Countries, Report Card 9" (Florence, Italy: UNICEF Innocenti Research Center, November 2010), accessed January 26, 2011, http://www.unicef-irc.org/publications/pdf/rc9_eng.pdf.
8. David K. Shipler, *The Working Poor: Invisible in America* (New York: Alfred A. Knopf, 2004), 300.
9. U.S. Census Bureau, "Gini Ratios for Families, by Race and Hispanic Origin of Householder [XLS]," Washington, DC, accessed August 19, 2012, http://www .census.gov/hhes/www/income/data/historical/inequality/index.html.
10. The World Bank, "Measuring Inequality," Washington, DC, accessed January 7, 2011, http://web.worldbank.org/WBSITE/EXTERNAL/TOPICS/EXTPOVERTY /EXTPA/0,,contentMDK:20238991~menuPK:492138~pagePK:148956 ~piPK:216618~theSitePK:430367,00.html; Richard Blundell, "From Income to Consumption: Understanding the Transmission of Inequality," *Focus* 28, no. 1 (Madison, WI: Institute for Research on Poverty, Spring/Summer 2011): 23–28, accessed June 29, 2011, http://www.irp.wisc.edu/publications/focus/pdfs/foc 281f.pdf.
11. World Bank, "Measuring Inequality"; The Equality Trust, "Income Inequality: Trends and Measures," *Equality Trust Research Digest*, no. 2 (London, 2011): 1–8.

208 NOTES

12. The jump between 1992 and 1993 is from a combination of changing survey methodology and a real increase, so the line in figure 2 is not joined at this point. Paul Ryscavage, *Monthly Labor Review,* August 1995 (Washington, DC: U.S. Bureau of Labor Statistics), accessed January 7, 2011, http://www.bls.gov /opub/mlr/1995/08/art5full.pdf; U.S. Census Bureau, "The Changing Shape of the Nation's Income Distribution: 1947–1998," Washington, DC, June 2000, accessed August 18, 2012, http://www.census.gov/prod/2000pubs/p60-204.pdf.

13. *The World Factbook* (Washington, DC: Central Intelligence Agency), accessed January 7, 2011, https://www.cia.gov/library/publications/the-world-factbook /index.html for the Gini coefficients; World Bank, Gross National Income (GNI) per capita, Washington, DC, accessed January 8, 2011, http://data.worldbank. org/indicator/NY.GNP.PCAP.cd.

14. GNI is the total value of all goods and services produced in a country (gross domestic product [GDP] plus income paid into the country by other countries for items such as interest and dividends, less similar payments to other countries. "Gross Domestic Product (GDP)/Gross National Product (GNP)/Gross National Income (GNI)," accessed January 26, 2011, http://www.solutionmatrix.com/gdp .html.

15. U.S. Congress Joint Economic Committee, "Income Inequality and the Great Recession," Representative Carolyn B. Maloney, chair; Senator Charles E. Schumer, vice chairman, September 2010, accessed January 7, 2011, http://jec.senate .gov/public/?a=Files.Serve&File_id=91975589-257c-403b-8093-8f3b584a088c.

16. Ibid., 2.

17. Arloc Sherman and Chad Stone, "Income Gaps between Very Rich and Everyone Else More than Tripled in Last Three Decades, New Data Show" (Washington, DC: Center on Budget and Policy Priorities, June 25, 2010), accessed January 7, 2011, http://www.cbpp.org/files/6-25-10inc.pdf; Avi Feller and Chuck Marr, "Tax Rate for Richest 400 Taxpayers Plummeted in Recent Decades, Even as Their Pre-Tax Incomes Skyrocketed" (Washington, DC: Center on Budget and Policy Priorities, February 23, 2010), accessed January 7, 2011, http://www.cbpp .org/files/2-23-10tax.pdf; Frank Levy and Peter Temin, "Inequality and Institutions in 20th Century America, Working Paper 07-17" (Cambridge, MA: Massachusetts Institute of Technology, Department of Economics, May 1, 2007), accessed January 17, 2011, http://papers.ssrn.com/sol3/papers.cfm?abstract _id=984330.

18. Robert B. Reich, *Aftershock: The Next Economy and America's Future* (New York: Alfred A. Knopf, 2010).

19. Carmen DeNavas-Walt, Bernadette D. Proctor, and Jessica C. Smith, U.S. Census Bureau Current Population Reports, P60–243, *Income, Poverty, and Health Insurance Coverage in the United States: 2011* (Washington, DC: U.S. Government Printing Office, 2012), 13, accessed September 12, 2012, http://www.census.gov /prod/2012pubs/p60-243.pdf.

20. Ibid., 13.

21. Ibid., 21.

22. Sam Dillon, "Line Grows Long for Free Meals at U.S. Schools," *New York Times,* November 29, 2011, accessed November 30, 2011, http://www.nytimes.com /2011/11/30/education/surge-in-free-school-lunches-reflects-economic-crisis .html?pagewanted=1&_r=1&nl=todaysheadlines&emc=tha2.

23. Alisha Coleman-Jensen, Mark Nord, Margaret Andrews, and Steven Carlson, *Household Food Security in the United States, 2011,* ERR-141 (Washington, DC: U.S. Department of Agriculture, Economic Research Service, September 2012), v,

10, accessed September 14, 2012, http://www.ers.usda.gov/media/884525/ERR141.pdf.

24. First Focus and the National Association for the Education of Homeless Children and Youth, *A Critical Moment: Child and Youth Homelessness in Our Nation's Schools* (Washington, DC: July 2010), accessed January 7, 2011, http://www.firstfocus.net/sites/default/files/HomelessEd_0.pdf.

25. For a comparison of taxation rates in Organization for Economic Cooperation and Development (OECD) countries, see Lauren Damme, "Losing Middle America: From Job Polarization to Wage Inequality," Next Social Contract Initiative Policy Brief, New America Foundation, September 2011, 7, accessed November 22, 2011, http://newamerica.net/sites/newamerica.net/files/policydocs/Losing%20Middle%20America%20-%20Wage%20Inequality%20-%20Damme%20-%2022%20Sept.pdf; historical U.S. taxation rates by income level are summarized in a chart from the *New York Times*, October 31, 2007, accessed November 22, 2011, http://www.nytimes.com/imagepages/2007/10/31/business/31Leonhardt.html; Sarah Anderson, Chuck Collins, Scott Klinger, and Sam Pizzigati, "The CEO Hands in Uncle Sam's Pocket: How Our Tax Dollars Subsidize Exorbitant Executive Pay, Executive Excess 2012, 19th Annual Executive Pay Survey" (Washington, DC: Institute for Policy Studies, August 16, 2012), 1–2.

26. Sarah Anderson, Chuck Collins, Scott Klinger, and Sam Pizzigati, "The Massive CEO Rewards for Tax Dodging, Executive Excess 2011, 18th Annual Executive Compensation Survey" (Washington, DC: Institute for Policy Studies, August 31, 2011), 2; Lawrence Mishel, Josh Bivens, Elise Gould, and Heidi Shierholz, *The State of Working America, 12th Edition*, A forthcoming Economic Policy Institute book (Ithaca, NY: Cornel University Press, 2012), 291, updated information available at http://stateofworking america.org/about/, accessed September 13, 2012.

27. Sarah Anderson, Chuck Collins, Sam Pizzigati, and Kevin Shih, "CEO Pay and the Great Recession, Executive Excess 2010, 17th Annual Executive Compensation Survey" (Washington, DC: Institute for Policy Studies, September 1, 2010), 4; Mishel et al., *The State of Working America 2008/2009*, 221.

28. Sarah Anderson, John Cavanagh, Scott Klinger, and Liz Stanton, "Executive Excess 2005: Defense Contractors Get More Bucks for the Bang" (Washington, DC: Institute for Policy Studies; and Boston, MA: United for a Fair Economy, 2005), 19, 20.

29. Jack T. Ciesielski, *The Analyst's Accounting Observer* 20, no. 7 (Baltimore, MD, May 23, 2011): 1–3; Greg Ruel and Paul Hodgson, "2011 Preliminary CEO Pay Survey" (New York: Governance Metrics International, June 7, 2011), 1–12.

30. U.S. Bureau of Labor Statistics, Employment Cost Index, Washington, DC, accessed September 3, 2011, http://data.bls.gov/timeseries/CIU1010000000000A.

31. R. Bruce Josten, "Letter Opposing H.R. 3962, the 'Affordable Healthcare for America Act'" (Washington, DC: U.S. Chamber of Commerce, November 5, 2009), accessed January 7, 2011, http://www.uschamber.com/issues/letters/2009/letter-opposing-hr-3962-affordable-healthcare-america-act.

32. Warren E. Buffett, "Stop Coddling the Super-Rich," *New York Times*, August 14, 2011, accessed August 15, 2011, http://www.nytimes.com/2011/08/15/opinion/stop-coddling-the-super-rich.html?_r=1&hp.

33. Muhammad Yunus, *Convocation Address*, University of the South, Sewanee, Tennessee, January 27, 1998.

34. Tommy Douglas, Great-Quotes.com, Gledhill Enterprises, 2011, accessed January 7, 2011, http://www.great-quotes.com/quote/851727.

35. Sam M. Intrator and Megan Scribner, *Leading from Within: Poetry That Sustains the Courage to Lead* (San Francisco: Jossey-Bass, 2007), 210.

Chapter 1. Integrating Needs So We All Benefit

1. Ron Elsdon, *Affiliation in the Workplace: Value Creation in the New Organization* (Westport, CT: Praeger, 2003), 24; describes the framework of relationship to work created by Betsy Brewer.
2. John B. Izzo and Pam Withers, *Values Shift* (Vancouver: Fair Winds Press, 2000), 89.
3. "Rethinking the Social Responsibility of Business," *Reason Magazine*, October 2005, accessed December 30, 2010, http://reason.com/archives/2005/10/01/rethinking-the-social-responsi (outlines John Mackey's perspective in conjunction with others); Terry Pearce, *Leading Out Loud* (San Francisco: Jossey-Bass, 2003), 22, 23, quotes from Howard Schultz's biography; "CEO Interview: Costco's Jim Sinegal," fastcompany.com, October 13, 2008, accessed December 30, 2010, http://www.fastcompany.com/magazine/130/thinking-outside-the-big-box.html.
4. Franklin D. Roosevelt, *Second Inaugural Address*, January 20, 1937, accessed December 30, 2010, http://www.bartleby.com/124/pres50.html.
5. Food Bank of Contra Costa and Solano, *2010 Annual Report*, accessed December 30, 2010, http://www.foodbankccs.org/docs-pdfs/2010%20Annual%20Report.pdf.
6. National Center for Charitable Statistics, "Number of Nonprofit Organizations by State, 2010," accessed December 30, 2010, http://nccsdataweb.urban.org/PugApps/profileDrillDown.php?rpt=US-STATE; OECD.StatExtracts, "National Accounts at a Glance," accessed October 3, 2011, http://stats.oecd.org/Index.aspx?DataSetCode=DECOMP; Bureau of Economic Analysis, U.S. Department of Commerce, "Current-Dollar and 'Real' Gross Domestic Product," Washington, DC, accessed October 3, 2011, www.bea.gov/national/xls/gdplev.xls.
7. Ron Elsdon, ed., *Building Workforce Strength: Creating Value through Workforce and Career Development* (Santa Barbara, CA: Praeger, 2010), xxi; includes reference to a 2005 paper by Frank Levy and Richard Murnane, "How Computerized Work and Globalization Shape Human Skill Demands," accessed January 23, 2009, www7.national academies.org/CFE/Educ_21st_Century_Skills_Levy_Paper.pdf.
8. Anthony P. Carnevale, Nicole Smith, and Jeff Strohl, "Help Wanted: Projections of Jobs and Education Requirements through 2018," Georgetown University Center on Education and the Workforce, Washington, DC, June 2010, 14, accessed January 7, 2011, http://www9.georgetown.edu/grad/gppi/hpi/cew/pdfs/FullReport.pdf.
9. Elsdon, *Building Workforce Strength*, 7, 8.
10. United Nations Economic and Social Commission for Asia and the Pacific, "What Is Good Governance?," accessed December 31, 2010, http://www.unescap.org/pdd/prs/ProjectActivities/Ongoing/gg/governance.asp.
11. Mishel et al., *The State of Working America, 12th Edition*, 286–91; Anderson et al., "Executive Excess 2005"; Anderson et al., "Executive Excess 2011" (examples of a series of Executive Excess reports).
12. Steven Greenhouse, "How Costco Became the Anti-Wal-Mart," *New York Times*, July 17, 2005, accessed November 29, 2011, http://www.nytimes.com/2005/07/17/business/yourmoney/17costco.html?pagewanted=all.
13. Elsdon, *Affiliation in the Workplace*, 228.
14. Lawrence Mishel, Jared Bernstein, and Sylvia Allegretto, *The State of Working America 2006/2007* (Ithaca, NY: ILR Press, 2007), 258–64.
15. Amy Galland, *Toward a Safe, Just Workplace: Apparel Supply Chain Compliance Programs* (San Francisco: As You Sow Foundation, 2010), accessed January 19, 2001, http://www.asyousow.org/human_rights/labor_transparency.shtml.

16. Simon Zadek, Peter Raynard, Cristiano Oliveira, Edna do Nascimento, and Rafael Tello, *Responsible Competitiveness*, AccountAbility in Association with FDC, London, December 2005, 80, 86, accessed January 3, 2011, http://www.account ability.org/images/content/1/1/110/Full%20Report%20(Compressed).pdf.
17. United Nations Global Compact, Caring for Climate Working Group on Climate Change and Development, accessed January 3, 2011, http://www.unglobalcom pact.org/Issues/Environment/Climate_Change/working_group_on_climate _change_and_development.html.
18. Zadek et al., *Responsible Competitiveness*, 83.
19. William B. Werther, Jr., and David Chandler, *Strategic Corporate Social Responsibility: Stakeholders in a Global Environment* (Los Angeles: SAGE, 2011), 35.
20. Elsdon, *Building Workforce Strength*, 9, citing Marc Saner, "Ethics Codes Revisited: A New Focus on Outcomes," Policy Brief no. 20, Institute on Governance, Ottawa, June 2004, accessed December 4, 2008, http://iog.ca/sites/iog/files /policybrief20.pdf .
21. Elsdon, *Building Workforce Strength*, 9.
22. Daniel Goleman, Richard Boyatzis, and Annie McKee, *Primal Leadership: Realizing the Power of Emotional Intelligence* (Boston: Harvard Business School Press, 2002), 39.
23. Ibid., 55.
24. Jim Collins, *Good to Great: Why Some Companies Make the Leap . . . and Others Don't* (New York: Harper Business, 2001), 39.
25. Larry C. Spears, "Practicing Servant Leadership," *Leader to Leader* 34 (Fall 2004): 7–11.
26. Elsdon, *Affiliation in the Workplace*, 169–76.
27. Management Research Group, "Leadership Best Practices for Senior Executives in North America, Report No. 260," Portland, ME, 2009.
28. IBM, "Capitalizing on Complexity: Insights from the Global Chief Executive Officer Study" (Somers, NY: IBM Global Business Services, 2010), 9–10.
29. Chuck Collins, Mike Lapham, and Scott Klinger, "I Didn't Do It Alone: Society's Contribution to Individual Wealth and Success" (Boston, MA: United for a Fair Economy, August 2004), 18.

Chapter 2. Corporate Social Responsibility: Lessons from Educational Practice in an Emerging Democracy

1. Authors are listed alphabetically. The views expressed by the authors of this chapter do not necessarily reflect those of the organizations discussed.
2. Kunal Basu and Guido Palazzo, "Corporate Social Responsibility: A Process Model of Sensemaking," *Academy of Management Review* 33, no. 1 (2008): 123.
3. Ibid., 124.
4. Lee G. Bolman and Terrence E. Deal, *Reframing Organizations* (San Francisco: Jossey-Bass, 1991), 9.
5. Ibid., 14.
6. Ibid., 11.
7. Basu and Palazzo, "Corporate Social Responsibility," 125.
8. Ibid., 126.
9. Ibid.
10. Ibid., 127.
11. Ibid.
12. BBC News, Georgia Country Profile, accessed November 21, 2011, http://news .bbc.co.uk/2/hi/europe/country_profiles/1102477.stm.

13. World Bank, *Doing Business 2011* (Washington, DC: The World Bank, 2010), 6.
14. Chemonics International, accessed November 9, 2011, http://www.chemonics .com/AboutUs/AboutUs.asp.
15. Bolman and Deal, *Reframing Organizations*, 12.
16. Basu and Palazzo, "Corporate Social Responsibility," 125.
17. Ibid., 127.
18. Felipe Barrera-Osorio, Tazeen Fasih, Harry Patrinos, and Lucrecia Santibáñez, *Decentralized Decision-Making in Schools: The Theory and Evidence on School-Based Management* (Washington, DC: The World Bank, 2009).
19. Basu and Palazzo, "Corporate Social Responsibility," 129.
20. Ibid., 130.
21. OECD Programme for International Student Assessment, accessed November 9, 2011, http://www.pisa.oecd.org/pages/0,2987, en_32252351_32235731_1_1 _1_1_1,00.html.

Chapter 3. Understanding and Assessing Corporate Social Responsibility in Organizations

1. Peter F. Drucker, *Management: Tasks, Responsibilities, Practices* (New York: Harper-Collins Publishers, 1973), 325.
2. Aneel Karnani, "The Case against Corporate Social Responsibility," *Wall Street Journal*, August 23, 2010, accessed July 8, 2011, http://online.wsj.com/article /SB10001424052748703338004575230112664504890.html.
3. Milton Friedman, "The Social Responsibility of Business Is to Increase Its Profits," *New York Times Magazine*, September 13, 1970, accessed November 30, 2011, http://www.colorado.edu/studentgroups/libertarians/issues/friedman-soc -resp-business.html.
4. "Deepwater: The Gulf Oil Disaster and the Future of Offshore Drilling," National Commission on the BP Deepwater Horizon Oil Spill and Offshore Drilling, January 11, 2011, 119, 125.
5. Ibid., 126.
6. "Gulf of Mexico Oil Spill (2010)," Times Topics, *New York Times,* updated October 17, 2011, accessed November 19, 2011, http://topics.nytimes.com/top /reference/timestopics/subjects/o/oil_spills/gulf_of_mexico_2010/index.html.
7. John Elkington, *Cannibals with Forks: The Triple Bottom Line of 21st Century Business* (London: New Society, 1998); John Elkington, *The Chrysalis Economy: How Citizen CEOs and Corporations Can Fuse Values and Value Creation* (Oxford, UK: Capstone Publishing Ltd [A John Wiley & Sons Co.], 2001); *Vision 2050: The New Agenda for Business* (Geneva: World Business Council for Sustainable Development, February 2010).
8. Ralph Stacey, *Complexity and Creativity in Organizations* (San Francisco: Berrett-Koehler, 1996); Richard Vicenzi, *Creating Conditions for Creativity and Innovation in Organizations*, Proceedings, ICMET 2000, Singapore.
9. *Encyclopedia of Business*, 2nd ed., accessed April 17, 2011, http://www.refer-enceforbusiness.com/management/Comp-De/Corporate-Social-Responsibility .html, quoting Archie B. Carroll and Ann K. Buchholtz, *Business and Society: Ethics and Stakeholder Management*, 5th ed. (Cincinnati, OH: Thomson South-Western, 2003), 36.
10. Ibid.
11. Marilyn Ferguson, "The Transformation of Values and Vocation," *The New Paradigm in Business: Emerging Strategies for Leaders and Organizational Change*, ed. Mi-

chael Ray and Alan Rinzler (New York: Jeremy P. Tarcher Books/Perigee Books, Putnam, 1993), 32–33.

12. Lorin J. B. Loverde, *Dynamic Markets Leadership: A Multi-Disciplinary Approach to Business and the Hidden Soul of Capitalism* (Glendale, CA: GDI Press, in press), 241–43.

13. *Embedding Ethics in Business and Higher Education: From Leadership to Management Imperative* (Washington, DC: Business-Higher Education Forum, 2005)—see chap. 2, where the ethical shortcomings of the cultures at Enron and WorldCom are treated extensively, and p. 27 for a brief review of Arthur Andersen; Simon Romero and Geraldine Fabrikant, "The Rise and Fall of Global Dreams," *New York Times*, March 3, 2002, Global Crossing; accessed November 21, 2011, http://www.nytimes.com/2002/03/03/business/the-rise-and-fall-of-global-dreams.html?pagewanted=all&src=pm; Gretchen Morgenson, "Inside the Countrywide Lending Spree," *New York Times*, August 26, 2007, accessed November 21, 2011, http://www.nytimes.com/2007/08/26/business/yourmoney/26country.html?adxnnl=1&pagewanted=all&adxnnlx=1321939435-Sh5NSpfU8J6CbWXKw5A ZJg; Mark Trumbull, "Lehman Bros. Used Accounting Trick amid Financial Crisis—and Earlier," *Christian Science Monitor*, March 12, 2010, accessed November 21, 2011, http://www.csmonitor.com/USA/2010/0312/Lehman-Bros.-used-accounting-trick-amid-financial-crisis-and-earlier.

14. Ken Thomas and Tomoko A. Hosaka (AP), "Toyota to Pay $32.4 Million in Extra Fines," December 21, 2010, accessed November 19, 2011, http://www.huffingtonpost.com/huff-wires/20101221/as-toyota-recall/.

15. Alex Taylor, "How Toyota Lost Its Way," *Fortune*, July 10, 2010, accessed February 27, 2011, http://money.cnn.com/2010/07/12/news/international/toyota_recall_crisis.fortune/index.htm.

16. Ibid.

17. Michael Connor, "Toyota Recall: Five Critical Lessons," *Business Ethics*, January 31, 2010, accessed February 27, 2011, http://business-ethics.com/2010/01/31/2123-toyota-recall-five-critical-lessons/.

18. James Hyatt, "Apple Expands Supplier Responsibility Program," *Business Ethics*, February 15, 2011, accessed November 19, 2011, http://business-ethics.com/2011/02/15/1030-apple-inc-expands-supplier-responsibility-program/.

19. Ibid.

20. Ibid.

21. Ibid.

22. Knut Haanaes, David Arthur, Balu Balagopal, Ming Teck Kong, Martin Reeves, Ingrid Velken, Michael S. Hopkins, and Nina Kruschwitz, "Sustainability: The 'Embracers' Seize Advantage," *MIT/Sloan Management Review* and the Boston Consulting Group, Research Report, Winter 2011.

23. Dow Jones Sustainability Index available at http://www.sustainability-index.com/; Boston College Center for Corporate Citizenship, available at http://www.bcccc.net/index.cfm.

24. Michael D. Greenberg, *Conference Proceedings: Perspectives of Chief Ethics and Compliance Officers on the Detection and Prevention of Corporate Misdeeds: What the Policy Community Should Know* (Santa Monica, CA: RAND, 2009), 29.

25. Global Reporting Initiative, accessed November 8, 2011, http://www.globalreporting.org/ReportingFramework/.

26. AccountAbility, accessed November 8, 2011, http://www.accountability.org/standards/aa1000aps.html.

27. Elkington, *The Chrysalis Economy*, 198–205.

28. London Benchmarking Group, accessed November 8, 2011, http://www.lbg -online.net/about-lbg/a-global-network.aspx.
29. Global Reporting Initiative, accessed November 8, 2011, http://www.global reporting.org; AccountAbility, accessed November 8, 2011, http://www.account ability.org/; London Benchmarking Group, accessed November 19, 2011, http://www.lbg-online.net/about-lbg/a-global-network.aspx.
30. Boston College Center for Corporate Citizenship, accessed November 8, 2011, http://www.bcccc.net/index.cfm?fuseaction=page.viewPage&pageID=2079 &nodeID=1#trends.
31. CorporateRegister.com, accessed November 8, 2011, http://www.corporate register.com/stats/.
32. Global Reporting Initiative, GRI reports list, accessed February 24, 2011, http: //www.globalreporting.org/ReportServices/GRIReportsList/.
33. *How To Read a Corporate Social Responsibility Report,* Boston College Center for Corporate Citizenship/Institute for Responsible Investment, January 26, 2010, accessed November 19, 2011, http://www.bcccc.net/index.cfm?fuseaction =document.showDocumentByID&DocumentID=1353.
34. To access reviews and analysis of company reports, see http://www.corporate register.com/reports/.
35. Ibid.
36. Jen Anderson, GreenBiz.com, accessed November 19, 2011, http://www.greenbiz .com/blog/2011/05/16/sustainability-surveys-buried-under-best-intentions.
37. Aaron Chatterji, David Levine, and Michael Toffel, "How Well Do Social Rat- ings Actually Measure Corporate Social Responsibility?," *Journal of Economics & Management Strategy* 18, no. 1 (Spring 2009): 125–69 (p. 130 outlines the investor motivational categories), accessed January 29, 2011, http://onlinelibrary.wiley .com/doi/10.1111/j.1530-9134.2009.00210.x/pdf.
38. Institutional Shareholder Services, accessed November 8, 2011, http://www.iss governance.com/about.
39. Global Reporting Initiative, GRI Sustainability Reporting Guidelines Version 3.1 (Amsterdam: Global Reporting Initiative 2011).
40. Lucian Bebchuk, Alma Cohen, and Allen Ferrell, *What Matters in Corporate Gover- nance?,* Discussion Paper no. 491 (Harvard Law School: John M. Olin Center for Law, Economics, and Business, 2004).
41. "Non-Financial Performance Metrics for Corporate Responsibility Reporting Revisited," Working Paper (Cranfield, UK: Doughty Centre for Corporate Re- sponsibility, Cranfield School of Management, 2008).
42. For a list of BCCCC's members, see http://www.bcccc.net/index.cfm?pageId=629.
43. Steven Rochlin, Kathleen Witter, and Phil Mirvis (BCCCC) and Stephan Jordan and D. Tomme Beevas (U.S. Chamber of Commerce Center for Corporate Citi- zenship), *The State of Corporate Citizenship in the U.S.: A View from Inside, 2003–2004* (Boston: Boston College Center for Corporate Citizenship, 2004).
44. Vesela Veleva, Peggy Connolly, Bradley K. Googins, Philip Mirvis, Christopher Pinney, and Kwang Ryu (BCCCC) and Barbara Dyer and Mark Popovich (Hita- chi Foundation), *The State of Corporate Citizenship 2007: Time to Get Real—Closing the Gap between Rhetoric and Reality* (Boston: Boston College Center for Corporate Citizenship, 2007).
45. Philip H. Mirvis, "What Do Surveys Say about Corporate Citizenship?," Working Paper (Boston: Boston College Center for Corporate Citizenship, 2007), accessed November 21, 2011, http://www.bcccc.net/index.cfm?fuseaction=document .showDocumentByID&DocumentID=1156.

46. McKinsey & Co., "Shaping the New Rules of Competition: UN Global Compact Participant Mirror," July 2007, accessed November 30, 2011, http://www.unglobal compact.org/docs/news_events/8.1/McKinsey.pdf.

47. Andrew Winston, *Bloomberg Businessweek*, July 14, 2009, "Wal-Mart Brazil Thinks Green," accessed February 26, 2011, http://www.businessweek.com/managing /content/jul2009/ca20090714_100756.htm.

48. George Pohle and Jeff Hittner, *Attaining Sustainable Growth through Corporate Social Responsibility*, IBM Institute for Business Value, February 2008, accessed February 17, 2011, http://www-935.ibm.com/services/us/gbs/bus/pdf/gbe 03019-usen-02.pdf.

49. Ibid.

50. Ilknur H. Tekin and Dundar F. Kocaoglu, "A Bibliometric Analysis on Green Innovations, Green Investments, and Green Venture Capital," in *2011 Proceedings of PICMET '11: Technology Management in the Energy Smart World* (Portland, OR: PICMET 2011).

51. Edward Soule, *Embedding Ethics in Business and Higher Education: From Leadership to Management Imperative* (Washington, DC: Business-Higher Education Forum, 2005), 30.

52. Ibid., 32.

53. "Deepwater" National Commission; David Glovin, "Bank of America $150 Million SEC Accord Is Approved," *Bloomberg.com*, February 22, 2010, accessed November 2, 2011, http://www.bloomberg.com/apps/news?pid=newsarchive&sid =aMU9F1952OHA; Zachary A. Goldfarb, "Bank of America to Pay $137 Million in State Fraud Cases," *Washington Post*, December 7, 2010, accessed November 19, 2011, http://www.washingtonpost.com/wp-dyn/content/article/2010/12/07 /AR2010120703314.html?hpid=topnews; Leslie Wayne, "Goldman Pays to End State Inquiry into Loans," *New York Times*, May 11, 2009, accessed November 19, 2011, http://www.nytimes.com/2009/05/12/business/12lend.html; Gretchen Morgenson and Louise Story, "Banks Bundled Bad Debt, Bet against It and Won," *New York Times*, December 23, 2009, accessed November 19, 2011, http: //www.nytimes.com/2009/12/24/business/24trading.html; Frederick Kaufman, "The Food Bubble: How Wall Street Starved Millions and Got Away with It," *Harper's Magazine*, July 2010, accessed November 30, 2011, http://harpers.org /archive/2010/07/0083022.

54. Pohle and Hittner, *Attaining Sustainable Growth*, 11.

55. Loverde, *Dynamic Markets Leadership*, 250–52.

56. Ibid.

Chapter 4. Partnerships between the For-Profit and Nonprofit Sectors

1. Walker Information, Inc., and Council on Foundations, "Measuring the Business Value of Corporate Philanthropy," National Benchmark Study, Indianapolis, May 2002.

2. Justmeans, *70% of Consumers Willing to Pay More for CSR*, March 21, 2010, accessed June 18, 2011, http://www.justmeans.com/70-of-Consumers-willing-pay -more-for-CSR/12007.html.

3. Ken Dami, private communication, May 10, 2011.

4. Michael Hannigan, private communication, April 8, 2011.

5. Dami, private communication.

6. Greg Coplans, private communication, March 28, 2011.

7. Daryl Lee, private communication, April 5, 2011.

8. John Bateson, private communication, April 5, 2011.

9. Charles F. Broom, private communication, March 31, 2011.

10. Michael Hannigan, private communication, April 8, 2011.
11. Dirk Fitzgerald, private communication, May 1, 2011.
12. Daryl Lee, private communication, April 6, 2011.
13. Stuart McCullough, private communication, April 8, 2011.
14. Elena Bicker, private communication, April 13, 2011.
15. Daryl Lee, private communication, April 6, 2011.
16. Charles F. Broom, private communication, July 14, 2011.
17. Points of Light Institute, Measuring Impact, accessed July 18, 2011, http://www .pointsoflight.org/research-center.
18. KidSource Online, *What Is Early Intervention?*, accessed July 8, 2011, http://www .kidsource.com/kidsource/content/early.intervention.html.

Chapter 5. Government as a Business Partner in the Pursuit of Social Responsibility

1. Robert Reich, *The Case against Corporate Social Responsibility*, Goldman School Working Paper Series (Berkeley: University of California–Berkeley, 2008), accessed September 28, 2011, http://ssrn.com/abstract=1213129.
2. Milton Friedman, "Social Responsibility of Business Is to Increase Its Profits," *New York Times Magazine*, September 13, 1970, accessed September 30, 2011, http:// www.colorado.edu/studentgroups/libertarians/issues/friedman-soc-resp -business.html.
3. Christopher Holshek, "The Power of Both," *Huffington Post*, May 23, 2011, accessed October 18, 2011, http://www.huffingtonpost.com/christopher-holshek /the-power-of-both_b_864645.html.
4. Ibid.
5. *Merriam-Webster Online*, Encyclopedia Britannica Co., s.v. "Business," accessed September 30, 2011, http://www.merriam-webster.com/dictionary/business.
6. Deval Patrick, Remarks to the 2008 Democratic National Convention, Denver, Colorado, August 26, 2008. Patrick attributes the line to Rep. Barney Frank of Massachusetts as something he is fond of saying.
7. Organisation for Economic Co-operation and Development (OECD), "About the Organisation for Economic Co-operation and Development" (Paris: OECD), accessed September 30, 2011, http://www.oecd.org/pages/0,3417,en_36734052 _36734103_1_1_1_1_1,00.html; OECD, "The Well-Being of Nations: The Role of Human and Social Capital" (Paris: OECD, 2001).
8. Ron Haskins, "Obama's Deficit Opportunity," *The Hill*, September 20, 2011, accessed September 30, 2011, http://thehill.com/opinion/op-ed/182773-obamas -deficit-opportunity.
9. Shannon Murphy, "Business and Philanthropy Partnerships for Human Capital Development in the Middle East: A Working Paper," *Corporate Social Responsibility Initiative*, April 2009, accessed September 30, 2011, http://www.hks.harvard.edu /m-rcbg/CSRI/publications/workingpaper_52_murphy.pdf.
10. Pam Fessler, "A Squash's Journey: From the Shelf to the Hungry," *All Things Considered*, June 23, 2011, compact disc, accessed November 11, 2011, http:// www.npr.org/2011/06/23/137319064/a-squashs-journey-from-the-shelf-to-the -hungry.
11. Stephanie Strom, "Wal-Mart Gives $2 Billion to Fight Hunger," *New York Times*, May 12, 2010, accessed September 30, 2011, http://www.nytimes.com/2010/05/13 /us/13gift.html.
12. U.S. Department of Agriculture (USDA), "A Citizen's Guide to Food Recovery,"

accessed February 1999 and October 11, 2012, http://hdl.handle.net/2027/umn .31951d016906487/.

13. Ibid.

14. This is referred to as the "Emerson law" because one of its sponsors, Representative Emerson, died before the bill was passed, and it was named after him.

15. U.S. Environmental Protection Agency (EPA), "Food Donation: Feed People— Not Landfills," accessed September 30, 2011, http://www.epa.gov/osw/conserve /materials/organics/food/fd-donate.htm.

16. Ibid.

17. Al Norman, "Wal-Mart's Rotten Hunger Campaign: Turning Trash into Tax Deductions," *Huffington Post* (blog), August 10, 2010, accessed November 11, 2011, http://www.huffingtonpost.com/al-norman/wal-marts-rotten-hunger-c_b _677857.html.

18. Al Norman, *The Case Against Wal-Mart* (Atlantic City: Raphel Marketing, 2004); Jessica Wohl, "Wal-Mart Trims Some U.S. Health Coverage," *Reuters*, October 21, 2011, accessed October 21, 2011, http://www.reuters.com/article/2011/10/21 /us-Wal-Mart-idUSTRE79K43Z20111021.

19. Chris Matthews, *Hardball* (New York: Touchstone, 1999), 188.

20. U.S. EPA, "Food Donation."

21. Sodexo, "Dining Management: Keeping Customers Satisfied," accessed September 30, 2011, http://www.sodexousa.com/usen/environments/military/food /diningmgmt/diningmgmt.asp.

22. U.S. EPA, "Food Donation."

23. "In Search of the Good Company: The Debate about the Social Responsibilities of Companies Is Heating Up Again," *Economist*, September 6, 2007, accessed September 30, 2011, http://www.economist.com/node/9767615/print.

24. Jeffrey B. Liebman, "Social Impact Bonds: A Promising New Financing Model to Accelerate Social Innovation and Improve Government Performance," Doing What Works (Washington, DC: Center for American Progress, February 2011), accessed November 11, 2011, http://www.americanprogress.org/issues /2011/02/pdf/social_impact_bonds.pdf.

25. U.S. Government Accountability Office, "Globalization: Numerous Federal Activities Complement U.S. Business's Global Corporate Social Responsibility Efforts," August 2005, accessed October 1, 2011, http://www.gao.gov/new.items/ d05744.pdf.

Chapter 6. Pro Bono Service: Driving Social Impact with Professional Skills

1. "St. Joseph's Villa for Children," accessed August 18, 2011, http://neverstop believing.org.

2. Capital One, "Capital One Corporate Citizenship," last modified 2011, accessed August 18, 2011, http://www.capitalone.com/about/corporate-citizenship /partnerships/virginia/.

3. Taproot Foundation, "Case Study: Capital One's Corporate Pro Bono Leadership," San Francisco, last modified 2011, accessed August 18, 2011, http://www .taprootfoundation.org/leadprobono/state/casestudies/co_leader.php.

4. Taproot Foundation, with Committee Encouraging Corporate Philanthropy, "Pro Bono Standards and Valuation," 2009, accessed August 18, 2011, http:// www.taprootfoundation.org/leadprobono/state/101/standards.php.

5. Nonprofit Finance Fund, "2012 State of the Sector Survey," April 2012, accessed August 18, 2012, http://nonprofitfinancefund.org/state-of-the-sector-surveys.

6. Deloitte & Touche USA LLP, "2009 Volunteer IMPACT Survey," last modified March 31, 2011, accessed August 18, 2011, http://www.deloitte.com/view/en US/us/About/Community-Involvement/7651773b93912210VgnVCM100000 ba42f00aRCRD.htm.

7. Taproot Foundation, "Taproot Foundation Survey of Nonprofits," San Francisco, 2009, accessed August 16, 2012, http://www.taprootfoundation.org/lead probono/professions/marketing.php.

8. Target Corp., "Targeting Volunteerism," accessed August 18, 2011, http://press-room.target.com/pr/news/targeting-volunteerism.aspx?ncid=24573.

9. IDEO, *Design for Social Impact: A How-To Guide* (2008), 115, http://www.ideo.com /images/uploads/news/pdfs/IDEO_RF_Guide.pdf.

10. Ashoka, "Our Partners," accessed August 18, 2011, http://www.ashoka.org/partners.

11. Taproot Foundation, "Case Study: Wells Fargo & Family Connections," San Francisco, last modified 2011, accessed August 18, 2011, http://www.taprootfound ation.org/leadprobono/state/casestudies/wf_fc.php.

12. James W. Shepard, Jr., and Alethea Hannemann, *Pro Bono Strategic Consulting: The $1.5 Billion Opportunity* (San Francisco: Taproot Foundation, 2008), 10, accessed November 30, 2011, http://www.taprootfoundation.org/docs/SM_White Paper_Oct2008.pdf.

13. Taproot Foundation, "Taproot Foundation Survey of Nonprofits."

14. Booz Allen Hamilton, Inc., "Wolf Trap Goes Green," accessed August 18, 2011, http://www.boozallen.com/consulting/better-our-world/sustainability/wolf -trap-goes-green.

15. Wolf Trap Foundation, "Go Green with Wolf Trap," accessed August 18, 2011, http://www.wolftrap.org/Learn_About_Wolf_Trap/Go_Green_with_Wolf _Trap.aspx.

16. Jim Collins, *Good to Great and the Social Sectors* (New York: HarperCollins, 2005), 17.

17. Accenture, *Identifying Enablers of Nonprofit High Performance* (2008), accessed November 30, 2011, http://www.accenture.com/SiteCollectionDocuments/PDF /Accenture_ExeIssuesNonProfits_ES_Final.pdf.

18. Taproot Foundation, "Taproot Foundation Survey of Nonprofits."

19. Jamie Hartman and Jane Park, with Natalya Matusova, *Making Pro Bono Work: 8 Proven Models for Community and Business Impact* (San Francisco: Taproot Foundation, last modified 2011), accessed November 30, 2011, http://www.taproot foundation.org/docs/8_Models_Whitepaper.pdf.

20. American Express, "Corporate Responsibility Initiatives," accessed August 18, 2011, http://about.americanexpress.com/csr/nla.aspx.

21. Accenture, *Identifying Enablers.*

22. Taproot Foundation, "Case Study: IBM & United Way's 2-1-1 Technology," San Francisco, last modified 2011, accessed August 18, 2011, http://www.taproot foundation.org/leadprobono/state/casestudies/ibm_211.php.

23. Taproot Foundation, "Case Study: Citi and Microfinance Institutions," San Francisco, last modified 2011, accessed August 18, 2011, http://www.taprootfound ation.org/leadprobono/state/casestudies/citi_microfinance.php.

24. KPMG, "Global Development Initiative," accessed August 18, 2011, http://www .kpmg.com/global/en/whoweare/corporatecitizenship/globaldevelopment /pages/global-development-initiative.aspx.

25. Taproot Foundation, with Committee Encouraging Corporate Philanthropy, "Pro Bono Standards and Valuation."

26. Deloitte & Touche USA LLP, "2007 Volunteer IMPACT Survey," last modified June 3, 2011, accessed August 18, 2011, http://www.deloitte.com/view/en_US

/us/About/Community-Involvement/f0d3264f0b0fb110VgnVCM100000
ba42f00aRCRD.htm.

27. LBG Associates, "Pro Bono Service: The Business Case," Stamford, CT, 2009.
28. Sylvia Reynolds, Wells Fargo, private communication, 2010.
29. Michael Porter and Mark Kramer, "Strategy and Society: The Link between Competitive Advantage and Corporate Social Responsibility," *Harvard Business Review*, December 2006, 1–15.

Chapter 7. Public/Private Sector Collaboration

1. Welfare Information, "US Welfare System—Help for US Citizens," accessed August 23, 2011, http://www.welfareinfo.org/.
2. "Welfare-to-Work Programs—History of Workfare," accessed August 23, 2011, http://www.libraryindex.com/pages/926/Welfare-Work-Programs-HISTORY-WORKFARE.html.
3. Ibid.
4. Vee Burke, "A Brief History of the AFDC Program," unpublished manuscript 1997, 6, accessed September 9, 2011, http://aspe.hhs.gov/hsp/afdc/baseline/1history.pdf.
5. "Welfare-to-Work Programs."
6. Ibid., 1.
7. Janice Peskin et al., *Staff Working Papers—Work and Welfare: The Family Support Act of 1988* (Washington, DC: Congressional Budget Office, January 1989).
8. Alan Weil and Kenneth Finegold, *Welfare Reform: The Next Act/Introduction*, accessed September 14, 2011, http:www.urban.org/books/welfare_reform/intro.cfm.
9. Michael B. Katz, "The American Welfare State," 2008, 1, accessed November 3, 2011, http://www.history.ac.uk/ihr/Focus/welfare/articles/katzm.html.
10. Health and Human Services News Release, ACF Press Office, November 25, 2002, accessed November 2, 2011, http://archive.hhs.gov/news/press/2002pres/20021125a.html.

Chapter 8. Healthcare as Social Responsibility: Implications for Business

1. Henry J. Kaiser Family Foundation, *The Uninsured: A Primer* (Menlo Park, CA: October 2011), 1, accessed November 15, 2011, http://www.kff.org/uninsured/upload/7451-07.pdf.
2. The new law is referred to as the Affordable Care Act (ACA) and includes two laws—the Patient Protection and Affordable Care Act (PL 111–148) as enacted on March 23, 2010, and amended by the Health Care and Education Affordability Reconciliation Act of 2010 (PL 111–152) as enacted on March 30, 2010.
3. House Republicans, *A Pledge to America*, September 23, 2010, 25, accessed November 26, 2011, http://www.gop.gov/resources/library/documents/solutions/a-pledge-to-america.pdf.
4. "HR 2, Repealing the Job-Killing Health Care Law Act," passed the House January 19, 2011, accessed November 27, 2011, http://thomas.loc.gov/cgi-bin/query/z?c112:H.R.2; House Committee on the Budget, "The Path to Prosperity: Restoring America's Promise: 47," passed the House April 15, 2011, accessed November 26, 2011, http://budget.house.gov/UploadedFiles/PathToProsperity FY2012.pdf.
5. U.S. Chamber of Commerce, "U.S. Chamber Marks One Year Anniversary of Health Care Law," Washington, DC, March 23, 2011, accessed November 22, 2011, http://www.uschamber.com/press/releases/2011/march/us-chamber-marks-one-year-anniversary-health-care-law.

6. Business Roundtable, *Health Care Reform: Creating a Sustainable Health Care Marketplace*, a Report to the Business Roundtable by Hewitt Associates, Washington, DC, November 2009, 18–19, accessed November 21, 2011, http://business roundtable.org/uploads/studies-reports/downloads/Health_Care_Reform _Creating_a_Sustainable_Health_Care_Marketplace.pdf.

7. Kaiser Family Foundation, *The Uninsured*, 1.

8. Andrew P. Wilper, Steffie Woolhandler, Karen E. Lasser, Danny McCormick, David H. Bor, and David U. Himmelstein, "Health Insurance and Mortality in US Adults," *American Journal of Public Health* 99, no. 12 (December 2009): 1–7, accessed November 21, 2011, http://www.pnhp.org/excessdeaths/health-insur ance-and-mortality-in-US-adults.pdf.

9. Kaiser Family Foundation, *The Uninsured*, 6; the federal poverty level for a family of four was $22,050 in 2010.

10. Cathy Schoen, Michelle M. Doty, Ruth H. Robertson, and Sara R. Collins, "Affordable Care Act Reforms Could Reduce the Number of Underinsured US Adults by 70 Percent," *Health Affairs* 30, no. 9 (September 2011): 1762–71.

11. David U. Himmelstein, Deborah Thorne, Elizabeth Warren, and Steffie Woolhandler, "Medical Bankruptcy in the United States: 2007: Results of a National Study," *American Journal of Medicine*, May 2009, 1–6, accessed November 21, 2011, http://www.pnhp.org/new_bankruptcy_study/Bankruptcy-2009.pdf.

12. Centers for Medicare and Medicaid Services, *National Health Expenditure Data, Historical*, 2009, table 1, accessed October 1, 2011, https://www.cms.gov /NationalHealthExpendData/downloads/tables.pdf; Paul Ginsburg, *High and Rising Health Care Costs: Demystifying U.S. Health Care Spending*, Policy Brief no. 16 (Princeton: Robert Wood Johnson Foundation, October 2008), 3, accessed November 15, 2011, http://www.rwjf.org/files/research/35368.highrisingcosts .brief.pdf.

13. Henry J. Kaiser Family Foundation, "Average Annual Premiums for Family Health Benefits Top $15,000 in 2011, Up 9 Percent, Substantially More than the Growth in Workers' Wages, Benchmark Employer Survey Finds," News Release, September 27, 2011, accessed September 28, 2011, http://www.kff.org /insurance/092311nr.cfm.

14. Congressional Budget Office (CBO), *Long-Term Budget Outlook: Summary*, June 2009, accessed November 21, 2011, http://www.cbo.gov/ftpdocs/102xx /doc10297/SummaryforWeb_LTBO.pdf.

15. David A. Squires, *The U.S. Health System in Perspective: A Comparison of Twelve Industrialized Nations* (New York: Commonwealth Fund, July 2011), 3, accessed November 17, 2011, http://www.commonwealthfund.org/~/media/Files/Pub lications/Issue%20Brief/2011/Jul/1532_Squires_US_hlt_sys_comparison_12 _nations_intl_brief_v2.pdf.

16. Commonwealth Fund Commission on a High Performance Health System, *Why Not the Best?*, October 2011, 13, accessed November 21, 2011, http://www .commonwealthfund.org/~/media/Files/Publications/Fund%20Report /2011/Oct/1500_WNTB_Natl_Scorecard_2011_web.pdf.

17. Business Roundtable, *Business Roundtable Health Care Value Index: Executive Summary*, May 23 2009, accessed November 27, 2011, http://businessroundtable .org/uploads/studies-reports/downloads/The_Business_Roundtable_Health _Care_Value_Index_Executive_Summary.pdf.

18. For citations to the annual analyses of OECD data sponsored by the Commonwealth Fund, see Squires, *U.S. Health System in Perspective*, 12.

19. Gerard F. Anderson and David A. Squires, *Measuring the U.S. Health Care System: A*

Cross-National Comparison (New York: Commonwealth Fund, June 2010), 2–3, accessed November 21, 2011, http://www.commonwealthfund.org/Publications/Issue-Briefs/2010/Jun/Measuring-the-US-Health-Care.aspx.

20. Ibid., 4.

21. Gerard F. Anderson, Uwe E. Reinhardt, Peter S. Hussey, and Varduhi Petrosyan, "It's the Prices, Stupid: Why the United States Is So Different from Other Countries," *Health Affairs* 22, no. 3 (May/June 2003): 89–105, accessed November 28, 2011, http://content.healthaffairs.org/content/22/3/89.full.pdf+html.

22. McKinsey Global Institute, *Accounting for the Cost of Health Care in the United States*, January 2007, 13, accessed November 22, 2011, http://www.mckinsey.com/mgi/rp/healthcare/accounting_cost_healthcare.asp.

23. Ibid., 70, 72.

24. Dante Morra, Sean Nicholson, Wendy Levinson, David N. Gans, Terry Hammons, and Lawrence P. Casalino, "US Physician Practices Versus Canadians: Spending Nearly Four Times as Much Money Interacting with Payers," *Health Affairs* 30, no. 8 (August 2011): 1443–50.

25. Paul Starr, in *The Social Transformation of American Medicine* (New York: Basic Books, 1982), provides a thorough analysis of the early evolution of our healthcare system.

26. James C. Robinson, "Physician-Hospital Integration and the Economic Theory of the Firm," *Medical Care Research and Review* 54, no. 1 (1997): 3–24, cited in Lawrence P. Casalino, Elizabeth A. November, Robert A. Berenson, and Hoangmai H. Pham, "Hospital-Physician Relations: Two Tracks and the Decline of the Voluntary Medical Staff Model," *Health Affairs* 27, no. 5 (September/October 2008): 1306.

27. Kelly J. Devers, Linda R. Brewster, and Lawrence P. Casalino, "Changes in Hospital Competitive Strategy: A New Medical Arms Race?," *HSR: Health Services Research* 38, no. 1, part II (February 2003): 449–450, accessed November 22, 2011, http://www.ncbi.nlm.nih.gov/pmc/articles/PMC1360894/pdf/hesr_124.pdf.

28. Ibid., 449.

29. Milton I. Roemer, "Hospital Utilization and the Supply of Physicians," *Journal of the American Medical Association* 178, no. 1 (December 1961): 933–89, quoted in Kent Patel and Mark E. Rushefsky, *Health Care Politics and Policy in America*, 2nd ed. (Armonk: M. E. Sharpe, 1999), 168.

30. Centers for Medicare and Medicaid Services, *National Health Expenditure Data*, table 1.

31. Arnold S. Relman, *A Second Opinion: Rescuing America's Health Care* (New York: Century Foundation, 2007), 69.

32. Cathie Jo Martin, "Markets, Medicare and Making Do: Business Strategies after National Health Care Reform," *Journal of Health Politics, Policy and Law* 22, no. 2 (April 1997): 561.

33. Jon R. Gabel, Gail A. Jensen, and Samantha Hawkins, "Self-Insurance in Times of Growing and Retreating Managed Care," *Health Affairs* 22, no. 2 (March/April 2003): 202–10.

34. James C. Robinson, "The Commercial Health Insurance Industry in an Era of Eroding Employer Coverage, *Health Affairs* 25, no. 6 (November/December 2006): 1478.

35. For a good explanation of both DRGs and RVUs, see Thomas S. Bodenheimer and Kevin Grumbach, *Understanding Health Policy: A Clinical Approach*, 2nd ed. (Stamford: Appleton & Lange, 1998), 49, 58.

36. Karen Davis, Karen S. Collins, and Cynthia Morris, "Managed Care: Promise and

Concerns," *Health Affairs* 13, no. 4 (Fall 1994): 178–85, accessed November 28, 2011, http://content.healthaffairs.org/content/13/4/178.full.pdf+html.

37. Martin, "Markets, Medicare and Making Do," 564.

38. Gabel et al., "Self-Insurance," 203; Henry J. Kaiser Family Foundation and Health Research & Educational Trust, *Employer Health Benefits: 2011 Summary of Findings* (Menlo Park, CA: September 2011), 2, accessed October 3, 2011, http://ehbs.kff .org/pdf/8226.pdf.

39. Davis et al., "Managed Care," 181.

40. Mark A. Peterson, "Introduction: Health Care into the Next Century," *Journal of Health Politics, Policy and Law* 22, no. 2 (April 1997): 298; American Medical Association (AMA), "Study Finds Lack of Competition among Health Insurers," February 23, 2011, accessed November 23, 2011, http://www.ama-assn.org/ama /pub/news/news/competition-health-insurers.page.

41. Kelly J. Devers, Lawrence P. Casalino, Liza S. Rudell, Jeffrey J. Stoddard, Linda R. Brewster, and Timothy K. Lake, "Hospitals' Negotiating Leverage with Health Plans: How and Why Has It Changed?," *HSR: Health Services Research* 38, no. 1, part II (February 2003): 422, accessed November 22, 2011, http://www.ncbi.nlm .nih.gov/pmc/articles/PMC1360893/pdf/hesr_123.pdf.

42. Centers for Medicare and Medicaid Services, *National Health Expenditure Data*, table 1.

43. Cara S. Lesser, Paul B. Ginsburg, and Kelly J. Devers, "The End of an Era: What Became of the 'Managed Care Revolution' in 2001?," *HSR: Health Services Research* 38, no. 1, part II (February 2003): 337, accessed November 23, 2011, http://www.ncbi.nlm.nih.gov/pmc/articles/PMC1360889/.

44. Robert Cunningham, "Hospital Finance: Signs of 'Pushback' among Resurgent Cost Pressures," *Health Affairs* 20, no. 2 (March/April 2001): 233–40, accessed November 28, 2011, http://content.healthaffairs.org/content/20/2/233.full .pdf+html.

45. Robert A. Berenson, Thomas Bodenheimer, and Hoangmai H. Pham, "Specialty Service Lines: Salvos in the New Medical Arms Race," *Health Affairs* 25, no. 5 (2006): 338.

46. Devers et al., "Changes in Hospital Competitive Strategy."

47. Debra A. Draper and Paul Ginsburg, *Health Care Costs and Access Challenges Persist: Initial Findings from HSC's 2007 Site Visits*, Center for Studying Health System Change, October 2007, 1, accessed November 23, 2011, http://www.hschange .org/CONTENT/947/947.pdf.

48. McKinsey Global Institute, *Accounting for the Cost of Health Care: A New Look at Why Americans Spend More*, December 2008, 13, accessed November 22, 2011, http:// www.mckinsey.com/mgi/reports/pdfs/healthcare/US_healthcare_Executive _summary.pdf.

49. Paul B. Ginsburg and Joy M. Grossman, "When the Price Isn't Right: How Inadvertent Payment Incentives Drive Medical Care," *Health Affairs* 24, w5.376 (August 9, 2005): 376–84, accessed November 28, 2011, http://content.healthaffairs .org/content/early/2005/08/09/hlthaff.w5.376.short.

50. Ibid., 376.

51. Medicare Payment Advisory Commission (MedPAC), *Report to the Congress: Medicare Payment Policy*, March 2006, 133–36, accessed November 23, 2011, http:// www.medpac.gov/documents/Mar06_EntireReport.pdf.

52. Quoted in John Iglehart, "The Policy Lessons of Health Care Cost Variations: A Roundtable with Bob Berenson, Elliott Fisher, Bob Galvin, and Gail Wilensky," *Health Affairs* blog, June 18, 2009, accessed November 12, 2011, http://

healthaffairs.org/blog/2009/06/18/the-policy-lessons-of-health-care-cost -variations-a-roundtable-with-bob-berenson-elliott-fisher-bob-galvin-and-gail -wilensky/.

53. Lawrence P. Casalino, Kelly J. Devers, and Linda R. Brewster, "Focused Factories? Physician-Owned Specialty Facilities," *Health Affairs* 22, no. 6 (November/December 2003): 56–67, accessed November 28, 2011, http://content.healthaffairs.org /content/22/6/56.full.pdf+html.

54. Draper and Ginsburg, *Health Care Costs*, 1; Casalino et al., "Focused Factories?," 61.

55. Casalino et al., "Focused Factories?," 59.

56. Bruce Hillman and Jeff Goldsmith, "Imaging: The Self-Referral Boom and the Ongoing Search for Effective Policies to Contain It," *Health Affairs* 29, no. 12 (December 2010): 2232.

57. Ibid.

58. Anderson et al., "It's the Prices, Stupid," 102.

59. U.S. Government Accountability Office (GAO), *Medicare Part B Imaging Services: Rapid Spending and Shift to Physician Offices Indicate Need for CMS to Consider Additional Management Practice*, June 2008, 5, accessed November 23, 2011, http:// www.gao.gov/new.items/d08452.pdf.

60. Jonathan Skinner and Elliott S. Fisher, *Reflections on Geographic Variations in U.S. Health Care* (Lebanon, NH: Dartmouth Institute for Health Policy and Clinical Practice, March 31, 2010; updated May 12, 2010); page 2 provides a brief description of the Dartmouth Atlas of Health Care, accessed November 23, 2011, http://www.dartmouthatlas.org/downloads/press/Skinner_Fisher_DA_05_10.pdf.

61. Ibid., 2.

62. Ibid., 9–12.

63. Dartmouth Institute, *An Agenda for Change: Improving Quality and Curbing Health Care Spending—Opportunities for the Congress and the Obama Administration*, Dartmouth Atlas White Paper, December 2008, 2, 5, accessed November 23, 2011, http://tdi.dartmouth.edu/documents/publications/An%20Agenda%20 for%20Change.pdf.

64. Elliott Fisher, David Goodman, Jonathan Skinner, and Kristen Bronner, *Health Care Spending, Quality, and Outcomes*, Dartmouth Atlas Project Topic Brief, February 27, 2009, 2, accessed November 23, 2011, http://www.dartmouthatlas.org /downloads/reports/Spending_Brief_022709.pdf.

65. Brenda Sirovich, Patricia M. Gallagher, David E. Wennberg, and Elliott S. Fisher, "Discretionary Decision Making by Primary Care Physicians and the Cost of U.S. Health Care," *Health Affairs* 27, no. 3 (May/June 2008): 813–23, accessed November 28, 2011, http://content.healthaffairs.org/content/27/3/813.full .pdf+html.

66. Elliott S. Fisher, Julie P. Bynum, and Jonathan S. Skinner, "Slowing the Growth of Health Care Costs—Lessons from Regional Variations," *New England Journal of Medicine* 360, no. 99 (February 26, 2009): 852, accessed November 28, 2011, http://www.dartmouth.edu/~jskinner/documents/Fisher-Bynum-SkinnerFeb 26NEJM.pdf.

67. Skinner and Fisher, *Reflections on Geographic Variations*, 13–14; McKinsey Global Institute, *Accounting for the Cost of Health Care: A New Look*, develops a similar estimate.

68. American Hospital Association, *Trendwatch Chartbook 2011: Trends Affecting Hospitals and Health Systems*, Aggregate Hospital Payment-to-Cost Ratios for Private Payers, Medicare and Medicaid, 1989—2009, table 4.4, Chicago, 2011, accessed November 23, 2011, http://www.aha.org/research/reports/tw/chartbook/2011/table4-4 .pdf. This data is frequently used in describing Medicare's lower payment rates.

69. See the analysis prepared by the Milliman consulting firm for the major insurance companies, Will Fox and John Pickering, *Hospital & Physician Cost Shift: Payment Level Comparison of Medicare, Medicaid, and Commercial Payers,* December 2008, accessed October 5 2011, http://publications.milliman.com/research /health-rr/pdfs/hospital-physician-cost-shift-RR12-01-08.pdf.
70. See Business Roundtable, *Health Care Reform,* 18.
71. James C. Robinson, "Hospitals Respond to Medicare Payment Shortfalls by Both Shifting Costs and Cutting Them, Based on Market Concentration," *Health Affairs* 30, no. 7 (July 2011): 1268.
72. Uwe Reinhardt, "A Modest Proposal on Payment Reform," *Health Affairs* blog, July 24, 2009, accessed November 14, 2011, http://healthaffairs.org /blog/2009/07/24/a-modest-proposal-on-payment-reform.
73. Paul B. Ginsburg, *Wide Variation in Hospital and Physician Payment Rates Evidence of Provider Market Power,* Center for Studying Health System Change, November 2010, accessed November 25, 2011, http://www.hschange.com/CON-TENT/1162/1162.pdf. For an excellent and succinct historical summary, see the 2010 MedPAC report, *Report to the Congress: Medicare Payment Policy,* March 2010, 54, accessed November 23, 2011, http://www.medpac.gov/documents /Mar10_EntireReport.pdf.
74. Robinson, "Hospitals Respond," 1269.
75. MedPAC, *Report to the Congress,* March 2010, 57.
76. MedPAC, *Report to the Congress: Medicare Payment Policy,* March 2011, 31, accessed October 5, 2011, http://www.medpac.gov/documents/mar11_entirereport.pdf.
77. Robinson, "Hospitals Respond," 1267.
78. Health Care for America Now! (HCAN), *Health Insurers Falsely Claim Rising Costs Justify Soaring Premiums,* Washington, DC, March 2010, accessed November 25, 2011, http://hcfan.3cdn.net/578b1f7456962bfa7a_r6m6bhcjn.pdf.
79. HCAN, *New Health Insurance Premium Rules Will Control Costs for Families, Businesses,* July 2010, 6, accessed November 25, 2011, http://hcfan.3cdn.net /415b606e9dc7b1655c_w2m6ibgwg.pdf; HCAN, *HCAN Analysis Shows Health Insurers Pocketed Huge Profits in 2010 Despite Weak Economy,* March 3, 2011, accessed November 25, 2011, http://hcfan.3cdn.net/b61802440a3b0e08a6_gum6bhxaw .pdf.
80. James C. Robinson, "The Commercial Health Insurance Industry in an Era of Eroding Employer Coverage," *Health Affairs* 25, no. 6 (November/December 2006): 1477, accessed November 28, 2011, http://content.healthaffairs.org /content/23/6/11.full.pdf.
81. James C. Robinson, "Consolidation and the Transformation of Competition in Health Insurance," *Health Affairs* 23, no. 6 (November/December 2004): 14–15, accessed November 28, 2011, http://content.healthaffairs.org/content/23/6/11 .full.pdf.
82. AMA, "Study Finds Lack of Competition."
83. Henry J. Kaiser Family Foundation, "Concentration of Health Care Spending in the U.S. Population," Fast Facts, 2008, accessed November 23, 2011, http:// facts.kff.org/chart.aspx?ch=1344.
84. Bruce C. Vladeck and Thomas Rice, "Market Failure and the Failure of Discourse," *Health Affairs* 28, no. 5 (September/October 2009): 1308.
85. McKinsey Global Institute, *Accounting for the Cost of Health Care,* 70, 72.
86. Robert Zirkelbach, quoted in Robert Pear, "Proposal Would Aid Deciphering of Benefits," *New York Times,* August 18, 2011, accessed November 28, 2011, http:// www.nytimes.com/2011/08/18/us/18insure.html.

87. Julie Ann Sakowski, James G. Kahn, Richard G. Kronick, Jeffrey M. Newman, and Harold S. Luft, "Peering into the Black Box: Billing and Insurance Activities in a Medical Group," *Health Affairs* web exclusive 28, no. 4 (May 14, 2009): w544.
88. Steffie Woolhandler, Terry Campbell, and David U. Himmelstein, "Health Care Administration in the United States and Canada: Micromanagement, Macro Costs," *International Journal of Health Services* 34, no. 1 (2004): 65–78.
89. Congressional Budget Office, "Long-Term Analysis of a Budget Proposal by Chairman Ryan," Washington, DC, April 5, 2011, 21, accessed November 25, 2011, http://www.cbo.gov/ftpdocs/121xx/doc12128/04-05-Ryan_Letter.pdf; regarding Medicaid cost-effectiveness, see Center on Budget and Policy Priorities, *Expanding Medicaid a Less Costly Way to Cover More Low-Income Uninsured Than Expanding Private Insurance*, Washington, DC, June 26, 2008, accessed November 25, 2011, http://www.cbpp.org/files/6-26-08health.pdf.
90. Centers for Medicare and Medicaid Services, *National Health Expenditure Data*, table 13; see also Christina Boccuti and Marilyn Moon, "Comparing Medicare and Private Insurers: Growth Rates in Spending over Three Decades," *Health Affairs* 22, no. 2 (March/April 2003): 230–237, accessed November 28, 2011, http://content.healthaffairs.org/content/22/2/230.full.pdf.
91. Karen Davis, Stuart Guterman, and Michelle M. Doty, "Meeting Enrollees' Needs: How Do Medicare and Employer Coverage Stack Up?," *Health Affairs* web exclusive, May 12, 2009, w521–w532, accessed November 28, 2011, http://www.commonwealthfund.org/Publications/In-the-Literature/2009/May/Meeting-Enrollees-Needs.aspx.
92. Sara R. Collins, Rachel Nuzum, Sheila D. Rustgi, Stephanie Mika, Cathy Schoen, and Karen Davis, *How Health Care Reform Can Lower the Costs of Insurance Administration* (New York: Commonwealth Fund, July 2009), 2, 4, accessed November 25, 2011, http://www.commonwealthfund.org/~/media/Files/Publications/Issue%20Brief/2009/Jul/Admin%20Costs/1299_Collins_how_hlt_care_reform_can_lower_costs_ins_admin_v2.pdf.
93. See, for example, Randall Brown, *Strategies for Reining in Medicare Spending through Delivery System Reforms: Assessing the Evidence and Opportunities*, Henry J. Kaiser Family Foundation, September 2009, accessed November 25, 2011, http://www.kff.org/medicare/upload/7984.pdf.
94. MedPAC, *Report to the Congress*, 2011, 12.
95. Harold Pollack, "Point-Counterpoint: Introduction," *Journal of Health Politics, Policy and Law* 36, no. 4 (August 2011): 774.
96. Greg Critser, *Generation Rx: How Prescription Drugs Are Altering American Lives, Minds, and Bodies* (Boston: Houghton Mifflin, 2005), 32–35, 53.
97. Ibid.; Maggie Mahar, *Money-Driven Medicine* (New York: Collins, 2006), 293–320.
98. Hillman and Goldsmith, "Imaging," 2232.
99. Kaiser Family Foundation, *Employer Health Benefits*, 1.
100. Ibid., 5; Paul Fronstin, *Sources of Health Insurance and Characteristics of the Uninsured: Analysis of the March 2011 Current Population Survey*, no. 362 (Washington, DC: Employee Benefits Research Institute, September 2011), 1, accessed November 26, 2011, http://www.ebri.org/pdf/briefspdf/EBRI_IB_09-2011_No362_Uninsured1.pdf.
101. Kaiser Family Foundation, *Employer Health Benefits*, 4.
102. Ibid., 5.
103. Ibid., 4.
104. David I. Auerbach and Arthur L. Kellerman, "A Decade of Health Care Cost

Growth Has Wiped Out Real Income Gains for an Average US Family," *Health Affairs* 30, no. 9 (September 2011): 1630–36.

105. Cathy Schoen, Michelle M. Doty, Ruth H. Robertson, and Sara R. Collins, "Affordable Care Act Reforms Could Reduce the Number of Underinsured US Adults by 70 Percent," *Health Affairs* 30, no. 9 (September 2011): 1765–67.

106. See Commonwealth Fund Commission, *Why Not the Best?*, 9–17.

107. Jonathan Oberlander, "Long Time Coming: Why Health Reform Finally Passed," *Health Affairs* 29, no. 6 (June 2010): 1112–16.

108. Relman, *Second Opinion*, 93–110.

109. Paul Ryan, *A Roadmap for America's Future*, version 2.0, House Budget Committee, January 2010, 27–30, accessed November 26, 2011, http://www.roadmap. republicans.budget.house.gov/UploadedFiles/Roadmap2Final2.pdf.

110. Ibid., 43; John McCain, Press Release—"Call to Action" on Health Care Reform, April 29, 2008, accessed November 26, 2011, the American Presidency Project at University of California–Santa Barbara, http://www.presidency.ucsb.edu/ws /index.php?pid=91532#axzz1eqy47HrA.

111. House Republicans, *Pledge to America*, 27.

112. House Committee on the Budget, "Path to Prosperity," 47.

113. Kenneth Arrow, "Uncertainty and the Welfare Economics of Medical Care," *American Economic Review* 53, no. 5 (1963): 941–73, cited and summarized in Relman, *Second Opinion*, 22–23.

114. Uwe E. Reinhardt, "The Pricing of U.S. Hospital Services: Chaos behind a Veil of Secrecy," *Health Affairs* 25, no. 1 (January–February 2006): 68, accessed November 28, 2011, http://ahca.myflorida.com/schs/pdf/pricingofhospitalservices. pdf.

115. Michelle M. Doty, Sara R. Collins, Jennifer L. Nicholson, and Sheila D. Rustgi, *Failure to Protect: Why the Individual Insurance Market Is Not a Viable Option for Most US Families* (New York: Commonwealth Fund, July 21, 2009), 2, accessed November 27, 2011, http://www.commonwealthfund.org/Publications/Issue -Briefs/2009/Jul/Failure-to-Protect.aspx.

116. Kaiser Family Foundation, "Concentration of Health Care Spending."

117. Jonathan Oberlander and Joseph White, "Public Attitudes Aren't the Problem, Prices Are," *Health Affairs* 28, no. 5 (September/October 2009): 1287.

118. Amelia M. Haviland, Neeraj Sood, Roland McDevitt, and M. Susan Marquis, "How Do Consumer-Directed Health Plans Affect Vulnerable Populations?," *Forum for Health Economics & Policy* 14, no. 2 (2011): 18; Amal N. Trivedi, Husein Moloo, and Vincent Mohr, "Increased Ambulatory Care Copayments and Hospitalizations among the Elderly," *New England Journal of Medicine* 362, no. 4 (January 28, 2010): 320–28, accessed November 26, 2011, http://www.nejm.org/doi /full/10.1056/NEJMsa0904533.

119. The most important sources of information used in this summary of the Affordable Care Act are the text of the legislation and the staff section-by-section summaries, at http://dpc.senate.gov/dpcissue-sen_health_care_bill.cfm; the analyses by the Commonwealth Fund, at http://www.commonwealthfund.org/Health - Reform/Health-Reform-Resource.aspx; and the Henry J. Kaiser Family Foundation analyses, at http://healthreform.kff.org; all accessed November 26, 2011.

120. Individuals earning more than $200,000 per year and couples earning more than $250,000 per year.

121. Congressional Budget Office, Washington, DC, March 31, 2011, *CBO's Analysis of the Major Health Care Legislation Enacted in March 2010*, 17, accessed November 11,

2011, http://www.cbo.gov/ftpdocs/121xx/doc12119/03-30-HealthCareLegisla tion.pdf.

122. JoAnn Volk and Sabrina Corlette, *The Role of Exchanges in Quality Improvement: An Analysis of the Options*, Georgetown University, Health Policy Institute, Washington, DC, September 28, 2011, accessed November 26, 2011, http://www.rwjf .org/files/research/72851qigeorgetownexchange20110928.pdf.

123. CBO, *CBO's Analysis of the Major Health Care Legislation*, 3–4.

124. Lewin Group, *The Health Care for All California Act: Cost and Economic Impacts Analysis*, Prepared for Health Care for All Education Fund, January 19, 2006, ix.

125. Karen Davis, Stuart Guterman, Sara R. Collins, Kristof Stremikis, Sheila Rustgi, and Rachel Nuzum, *Starting on the Path to a High Performance Health System: Analysis of Health System Reform Provisions of Reform Bills in the House of Representatives and Senate* (New York: Commonwealth Fund, December 2009, updated January 7, 2010), 34, accessed November 22, 2011, http://www.commonwealthfund.org /Publications/Fund-Reports/2009/Nov/Starting-on-the-Path-to-a-High-Per formance-Health-System.aspx?page=all.

126. Lewin Group, *Cost Impact Analysis for the "Health Care for America" Proposal*, Final Report, Prepared for the Economic Policy Institute, February 15, 2008, accessed November 27, 2011, http://www.sharedprosperity.org/hcfa/lewin.pdf.

127. Jane Sasseen and Catherine Arnst, "Why Business Fears the Public Option," *Bloomberg Businessweek*, October 1, 2009, accessed November 26, 2011, http:// www.businessweek.com/magazine/content/09_41/b4150026723556.htm.

128. Vladeck and Rice, "Market Failure," 1312–13.

129. Uwe E. Reinhardt, "The Many Different Prices Paid to Providers and the Flawed Theory of Cost Shifting: Is It Time for a More Rational All-Payer System?," *Health Affairs* 30, no. 11 (November 2011): 2125–33.

130. Robert Murray, "Setting Hospital Rates to Control Costs and Boost Quality: The Maryland Experience," *Health Affairs* 23, no. 5 (September/October 2009): 1395–1405.

131. Reinhardt, "Many Different Prices," 2125; Vladeck and Rice, "Market Failure," 1312; Peter Lee, Pacific Business Group on Health (PBGH), Testimony, House Committee on Ways and Means, Hearing on Health Reform in the 21st Century: Proposals to Reform the Health System, June 24, 2011, accessed November 26, 2011, http://democrats.waysandmeans.house.gov/Hearings/Testimony .aspx?TID=2198; Business Roundtable, *Health Care Reform*, 8.

132. Vermont Act 48, an act related to a universal and unified health system, approved May 26, 2011, accessed November 26, 2011, http://www.leg.state.vt.us /docs/2012/Acts/ACT048.pdf.

133. Vermont Legislative Joint Fiscal Office and the Department of Banking, Insurance, Securities and Health Care Administration, *Costs of Vermont's Health Care System: Comparison of Baseline and Reformed System, Final Report*, November 1, 2011, 3, accessed November 26, 2011, http://leg.state.vt.us/jfo/healthcare/November %20Report%20-%20Final.pdf.

134. Bruce Josten, "Repeal the Job-Killing Employer Mandate," *ChamberPost*, September 14, 2011, accessed September 20, 2011, http://www.chamberpost.com /2011/09/repeal-the-job-killing-employer-mandate/.

135. Tom Donohue, "The Right Way to Reduce Health Care Costs," *ChamberPost*, July 12, 2011, accessed November 27, 2011, http://www.chamberpost.com/2011/07 /the-right-way-to-reduce-health-care-costs.

136. Lee, Testimony, 4.

137. Ibid.; Business Roundtable, *Health Care Reform*, 8.
138. Helen Darling, National Business Group on Health, "Health Care Reform: Perspectives from Large Employers," *Health Affairs* 29, no. 6 (June 2010): 1221–24; Business Roundtable, *Health Care Reform*, 8, 14.
139. Business Roundtable, *Health Care Reform*, 19, 18.
140. Dartmouth Institute, *Agenda for Change*, 5.
141. Vladeck and Rice, "Market Failure," 1314.
142. Jane Mayer, "Covert Operations," *New Yorker*, August 30, 2010, accessed November 26, 2011, http://www.newyorker.com/reporting/2010/08/30/100830fa _fact_mayer; Jeremy W. Peters, "Television Attack Ads Aim at Obama Early and Often," *New York Times*, November 27, 2011, accessed November 27, 2011, http://www.nytimes.com/2011/11/27/us/politics/television-attack-ads-aim -at-obama-early-and-often.html?scp=2&sq=Jeremy%20Peters&st=cse.

Chapter 9. Social Responsibility, Healthcare Equity, and Workforce Planning

1. Martin Luther King Jr., Presentation at the Second National Convention of the Medical Committee for Human Rights, Chicago, March 25, 1966.
2. U.S. Department of Health and Human Services, Office of Minority Health, National Partnership for Action to End Health Disparities, accessed November 16, 2011, http://minorityhealth.hhs.gov/npa/.
3. Fast Facts about Kaiser Permanente, accessed, November 9, 2011, http://xnet.kp .org/newscenter/aboutkp/fastfacts.html.
4. Henry J. Kaiser Family Foundation, "The Uninsured: A Primer," December 2010, 5–9.
5. Institute for the Future and Kaiser Permanente Northern California Region, "Mastering Cultural Agility, Future Impacts of Diversity on Health and Health Care," Oakland, CA, 2011.
6. Kaiser Permanente National Diversity Council, "A Provider's Handbook on Culturally Competent Care," Oakland, CA, 1996, 1.
7. "Beyond Language: The Challenge of Delivering Culturally Competent Care," LMP partnership stories-videos, January 7, 2011, accessed November 16, 2011, http:// www.lmpartnership.org/stories-videos/beyond-language-challenge-delivering -culturally-competent-care.
8. Kaiser Permanente National Diversity Council, "Provider's Handbook on Culturally Competent Care: Latino Population," Oakland, CA, 1996.
9. DiversityInc, "DiversityInc Top 50 Companies for Diversity: #1 Kaiser Permanente," accessed November 16, 2011, http://diversityinc.com/the-2011-diversity inc-top-50/no-1-kaiser-permanente/.
10. Bob Redlo and Ron Elsdon, "Creating Value with Workforce Planning and Development," in *Building Workforce Strength: Creating Value through Workforce and Career Development*, ed. Ron Elsdon (Santa Barbara, CA: Praeger, 2010), 63.
11. Kaiser Permanente Human Resource Information System, 2011 Demographic Data, Oakland, CA.
12. Kaiser Family Foundation, "The Uninsured."
13. George Halvorson, Kaiser Permanente Diversity Overview, Message from Leadership, internal website.
14. American Hospital Association, "Issue Paper: Workforce," March 29, 2011, accessed November 9, 2011, http://www.aha.org/content/11/11-Workforce.pdf.
15. Brian D. Smedley, Adrienne Stith Butler, and Lonnie R. Bristow, eds., Institute of Medicine, Committee on Institutional and Policy-Level Strategies for Increas-

ing the Diversity of the U.S. Healthcare Workforce, "In the Nation's Compelling Interest: Ensuring Diversity in the Health Care Workforce" (Washington, DC: National Academy Press, 2004), 31–33.

16. Ibid.
17. Gary Orfield, Daniel Losen, and Johanna Wald, "Losing Our Future: How Minority Youth Are Being Left Behind by the Graduation Rate Crisis," February 25, 2004, accessed November 16, 2011, http://www.urban.org/UploadedPDF/410936_LosingOurFuture.pdf.
18. Ibid.
19. The American Registry of Radiologic Technologists (ARRT) Associate Degree Requirements FAQs, accessed November 7, 2011, www.arrt.org/FAQ/Associate-Degree-Requirement.
20. Richard Oliver, dean of the School of Health Professions, University of Missouri, at the HRSA/IOM Workshop on Allied Health Workforce Services, Washington, DC, May 9–10, 2011.
21. Colleen Moore and Nancy Shulock, "Divided We Fail: Improving Completion and Closing Racial Gaps in California's Community Colleges," Institute for Higher Education Leadership and Policy, California State University, Sacramento, October 2010.
22. Victoria Choitz, *Strategies for Success* (Boston: Jobs for the Future, April 2006), accessed December 1, 2011, http://registration.jff.org/~jff/Documents/StratSucc ML2004.pdf.
23. Laura Long, unpublished presentations, allied health presentations to high school students in California's Central Valley, 2010–2011.
24. Elsdon, *Building Workforce Strength*, chaps. 4 and 9.

Chapter 10. Labor-Management Partnerships: A Collaborative Path toward Improved Business Results and Employee Satisfaction

1. Steven Greenhouse, "Union Membership in U.S. Fell to a 70-Year Low Last Year," *New York Times*, January 21, 2011, accessed November 12, 2011, http://www.nytimes.com/2011/01/22/business/22union.html.
2. Mary DeWolf, "We the People: Workers Need Reason to Celebrate," Opinion, *Crossville Chronicle*, September 6, 2011, accessed November 12, 2011, http://crossville-chronicle.com/opinion/x1095937837/WE-THE-PEOPLE-Workers -need-reason-to-celebrate.
3. Bureau of Economic Analysis, U.S. Department of Commerce, "Current-Dollar and 'Real' Gross Domestic Product," Washington, DC, accessed October 1, 2011, www.bea.gov/national/xls/gdplev.xls.
4. Gerald Friedman, "Labor Unions in the United States," Economic History Association, February 1, 2010, accessed November 12, 2011, http://eh.net/encyclopedia /article/friedman.unions.us.
5. Hendrik Hertzberg, "Union Blues," *New Yorker Magazine*, March 7, 2011, accessed November 12, 2011, http://www.newyorker.com/talk/comment/2011 /03/07/110307taco_talk_hertzberg.
6. Richard McCormack, ed., *Manufacturing a Better Future for America* (Washington, DC: The Alliance for American Manufacturing, 2009).
7. Taft-Hartley Act, 1947, accessed October 1, 2011, http://vi.uh.edu/pages/ buzzmat/tafthartley.html.
8. Richard S. Belous, "How Human Resource Systems Adjust to the Shift toward Contingent Workers," *Monthly Labor Review*, March 1989, 7–12.

9.   Thomas A. Kochan, Adrienne E. Eaton, Robert B. McKersie, and Paul S. Adler, *Healing Together: The Labor-Management Partnership at Kaiser Permanente* (Ithaca, NY: Cornell University Press, 2009), 18.

10. Harley Shaiken, "State of the Unions," *Los Angeles Times*, February 17, 2007, accessed November 12, 2011, http://articles.latimes.com/2007/feb/17/opinion/oe-shaiken17.

11. Steven Greenhouse, "Most U.S. Union Workers Are Now Working for the Government, New Data Shows," *New York Times*, January 23, 2010, accessed November 12, 2011, http://www.nytimes.com/2010/01/23/business/23labor.html. According to the labor bureau, 7.2 percent of private-sector workers were union members in 2009, down from 7.6 percent the previous year. That, labor historians said, was the lowest percentage of private-sector workers in unions since 1900. Among government workers, union membership grew to 37.4 percent in 2009, from 36.8 percent in 2008.

12. Ezra Klein, "Do We Still Need Unions? Yes," *Newsweek*, February 27, 2011, accessed November 12, 2011, http://www.thedailybeast.com/newsweek/2011/02/27/do-we-still-need-unions-yes.html.

13. Hertzberg, "Union Blues."

14. "Since the end of World War II, real wages for production workers have risen by more than half. Most of this growth occurred, however, in the 1950s and 1960s. After reaching a peak in 1973, real hourly earnings for production workers either fell or stagnated for two decades." Alexis M. Herman, U.S. Department of Labor Report, "Future Work: Trends and Challenges for Work in the 21st Century," 1999, accessed November 12, 2011, http://digitalcommons.ilr.cornell.edu/key_workplace/65/.

15. Robert Reich, "A Good Fight," robertreich.org, September 19, 2011, accessed November 12, 2011, http://robertreich.org/post/10413056931.

16. DeWolf, "We the People."

17. Robert B. Reich, "The Limping Middle Class," *New York Times*, September 3, 2011, accessed November 12, 2011, http://www.nytimes.com/2011/09/04/opinion/sunday/jobs-will-follow-a-strengthening-of-the-middle-class.html?pagewanted=all.

18. Carmen DeNavas-Walt, Bernadette D. Proctor, and Jessica C. Smith, U.S. Census Bureau Current Population Reports, P60-243, *Income, Poverty, and Health Insurance Coverage in the United States: 2011* (Washington, DC: U.S. Government Printing Office, 2012), 5.

19. Jared Bernstein, "The Lost Decade for the Middle Class," *Christian Science Monitor*, September 15, 2011, accessed October 26, 2011, http://www.csmonitor.com/Business/On-the-Economy/2011/0915/The-lost-decade-for-the-middle-class.

20. Paul Krugman, "Wisconsin Power Play," *New York Times*, February, 20, 2011, accessed November 12, 2011, http://www.nytimes.com/2011/02/21/opinion/21krugman.html.

21. Steven Greenhouse, "A Challenge for Unions in Public Opinion," *New York Times*, Economix, September 2, 2011, accessed November 12, 2011, http://economix.blogs.nytimes.com/2011/09/02/a-challenge-for-unions-in-public-opinion/.

22. Patrick O'Conner, "Strong Support for Bargaining Rights," *Wall Street Journal Online*, accessed September 23, 2011, http://blogs.wsj.com/washwire/2011/03/02/wsjnbc-poll-strong-support-for-bargaining-rights/.

23. Lawrence Mishel and Matthew Walters, "How Unions Help All Workers," Economic Policy Institute Briefing Paper (Washington, DC: Economic Policy Insti-

tute, August 2003). In a separate study, union wages in the private sector in the year 2006 were about 19 percent higher than those in comparable nonunion firms. Barry T. Hirsch, "Sluggish Institutions in a Dynamic World: Can Unions and Industrial Competition Coexist?" Discussion Paper no. 2930 (Bonn: Institute for the Study of Labor, July 2007).

24. David Madland and Karla Walter, "Unions Are Good for the American Economy," Center for American Progress Action Fund, February 18, 2009, accessed November 12, 2011, http://www.americanprogressaction.org/issues/2009/02/efca_factsheets.html.

25. Kochan et al., *Healing Together*, 32–33, referencing worker views as reported by Richard B. Freeman and Joel Rogers.

26. Art Levine, "GOP Blocks Obama's Labor Nominee, Pushes Big Lie on 'Card Check,'" *Huffington Post*, January 24, 2009, accessed November 12, 2011, http://www.huffingtonpost.com/art-levine/gop-blocks-obamas-labor-n_b_160539.html.

27. Jim Newton, "Newton: Labor on the Wane? Not in L.A.," *Los Angeles Times*, September 5, 2011, accessed November 12, 2011, http://www.latimes.com/news/opinion/commentary/la-oe-newton-column-labor-20110905,0,244942.column.

28. Michael R. Bloomberg, "Limit Pay, Not Unions," *New York Times*, February 27, 2011, accessed November 14, 2011, http://www.nytimes.com/2011/02/28/opinion/28mayor.html.

29. Kochan et al., *Healing Together*, 22.

30. Peter diCicco, Coalition of Kaiser Permanente Unions, private communication, provided by Richard Parker, Kaiser Permanente, October 3, 2011.

31. Richard B. Freeman and Joel Rogers, *What Workers Want*, Russell Sage Foundation (Ithaca, NY: Cornell University Press, 1999), 33.

32. Daniel P. O'Meara and Adam J. Taliaferro, "Six Steps to an Effective Labor Management Partnership," Report for Corporate Counsel, August 19, 2009, accessed November 12, 2011, http://www.law.com/jsp/cc/PubArticleCC.jsp?id=1202433126509.

33. Kochan et al., *Healing Together*, 19–22.

34. Teri Ann Allen, *SCPMG . . . The First Fifty Years: History of the Southern California Permanente Medical Group, 1953–2003* (Pasadena, CA: SCPMG, 2003).

35. Rickey Hendricks, *A National Model for Health Care: The History of Kaiser Permanente* (New Brunswick, NJ: Rutgers University Press, 1993), 35.

36. Kochan et al., *Healing Together*, 33–35.

37. Ibid., 34.

38. Ibid., 37.

39. From the LMP website (http://www.lmpartnership.org/home): "Interest-based problem solving involves participants working together to reach agreement by sharing information and remaining creative and flexible, instead of taking adversarial positions. Consensus decision making is a form of group decision making. All involved discuss the issues to be decided so the group benefits from the knowledge and experience of all members. Consensus occurs when every member of the group supports the decision."

40. Richard Parker, UBT practice leader, Southern California KP Labor Management Partnership, private communication, October 27, 2011.

41. Daniel Hong, senior consultant at the labor-management partnership in KP Southern California, compiled employee survey results into a report for the LMP Council. The 2011 results point to employees identifying LMP UBTs as

helping to improve working conditions and organizational performance and as encouraging people to speak up about problems. Data also suggest a correlation between high-performing UBTs and lower workplace injury rates.

42. Ben Chu, president, Kaiser Foundation Health Plan and Hospitals, Southern California, 2010, accessed November 17, 2011, http://www.bargaining2010.org/aboutlmp.

43. Oliver Goldsmith, interview regarding the KP LMP, *Permanente Journal*, Permanente Journal dialogue, March 19, 2001.

44. Kochan et al., *Healing Together*, 219.

45. Marick F. Masters, Christina Sickles Merchant, and Robert Tobias, "Engaging Federal Employees through Their Union Representatives to Improve Agency Performance," Wayne State University, February 2, 2010, accessed November 12, 2011, http://www.govexec.com/pdfs/021010ar1.pdf.

46. Kochan et al., *Healing Together*, 233.

47. Barbara Martinez, "Teacher Seniority Rules Challenged," *Wall Street Journal*, February 19, 2010, accessed November 12, 2011, http://online.wsj.com/article/SB10001424052748703315004575073561669221720.html.

48. Abigail Paris, "Partnership in Education: How Labor-Management Collaboration Is Transforming Public Schools" (Washington, DC: America Rights at Work Education Fund, May 2011), accessed November 12, 2011, http://www.americanrightsatwork.org/dmdocuments/ARAWReports/partnershipsineducation_final.pdf.

Chapter 11. Financial Institutions and Social Responsibility

1. ThinkExist.com, accessed October 19, 2011, http://thinkexist.com/quotation/capitalism-requires-a-structure-and-value-system/1173123.html.

2. National Commission on the Causes of the Financial and Economic Crisis in the United States, "The Financial Crisis Inquiry Report," January 2011, xv–xxvii.

3. Ibid.

4. Investopedia, "The Greatest Investors: Ralph Wanger," accessed October 19, 2011, http://www.investopedia.com/university/greatest/ralphwanger.asp#axzz1bHTUQYAS.

5. Annamaria Lusardi and Olivia S. Mitchell, "Financial Literacy and Retirement Planning in the United States," February 1, 2011, accessed October 24, 2011, http://www.financialliteracyfocus.org/files/FLatDocs/Paper_USdata.pdf, 5.

6. U.S. Government Accountability Office, "Defined Benefit Pensions: Survey Results of the Nation's Largest Private Defined Benefit Plan Sponsors," Washington, DC, March 2009, accessed August 18, 2012, http://www.gao.gov/assets/290/288087.pdf; U.S. Department of Labor, U.S. Bureau of Labor Statistics, "National Compensation Survey: Employee Benefits in the United States, March 2008," Washington, DC, September 2008, accessed August 18, 2012, http://www.bls.gov/ncs/ebs/benefits/2008/ebbl0041.pdf.

7. Consumer Search, March 2011, accessed September 15, 2011, http://www.consumersearch.com/online-brokers.

8. Adam Smith, *The Wealth of Nations* (University Park: Pennsylvania State University, 2005), 606–7.

9. James J. Green, "New Institute to Educate, Advocate on Fiduciary Standard," AdvisorOne, August 23, 2011, accessed October 1, 2011, http://www.advisorone.com/2011/08/23/new-institute-to-educate-advocate-on-fiduciary-sta.

10. Roy Diliberto, "A Good Business Model," *Financial Advisor* magazine, February 2011, 52.

11. Bob Clark, "New Institute for Fiduciary Standard Elevates the Conversation," AdvisorOne, August 23, 2011, accessed October 3, 2011, http://www.advisorone .com/2011/08/23/new-institute-for-fiduciary-standard-elevates-the?page=2.

12. John Turner and Sophie Korczyk, "Pension Participant Knowledge about Plan Fees, Data Digest" (Washington, DC: AARP Public Policy Institute, November 2004).

13. Special Committee on Aging, U.S. Senate, "401(k) Plans: Several Factors Can Diminish Retirement Savings, but Automatic Enrollment Shows Promise for Increasing Participation and Savings" (Washington, DC: U.S. Government Accountability Office, October 28, 2009).

14. Jesse Livermore, *How to Trade in Stocks* (New York: Duell, Sloan and Pierce, 1940).

15. Charles MacKay, *Extraordinary Popular Delusions and the Madness of Crowds* (New York: Broadway, 1995).

16. Kevin McCoy, "Pursuer of Madoff Blew a Whistle for Nine Years," *USA Today*, February 2, 2009, accessed December 2, 2011, http://www.usatoday.com/money /markets/2009-02-12-markopolos-madoff-ponzi_N.htm.

17. Robert Chew, "A Madoff Whistle-Blower Tells His Story," *Time Business*, February 4, 2009, accessed October 4, 2011, http://www.time.com/time/business /article/0,8599,1877181,00.html.

18. *Business Dictionary*, accessed October 4, 2011, http://www.businessdictionary .com/definition/due-diligence.html.

19. William K. Rasbaum and Diana B. Henriques, "Accountant for Madoff Is Arrested and Charged with Securities Fraud," *New York Times*, March 18, 2009, accessed December 2, 2011, http://www.nytimes.com/2009/03/19/business/19madoff. html.

20. Liz Skinner, "Stifel Defrauded School Districts: SEC," *Investment News*, August 10, 2011, accessed August 17, 2012, http://www.investmentnews.com/article /20110810/FREE/110819989

21. White Law Group, "Stifel Nicolaus Investigated by SEC over Risky Investments, CDOs," August 10, 2011, accessed September 29, 2011, from the White Law Group, http://www.whitesecuritieslaw.com/2011/08/10/stifel-nicolaus-invest igated-by-sec-over-risky-investments-cdos/.

22. Ibid.

23. Steve Goldstein, "Citi to Pay $285 Million over SEC Charges," *Market Watch*, accessed October 18, 2011, http://www.marketwatch.com/story/citi-to-pay-285 -million-over-sec-charges-2011-10-19?link=MW_home_latest_news.

24. Jess Cornaggia, Kimberly Rodgers Cornaggia, and John Hund, "Credit Ratings across Asset Classes: A A?," SSRN, August 31, 2011, available at http://ssrn.com /abstract=1909091.

25. Richard Esposito, "Raj Rajaratnam Indicted for Insider Trading," *ABC News*, December, 15, 2009, accessed December 2, 2011, http://abcnews.go.com/Blotter /raj-rajaratnam-indicted-insider-trading/story?id=9346142.

26. Nathaniel Popper and Walter Hamilton, "Raj Rajaratnam Sentenced to 11 Years for Insider Trading," *Los Angeles Times*, October 14, 2011, accessed October 20, 2011, http://articles.latimes.com/2011/oct/14/business/la-fi-raj-prison -20111014.

27. Patricia Hurtado, David Glovin, and Bob Van Voris, "Rajaratnam Odds Seen as Slim for Overturning Conviction," *Bloomberg News*, May 12, 2011, accessed October 3, 2011, http://www.bloomberg.com/news/2011-05-12/galleon-s-rajaratnam -may-face-uphill-battle-to-overturn-verdict-on-appeal.html.

28. Investopedia, "The Greatest Investors: Thomas Rowe Price, Jr.," accessed October

19, 2011, http://www.investopedia.com/university/greatest/thomasroweprice
.asp#axzz1bHTUQYAS.

29. Monika Mitchell, "John Bogle: The Conscience of Capitalism," *Good Business International, Inc.*, accessed October 18, 2011, http://good-b.com/?p=5481.

30. "Financial Planning Association of MA Member Rick Fingerman Named National Pro Bono Planner of the Year," citybizlist, November 14, 2011, accessed December 3, 2011, http://boston.citybizlist.com/7/2011/11/14 /Financial-Planning-Association-of-MA-member-Rick-Fingerman-named -national-Pro-Bono-Planner-of-the-Year.aspx.

31. Kristina Zucchi, "Derivatives 101," accessed September 28, 2011, from Investopedia, http://www.investopedia.com/articles/optioninvestor/10/derivatives-101 .asp#axzz1ZOPAjdzg.

32. Riverside Risk Advisors, "Derivatives Advisory Firm Offers Pro-Bono Services for Non-Profits," January 6, 2011, accessed September 25, 2011, http://riverside advisors.com/pressrelease010611.pdf.

33. Clark, "New Institute for Fiduciary Standard."

34. Carol J. Loomis, *CNN Money/Fortune Magazine*, "Warren Buffet Gives Away His Fortune," June 25, 2006, accessed October 25, 2011, http://money.cnn. com/2006/06/25/magazines/fortune/charity1.fortune/.

35. *Philanthropy News Digest*, "Top Philanthropists Attach Ambitious Goals to Mega-Gifts," November 20, 2006, accessed December 2, 2011, http://foundationcenter .org/pnd/news/story.jhtml?id=162500029.

36. Robert Langreth and Alex Nussbaum, "Mogul Using $100 Million in Race to Cure Daughter Lures Novartis," *Bloomberg Markets Magazine*, accessed December 2, 2011, http://www.bloomberg.com/news/2011-09-07/mogul-using-own-100 -million-in-race-to-cure-daughter-prompts-novartis-aid.html.

37. G. Bresiger, "Why Hedge Funds Care," *Traders Magazine*, May 2011, 7.

38. Carol J. Loomis, *CNN Money/Fortune*, "Charity on a Grand Scale," June 20, 2011, accessed October 22, 2011, http://features.blogs.fortune.cnn.com/2011/06/20 /charity-on-a-grand-scale/.

39. Investopedia, "The Greatest Investors: Geroge Soros," accessed October 25, 2011, http://www.investopedia.com/university/greatest/georgesoros.asp#axzz 1bHTUQYAS.

40. Securities and Exchange Commission (SEC), "The Investor's Advocate: How the SEC Protects Investors, Maintains Market Integrity, and Facilitates Capital Formation," Washington, DC, July 25, 2011, accessed October 1, 2011, http://www.sec .gov/about/whatwedo.shtml#create.

41. Ibid.

42. SEC, "SEC Enforcement Actions," Washington, DC, accessed October 22, 2011, http://www.sec.gov/spotlight/enf-actions-fc.shtml.

43. Jesse Eisinger and Jake Bernstein, "From Dodd-Frank to Dud: How Financial Reform May Be Going Wrong," Pro Publica, June 3, 2011, accessed October 4, 2011, http://www.propublica.org/article/from-dodd-frank-to-dud.

44. ThinkExist.com, accessed October 19, 2011, http://thinkexist.com/quotes /john_m._richardson,_jr./.

45. Verena Dobnik, "Wall Street Protesters: We're in for the Long Haul," *Business Week*, October 2, 2011, accessed October 22, 2011, http://www.businessweek .com/ap/financialnews/D9Q4CNR81.htm.

46. Livermore, *How to Trade in Stocks.*

47. John F. Kennedy, *The Uncommon Wisdom of JFK: A Portrait in His Own Words*, ed. Bill Adler and Tom Folsom (New York: Rugged Land, 2003).
48. Clark, "New Institute for Fiduciary Standard."

Concluding Thoughts

1. Dominique Browning, "Losing It," *New York Times*, March 25, 2010, accessed January 17, 2011, http://www.nytimes.com/2010/03/28/magazine/28fasttrack-t .html.
2. William Sloane Coffin, *Credo* (Louisville, KY: Westminster John Knox Press, 2004), 47.
3. Ibid., 53.
4. Ron Elsdon, *Affiliation in the Workplace: Value Creation in the New Organization* (Westport, CT: Praeger, 2003), 21; describes questions posed by Lynn Rhodes.
5. Floyd Norris, "For Business, Golden Days; for Workers, the Dross," *New York Times*, November 25, 2011, accessed December 2, 2011, http://www.nytimes. com/2011/11/26/business/for-companies-the-good-old-days-are-now.html.
6. Heidi Shierholz, "Labor Force Smaller than before Recession Started" (Washington, DC: Economic Policy Institute, January 7, 2011), accessed January 17, 2011, http://www.epi.org/publications/entry/labor_force_smaller_than_before _recession_started1/.
7. Franklin Delano Roosevelt, "State of the Union Message to Congress," accessed January 17, 2011, http://www.fdrlibrary.marist.edu/archives/address_text.html.
8. Richard Wilkinson and Kate Pickett, *The Spirit Level: Why Greater Equality Makes Societies Stronger* (New York: Bloomsbury Press, 2009); chap. 3 focuses on the reasons inequality affects us.
9. Ibid., 177.
10. Andrew Fieldhouse and Ethan Pollack, "Tenth Anniversary of the Bush-Era Tax Cuts," Policy Memorandum no. 184 (Washington, DC: Economic Policy Institute, June 1, 2011), accessed June 3, 2011, http://www.epi.org/page/-/EPI _PolicyMemorandum_184.pdf.
11. U.S. Census Bureau, "Gini Ratios for Families, by Race and Hispanic Origin of Householder [XLS]" (Washington, DC), accessed August 19, 2012, http://www .census.gov/hhes/www/income/data/historical/inequality/index.html.
12. Paula Braveman, "Social Conditions, Health Equity, and Human Rights," *Health and Human Rights* 12, no. 2 (2010), accessed February 8, 2011, http://www .hhrjournal.org/index.php/hhr/article/view/367/563; Commission on Social Determinants of Health, "Closing the Gap in a Generation: Health Equity through Action on the Social Determinants of Health, Final Report of the Commission on Social Determinants of Health" (Geneva, Switzerland: World Health Organization, 2008), accessed February 8, 2011, http://whqlibdoc.who.int/publications /2008/9789241563703_eng.pdf.
13. World Health Organization, "The World Health Organization's Ranking of the World's Health Systems," Geneva, Switzerland, 2000, accessed February 5, 2011, http://www.photius.com/rankings/healthranks.html.
14. Cathy Schoen, Robin Osborn, David Squires, Michelle M. Doty, Roz Pierson, and Sandra Applebaum, "How Health Insurance Design Affects Access to Care and Costs, by Income, in Eleven Countries" (New York: Commonwealth Fund, November 18, 2010), *Health Affairs* Web First, accessed February 5, 2011, http:// www.commonwealthfund.org/Content/Publications/In-the-Literature/2010 /Nov/How-Health-Insurance-Design-Access-Care-Costs.aspx.

15. Ed Diener and Martin E. P. Seligman, "Beyond Money: Toward an Economy of Well-Being," *Psychological Science in the Public Interest* 5, no. 1 (2004): 1–31, accessed January 18, 2011, http://www.psychologicalscience.org/pdf/pspi/pspi 5_1.pdf.

16. Daniel Kahneman, Alan B. Krueger, David Schkade, Norbert Schwartz, and Arthur A. Stone, "Would You Be Happier If You Were Richer? A Focusing Illusion," CEPS Working Paper no. 125, Princeton University Center for Economic Policy Studies, May 2006, 1–14, accessed January 18, 2011, http://www.princeton.edu/~ceps/workingpapers/125krueger.pdf; Richard A. Easterlin, "The Income-Happiness Relationship," University of Southern California, February 2002, 1–30, accessed January 18, 2011, http://www-bcf.usc.edu/~easterl/papers/Inchap prelat.pdf.

17. Diener and Seligman, "Beyond Money," 10.

18. Ed Diener, Weiting Ng, James Harter, and Raksha Arora, "Wealth and Happiness across the World: Material Prosperity Predicts Life Evaluation, Whereas Psychosocial Prosperity Predicts Positive Feeling," *Journal of Personality and Social Psychology* 99, no. 1 (2010): 52–61.

19. The curve is based on the data provided in Kahneman et al.'s May 2006 paper (2004 data) and Easterlin's February 2002 paper (1994 data), converting all data to Easterlin's happiness scale, using the Census Bureau mean family income of $43,133 for the 1994 data and $60,466 for the 2004 data, and setting the upper multiple of mean family income to a value of 3 in each study.

20. Jeni Klugman, *Human Development Report 2010: The Real Wealth of Nations: Pathways to Human Development* (New York: United Nations Development Program, 2010), 13, 152, 215.

21. Michael I. Norton and Dan Ariely, "Building a Better America—One Wealth Quintile at a Time," *Perspectives on Psychological Science* 6, no. 9 (2011): 9–12, accessed May 2, 2011, http://www.people.hbs.edu/mnorton/norton%20ariely.pdf.

22. David K. Shipler, *The Working Poor: Invisible in America* (New York: Alfred A. Knopf, 2004), 300.

23. Brian Barry, *Why Social Justice Matters* (Cambridge, UK: Polity Press, 2005), 1.

24. Lisa Simeone, "The Lonely Funeral," *Soundprint*, Laurel, MD, broadcast on KQED public radio, January 29, 2011, accessed February 5, 2011, http://soundprint.org/radio/display_show/ID/808/name/The+Lonely+Funeral.

25. Brian Stelter, "Protest Puts Coverage in Spotlight," *New York Times*, November 20, 2011, accessed November 21, 2011, http://www.nytimes.com/2011/11/21/business/media/occupy-wall-street-puts-the-coverage-in-the-spotlight.html?_r=1&nl=todaysheadlines&emc=tha25.

26. Andrew Webber, "Businesses as Partners to Improve Community Health," *American Journal of Preventive Medicine* 40, no. 1S1 (2011): S84–S85, accessed February 8, 2011, http://www.rwjf.org/files/research/4953.pdf; Joel Berg and Joy Moses, "The Case for State Food Action Plans" (Washington, DC: Center for American Progress, February 2011), accessed February 23, 2011, http://www.americanprogress.org/issues/2011/02/pdf/hunger_report.pdf/.

27. Jeffrey B. Liebman, "Social Impact Bonds" (Washington, DC: Center for American Progress, February 2011), accessed February 17, 2011, http://www.americanprogress.org/issues/2011/02/pdf/social_impact_bonds.pdf; Todd Wallack, "Investors May Fund Social Programs," Boston.com, June 27, 2011, accessed July 1, 2011, http://articles.boston.com/2011-06-27/business/29709425_1_non profits-intervention-program-social-finance.

28. Stephanie Strom, "A Quest for Hybrid Companies That Profit, but Can Tap Charity," *New York Times*, October 11, 2011, accessed October 13, 2011, http://www.nytimes.com/2011/10/13/business/a-quest-for-hybrid-companies-part-money-maker-part-nonprofit.html?pagewanted=1&_r=1&nl=todaysheadlines&emc=tha25.

29. David Bornstein, "Health Care for a Changing Workforce," *New York Times*, December 1, 2011, accessed December 2, 2011, http://opinionator.blogs.nytimes.com/2011/12/01/health-care-for-a-changing-work-force/?nl=todaysheadlines&emc=thab1.

30. Richard D. Kahlenberg, *America's Untapped Resource: Low-Income Students in Higher Education* (New York: Century Foundation Press, 2004), 106.

31. U.S. Census Bureau, "Voting and Registration in the Election of November 2008," Washington, DC, May 2010, accessed January 18, 2011, http://www.census.gov/prod/2010pubs/p20-562.pdf.

32. Joan D. Chittister, *Scarred by Struggle, Transformed by Hope* (Grand Rapids, MI: Wm. B. Eerdmans, 2003), 52.

Appendix A. Income Inequality and Gross National Income per Capita

1. Gross National Income (GNI) per capita in 2009 in U.S.$ from the World Bank (Washington, DC), accessed January 8, 2011, http://data.worldbank.org/indicator/NY.GNP.PCAP.cd.

2. Gini coefficients from the CIA's *The World Factbook* (Washington, DC: Central Intelligence Agency), accessed January 7, 2011, https://www.cia.gov/library/publications/the-world-factbook/index.html.

Appendix B. Modeling Income, Spending, and Inequality

1. Carmen DeNavas-Walt, Bernadette D. Proctor, and Jessica C. Smith, U.S. Census Bureau Current Population Reports, P60-238, *Income, Poverty, and Health Insurance Coverage in the United States: 2009* (Washington, DC: U.S. Government Printing Office, 2010), 55, accessed January 7, 2011, http://www.census.gov/prod/2010pubs/p60-238.pdf.

2. Internal Revenue Service, 2010 Tax Table, Washington, DC, accessed April 25, 2011, http://www.irs.gov/pub/irs-pdf/i1040tt.pdf.

3. Internal Revenue Service, "Ten Important Facts about Capital Gains and Losses," Washington, DC, accessed September 21, 2011, http://www.irs.gov/newsroom/article/0,,id=106799,00.html.

4. Dorothy S. Brady and Rose D. Friedman, *Part IV Savings and the Income Distribution from Studies in Income and Wealth* (Cambridge, MA: National Bureau of Economic Research, 1947), 253, accessed April 25, 2011, http://www.nber.org/chapters/c5687.pdf; David Bunting, "Savings and the Distribution of Income," *Journal of Post Keynesian Economics* 14, no. 1 (Fall 1991): 3–22, accessed April 25, 2011, http://access.ewu.edu/Documents/Faculty/David%20Bunting/savings.pdf; Karen E. Dynan, Jonathan Skinner, and Stephen P. Zeldes, "Do the Rich Save More?," *Journal of Political Economy* 112, no. 2 (2004): 397–438, accessed April 25, 2011, http://www.dartmouth.edu/~jskinner/documents/DynanKEDotheRich.pdf.

5. Dynan et al., "Do the Rich Save More?," 416.

6. U.S. Census Bureau, *Statistical Abstract of the United States: 2011*, Washington, DC, table 693, p. 454, accessed April 25, 2011, http://www.census.gov/prod/2011pubs/11statab/income.pdf.

7. U.S. Census Bureau, *Statistical Abstract*, table 692, p. 454.
8. U.S. Census Bureau, "Gini Ratios for Families, by Race and Hispanic Origin of Householder [XLS]," Washington, DC, accessed August 19, 2012, http://www.census.gov/hhes/www/income/data/historical/inequality/index.html.

SELECTED BIBLIOGRAPHY

Anderson, Sarah, Chuck Collins, Scott Klinger, and Sam Pizzigati. "The CEO Hands in Uncle Sam's Pocket: How Our Tax Dollars Subsidize Exorbitant Executive Pay, Executive Excess 2012, 19th Annual Executive Pay Survey." Washington, DC: Institute for Policy Studies, August 16, 2012.

Barry, Brian. *Why Social Justice Matters*. Cambridge, UK: Polity Press, 2005.

Basu, Kunal, and Guido Palazzo. "Corporate Social Responsibility: A Process Model of Sensemaking." *Academy of Management Review* 33, no. 1 (2008): 122–36.

Chittister, Joan D. *Scarred by Struggle, Transformed by Hope*. Grand Rapids, MI: Wm. B. Eerdmans, 2003.

Coffin, William Sloane. *Credo*. Louisville, KY: Westminster John Knox Press, 2004.

Collins, Jim. *Good to Great: Why Some Companies Make the Leap . . . and Others Don't*. New York: Harper Business, 2001.

The Dartmouth Institute. *An Agenda for Change: Improving Quality and Curbing Health Care Spending: Opportunities for the Congress and the Obama Administration*. A Dartmouth Atlas White Paper. Lebanon, NH: Dartmouth Institute, December 2008. http://tdi.dartmouth.edu/documents/publications/An%20Agenda%20for%20Change.pdf.

DeNavas-Walt, Carmen, Bernadette D. Proctor, and Jessica C. Smith. U.S. Census Bureau Current Population Reports, P60–243, *Income, Poverty, and Health Insurance Coverage in the United States: 2011*. Washington, DC: U.S. Government Printing Office, 2012.

Diener, Ed, and Martin E. P. Seligman. "Beyond Money: Toward an Economy of Well-Being." *Psychological Science in the Public Interest* 5, no. 1 (2004): 1–31.

Elsdon, Ron. *Affiliation in the Workplace: Value Creation in the New Organization*. Westport, CT: Praeger, 2003.

———, ed. *Building Workforce Strength: Creating Value through Workforce and Career Development*. Santa Barbara, CA: Praeger, 2010.

Galland, Amy. *Toward a Safe, Just Workplace: Apparel Supply Chain Compliance Programs*. San Francisco: As You Sow Foundation, 2010.

Goleman, Daniel, Richard Boyatzis, and Annie McKee. *Primal Leadership: Realizing the Power of Emotional Intelligence*. Boston: Harvard Business School Press, 2002.

Institute of Medicine, Committee on Institutional and Policy-Level Strategies for Increasing the Diversity of the U.S. Healthcare Workforce. "In the Nation's Compelling Interest: Ensuring Diversity in the Health Care Workforce." Washington, DC: National Academy Press, 2004.

Intrator, Sam M., and Megan Scribner. *Leading from Within: Poetry That Sustains the Courage to Lead.* San Francisco: Jossey-Bass, 2007.

Izzo, John B., and Pam Withers. *Values Shift.* Vancouver: Fair Winds Press, 2000.

Kaiser Family Foundation. *The Uninsured: A Primer.* Menlo Park, CA, October 2011. http://www.kff.org/uninsured/upload/7451-07.pdf.

Katz, Michael B. "The American Welfare State," 2008. http://www.history.ac.uk /ihr/Focus/welfare/articles/katzm.html.

Klugman, Jeni. *Human Development Report 2010: The Real Wealth of Nations: Pathways to Human Development.* New York: United Nations Development Program, 2010.

Kochan, Thomas A., Adrienne E. Eaton, Robert B. McKersie, and Paul S. Adler. *Healing Together: The Labor-Management Partnership at Kaiser Permanente.* Ithaca, NY: Cornell University Press, 2009.

Miller, David. *Principles of Social Justice.* Cambridge, MA: Harvard University Press, 1999.

Mitchell, Monika, "John Bogle: The Conscience of Capitalism." *Good Business International, Inc.* Accessed October 18, 2011. http://good-b.com/?p=5481.

Porter, Michael, and Mark Kramer. "Strategy and Society: The Link between Competitive Advantage and Corporate Social Responsibility." *Harvard Business Review,* December 2006, 1–15.

Reich, Robert B. *Aftershock: The Next Economy and America's Future.* New York: Alfred A. Knopf, 2010.

Relman, Arnold S. *A Second Opinion: Rescuing America's Health Care.* New York: Century Foundation, 2007.

Shipler, David K. *The Working Poor: Invisible in America.* New York: Alfred A. Knopf, 2004.

Smedley, Brian D., Adrienne Stith Butler, and Lonnie R. Bristow, eds. Institute of Medicine, Committee on Institutional and Policy-Level Strategies for Increasing the Diversity of the U.S. Healthcare Workforce. "In the Nation's Compelling Interest: Ensuring Diversity in the Health Care Workforce." Washington, DC: National Academy Press, 2004.

Squires, David A. *The U.S. Health System in Perspective: A Comparison of Twelve Industrialized Nations.* New York: Commonwealth Fund, July 2011. http://www.common wealthfund.org/~/media/Files/Publications/Issue%20Brief/2011/Jul/1532 _Squires_US_hlt_sys_comparison_12_nations_intl_brief_v2.pdf.

U.S. Government Accountability Office. "Globalization: Numerous Federal Activities Complement U.S. Business's Global Corporate Social Responsibility Efforts." Accessed October 1, 2011. http://www.gao.gov/new.items/d05744.pdf.

Walker Information. *Measuring the Business Value of Corporate Philanthropy.* Report prepared for Council on Foundations. Indianapolis: Walker Information, May 2002.

Werther, William B., Jr., and David Chandler. *Strategic Corporate Social Responsibility: Stakeholders in a Global Environment.* Los Angeles: SAGE, 2011.

Wilkinson, Richard, and Kate Pickett. *The Spirit Level: Why Greater Equality Makes Societies Stronger.* New York: Bloomsbury Press, 2009.

Zadek, Simon, Peter Raynard, Cristiano Oliveira, Edna do Nascimento, and Rafael Tello. *Responsible Competitiveness, 2005.* AccountAbility in Association with FDC, London, December 2005. Accessed January 3, 2011. http://www.accountability .org/images/content/1/1/110/Full%20Report%20(Compressed).pdf.

INDEX

ABOUT THE CONTRIBUTORS

Zeth Ajemian, MA, is the director of workforce planning and development for Kaiser Permanente's Southern California region. In this capacity Zeth leads a labor and management program initiative that provides strategic staff planning and career upgrade services for more than 50,000 workers in the region. Before coming to Kaiser Permanente, Zeth was the associate director for workforce development and research at the Los Angeles County Federation of Labor, where he developed training and career ladder programs for member American Federation of Labor–Congress of Industrial Organizations (AFL-CIO) unions. Zeth's background is in industry sector and labor market analysis with the intent of identifying and supporting growth industries that provide opportunities for high-wage jobs with career ladder potential. Zeth received his bachelor's in political science from Pitzer College and his master's in urban planning with an emphasis on economic development from the University of California–Los Angeles (UCLA) School of Public Policy. He can be reached at zeth.ajemian@kp.org.

Allyne Beach, MA, is a senior workforce analyst with Kaiser Permanente in national workforce planning and development. There she is responsible for workforce forecasting, evaluation and metrics, and program development. Prior to her work at Kaiser Permanente, Allyne was executive director of the Public Sector Labor Management Committee in Washington, D.C., developing and executing quality improvement initiatives in the public sector industries: water and wastewater, education, police, and social services.

251

Allyne also conceptualized, negotiated, and implemented the joint labor-management workforce development trust of the state of Ohio/Ohio Civil Service Employees Association. This is a $36 million joint labor-management education trust for state of Ohio employees. Allyne received her bachelor's in sociology from Ohio State University and her master's in social development/policy from the University of Chicago School of Social Science Administration. She can be reached at allyne.beach@kp.org.

Andrew "Andy" Domek, MA, is a senior consultant with the California Assembly Democratic Caucus. In this capacity, he has worked for three California assembly speakers, consulting on communications, media relations, and constituent outreach. Prior to this, he worked for the Association of California Water Agencies and the California Secretary of State's Office and served as an executive fellow at the California Fair Political Practices Commission. In 2010, Andy took a leave of absence from his state service to be a part of the team that helped add to the Democratic majority in the California assembly, the only legislative body in the country to do so. He has a master's in communication studies, with an emphasis in public and political communication, from Sacramento State University and a bachelor's in political science from the University of California at Davis. Andy can be reached at agdomek60@gmail.com.

Ron Elsdon, PhD, is a founder of organizations that specialize in career and workforce development for organizations and individuals. He has also been active in speaking and writing about and promoting a range of social causes. Ron has more than twenty-five years of leadership experience at diverse organizations in a broad range of sectors and has been an adjunct faculty member at, or affiliated with, several universities. He has authored numerous publications and has spoken regularly at national and regional events. Ron is the author of *Affiliation in the Workplace: Value Creation in the New Organization* (Praeger, 2003) and editor of *Building Workforce Strength: Creating Value through Workforce and Career Development* (Praeger, 2010). With his coauthor Ron was awarded the Walker Prize by the Human Resource Planning Society for a paper that best advances state-of-the-art thinking or practices in human resources. Ron received his PhD in chemical engineering from

Cambridge University, his master's in career development from John F. Kennedy University, and a first-class honors degree in chemical engineering from Leeds University. Ron can be reached at renewal@elsdon.com.

Aaron Hurst, BGS, president and founder of the Taproot Foundation, is a globally recognized social innovator and leading architect of the growing pro bono services movement. Launched in 2001, the Taproot Foundation has served more than 1,300 nonprofit organizations through its award-winning Service Grant program, which has touched the lives of nearly 19 million people across the United States, recruiting more than 10,000 business professionals as pro bono consultants. Widely known for his thought leadership in civic engagement, nonprofit management, and corporate social responsibility, Aaron is both an Ashoka and Draper Richards Kaplan Foundation fellow. He has been formally recognized as a leading social innovator by a number of institutions and in 2009 received the College of Literature, Science, and the Arts Humanitarian Service Award, the highest honor for University of Michigan alumni. Aaron currently sits on the international advisory board of directors of CiYuan, a three-year initiative to increase social investment in China, and serves on the boards of Reimagining Service and BoardSource. With his wife, Kara Hurst, he coauthored the children's book *Mommy and Daddy Do It Pro Bono.* Aaron has a BGS in service learning from the University of Michigan, and can be reached at aaron@taprootfoundation.org.

Megan Roberts Koller, MEd, contributed to this book as a graduate student at Vanderbilt University's Peabody College. In 2012, she earned a master's in human resource (HR) development, which focuses on the relationship between individual and organizational performance. Before enrolling at Vanderbilt University, Megan worked as an education fellow and then director of special projects for the Institute of Southern Jewish Life in Jackson, Mississippi. She graduated with a bachelor's in history from Indiana University–Bloomington in 2006.

Barbara Langsdale, BS, is the vice president of marketing and communications for We Care Services for Children. Barbara became interested in early intervention programs when her daughter was diagnosed with many of the developmental disabilities children at We Care have. After taking a leave from her for-profit job in the oil industry, she started as a volunteer at We Care and soon realized that nonprofit work was her passion. Barbara is active in a variety of local organizations, including as a member of the board of directors of the Concord Chamber of Commerce that mentors small nonprofits in developing their fund-raising capabilities, and she has volunteered for Habitat for Humanity. In recognition of her community work Barbara has received the Woman of the Year award by the Soroptimist International Diablo Vista chapter and the Rotary International Paul Harris Fellow award. She has a bachelor's in management and a certificate in nonprofit management from California State University–East Bay. Barbara can be reached at blangsdale@wecarechildren.org.

Jim Leatherberry, MBA, is the founder and chief executive officer (CEO) of Santa Fe Partners LLC, a hedge fund that trades U.S. equities for institutional clients. Jim's professional career has encompassed a variety of financial markets and products. He has extensive experience with major banks and investment companies in the equity, foreign exchange, fixed income, and commodity markets. Jim's responsibilities have included trading, portfolio management, institutional sales, financial engineering, and research. He has held memberships at the Philadelphia Stock Exchange and the International Monetary Market division of the Chicago Mercantile Exchange, and also taught as an adjunct professor at the College of Santa Fe. Jim holds a bachelor's in international finance from Ohio State University and an MBA from George Washington University in international finance. He can be reached at jim@santafepartnersllc.com.

Deborah LeVeen, PhD, is a professor emerita from San Francisco State University, where she was a member of the urban studies program. She taught health policy for more than twenty-five years, allowing her to look closely at the ongoing evolution of the U.S. healthcare system. Deborah has also been active in health policy advocacy efforts, researching, writing, and making presentations; she has worked with the women's health movement, the California single-payer campaign, and the ongoing effort to protect and strengthen the 2010 national healthcare legislation. Deborah earned a PhD in political science from the University of Chicago, an MA in political science from UCLA, and a BA magna cum laude in religion from Smith College. She also served in one of the first Peace Corps groups in Ghana. Deborah can be reached at dleveen@earthlink.net.

Laura Long, MBA, is the director of national workforce planning and development for Kaiser Permanente and codirector of the Ben Hudnall Memorial Trust, which provides education and training funding to union members at Kaiser Permanente. Her expertise is in strategic planning, grant writing, project development, and program management. Laura's professional experience includes leading local and state public health and community-based projects to improve health outcomes and eliminate health disparities. Prior to coming to Kaiser Permanente, she was a project director with a local health department and California training coordinator with the National Cancer Institute's cancer information service. Laura received her bachelor's in integrative biology from the University of California–Berkeley and her MBA from St Mary's College of California. She can be reached at Laura.I.Long@kp.org.

Emet Mohr, BA, is the senior vice president for the Caucasus and Central Asia region at Chemonics International. He has broad experience leading program design and implementation throughout Europe and Eurasia, particularly in Georgia, where he led the Education Management Project, a U.S. Agency for International Development activity dedicated to improving the Georgian educational system. As an education development specialist, Emet has conducted technical assignments on numerous projects, from Jordan to Peru, and has helped build the education practice at Chemonics. In addition to serving as a Peace Corps volunteer in Morocco, he has a bachelor's from Cornell University in American Studies and has completed graduate coursework in education at the University of Virginia and George Mason University.

Bob Redlo, MA, is the vice president of patient relations, labor relations, and workforce development for Doctors Medical Center, San Pablo, California.

In this role Bob is responsible for key patient and workforce relationships. Previously Bob was the director of national workforce planning and development for Kaiser Permanente and a codirector of the Ben Hudnall Memorial Trust, which provides education and training funding to union members at Kaiser Permanente. Bob and his team, with labor's partnership, initiated the groundwork for a national workforce development program at Kaiser Permanente. Prior to this, Bob was the senior HR consultant at Kaiser Permanente's San Francisco medical facility and previously served as an HR consultant at other Northern California medical facilities. Bob works with a number of community organizations, for example, committees for the California Community Colleges and the California Hospital Association. Before joining Kaiser Permanente, he was chair at the Center for Labor Research and Education at the University of California–Berkeley. Bob has a bachelor's in political science from State University College at Oswego, New York, and a master's from the Rockefeller College of Public Affairs and Policy at the University at Albany (State University of New York [SUNY]); he has also completed doctoral coursework at the University at Albany–SUNY.

Pearl Sims, EdD, is a faculty member in the Department of Leadership, Policy, and Organizations at Vanderbilt University, where she teaches courses in public and international leadership. She has been awarded more than $11 million in grants for her work in the use of technology for leadership and organizational development, including leading a major leadership development effort by the Gates Foundation in Tennessee, conducting an international study of U.S. Department of Defense schools, and designing a multimillion-dollar project in Tennessee aimed at using technology for large-scale organizational change. Pearl has served as an educational public policy and leadership expert in multiple international settings including China, Abu Dhabi, Vietnam, Republic of Georgia, Guatemala, and the European Union. As a former cabinet member of two elected officials, Pearl has served in a wide variety of roles. She has lived and worked in urban communities for more than twenty years and is active in many civic and education organizations; she is also the recipient of multiple leadership awards. Pearl has her bachelor's from Middle Tennessee State University in secondary education and her doctorate from Vanderbilt University in educational leadership. She can be reached at pearl.g.sims@vanderbilt.edu.

Richard Vicenzi, MS, has more than twenty years of experience in designing and implementing interventions and advising clients in organizational culture change issues, organizational effectiveness, staffing and recruitment, workplace diversity, executive coaching, and career management. His corporate clients have included Fortune 100 companies, privately held businesses, and nonprofit organizations. Richard's interest in sustainability and corporate social responsibility is an outgrowth of his research into organizations as complex adaptive systems where actions are recognized to have distant and unforeseen ramifications. He received a bachelor's in economics from the University of California–Riverside and an MBA from the University of California–Los Angeles. In addition, Richard received an MS in advanced management from the Drucker School of Management at Claremont Graduate University, where he also completed doctoral coursework in organization design and strategic management. He can be reached at rvicenzi@yahoo.com.

Linda Williams, MSSW, is the president and CEO of the RISE (Responsibility. Initiative. Solutions. Empowerment.) Foundation. The mission of RISE is to empower low-income families to become self-sufficient by building and sustaining human and financial assets. Previously Linda devoted thirty-two years of her career to working with the Tennessee Department of Human Services in positions ranging from welfare specialist to the administrative director of Shelby County, the largest urban county in the state. She received her undergraduate degree in social work from Southern Illinois University at Carbondale, and her master of science in social work from the University of Tennessee at Knoxville with a concentration in administration and planning. Linda can be reached at llwill02@bellsouth.net.